The
Modern Language
Review

OCTOBER 2024   VOLUME 119   PART 4

MODERN HUMANITIES RESEARCH ASSOCIATION

The Modern Humanities Research Association

was founded in Cambridge in 1918 and has become an international organization with members in all parts of the world. It is a registered charity number 1064670, and a company limited by guarantee, registered in England number 3446016. Its main object is to encourage advanced study and research in modern and medieval European languages, literatures, and cultures by its publication of journals, book series, and its Style Guide.

Further information about the activities of the Association and individual membership may be obtained by post from the MHRA Membership Secretary, Peters, Elworthy & Moore, Salisbury House, Station Road, Cambridge, CB1 2LA, UK, email membership@mhra.org.uk, or from the website at www.mhra.org.uk

The Association's publications, including most back volumes, are available in print or electronically. Full details are available from www.mhra.org.uk

For institutional subscription rates and information, contact subscriptions@mhra.org.uk

The Modern Language Review

The *Modern Language Review* is available to members of the Modern Humanities Research Association at a discounted rate. Membership is by application to the Membership Secretary; free associateship is also available to postgraduates (subject to terms and conditions). Some other publications of the MHRA are available to members at special rates.

ISSN 0026–7937 (Print)
ISSN 2222–4319 (Online)
ISBN 978–1–83954–271–8
© 2024 The Modern Humanities Research Association

DISCLAIMER

Views expressed in the content of the *Modern Language Review* are those of the respective authors and contributors and not of the journal editors or of the Modern Humanities Research Association (MHRA). MHRA makes no representation, express or implied, in respect of the accuracy of the material in this journal and cannot accept any legal responsibility or liability for views expressed or for any errors or omissions that may be made.

TYPESET BY JOHN WAŚ, OXFORD

Guidelines for Contributors to *MLR*

The *Modern Language Review* publishes articles and book reviews on modern and medieval European languages, literatures, and cultures around the globe where European languages are spoken. The journal welcomes scholarship that takes a global or comparative approach as well as articles that appeal to a broad cross-section of scholars working on areas including, but not limited to, literature, the visual and performing arts, sociolinguistics, cultural history, and Translation Studies. We encourage submissions from scholars at all stages, including postgraduate researchers. If you are in any doubt about the appropriateness of your paper for *MLR*, please take a moment to review previous volumes of the journal. The contents of these issues will give you a good sense of the areas of research which are of interest to us. The complete back issues of the journal can be found at https://www.jstor.org/journal/modelangrevi (pre-2001) and https://muse.jhu.edu/journal/822.

Articles should be submitted to the appropriate section editor in electronic copy sent as an email attachment. Articles should conform precisely to the conventions of the *MHRA Style Guide*, 4th edn, 2024 (ISBN 978-1-83954-248-0), obtainable in print or online at www.mhra.org.uk/style. Authors should provide an abstract of their articles with keywords highlighted in bold type. This abstract should not exceed 100 words. At the end of articles and reviews contributors should include, in this order, their affiliation or location; name as it is to be printed; name and postal address for correspondence; and email address. Simple references should be incorporated into the text (see *MHRA Style Guide*, §7.3). Double spacing should be used throughout, including quotations and footnotes, which should be in the same large size of type as the rest of the article. Articles are typically about 8000 words in length including footnotes, but longer and shorter ones are also welcome. Quotations and references should be carefully checked. Quotations from languages covered by the journal, and from Latin and Greek, should be given in the original language. Latin and Greek passages should normally be translated or at least paraphrased; usually this is not required in the case of modern languages, though it may be helpful where dialects or early forms of the language are cited. However, since the journal has a broad readership, please provide translations or paraphrases of quotations within comparative or general articles (except for modern French). If in doubt, consult the appropriate section editor.

It is a condition of publication in this journal that authors of articles and reviews assign copyright, including electronic copyright, to the MHRA. Permission, without fee, for authors to use their own material in other publications, after a reasonable period of time has elapsed, is not normally withheld. The MHRA offers several options for Open Access via the Green route. Please see our website or contact mail@mhra.org.uk for more details.

On publication of each issue of the journal authors will receive, by email, the finalized PDF of their contribution as it appears in the printed volume. Physical offprints are not supplied.

Articles and books for review should be sent to the Editor concerned:

General and Comparative. Professor Duncan Wheeler, School of Languages, Cultures and Societies, University of Leeds, Leeds LS2 9JT (d.wheeler@leeds.ac.uk).

English. Dr Adam Hansen, 123, Lipman Building, City Campus, Northumbria University, Newcastle upon Tyne NE1 8ST (adam.hansen@northumbria.ac.uk).

French. Dr Claire Moran, School of Arts, English and Languages, Queen's University Belfast, 2 University Square, BT7 1NN, Belfast (c.moran@qub.ac.uk).

Italian. Professor Guido Bonsaver, Pembroke College, Oxford OX1 1DW (guido.bonsaver@pmb.ox.ac.uk).

Hispanic. Professor Duncan Wheeler, School of Languages, Cultures and Societies, University of Leeds, Leeds LS2 9JT (d.wheeler@leeds.ac.uk).

German, Dutch, and Scandinavian. Dr Seán Williams, School of Languages and Cultures, University of Sheffield, Jessop West, 1 Upper Hanover Street, Sheffield S3 7RA (s.m.williams@sheffield.ac.uk).

Slavonic and Eastern European. Professor Muireann Maguire, Department of Modern Languages, University of Exeter, Queen's Building, The Queen's Drive, Exeter EX4 4QH (muireann.maguire@exeter.ac.uk).

CONTENTS

Contents

'MORE LOVE LETTERS, PLEASE!': PORTUGUESE LOVE AND THE LITERARY LEGACY OF SINCERE FEELING

Since 2004, the *New York Times* has run a very successful column entitled 'Modern Love'.[1] Exploring what love can be in a time when swiping right seems to be the preferred method for meeting romantic prospects, the column and its many offshoots suggest that despite an ostensible cultural preference for keeping it casual, ideal love remains a tantalizing idea. Indeed, as cultural critics have shown, there remains a significant pull to the notion of true love, its potentially disempowering ideological pressures notwithstanding.[2] Moreover, the disaffected, ironic position vis-à-vis love that has prevailed in mainstream culture for some generations—what Linda Kauffman terms 'the devaluation of the sentimental' and denounces as 'another form of repression, with ramifications as serious at the end of the twentieth century as sexual repression was at the end of the nineteenth'—is not without its own ideological pressures and detrimental effects.[3]

Kauffman's assertion of this devaluation acknowledges Roland Barthes's similar insight in *Fragments d'un discours amoureux* (*A Lover's Discourse: Fragments*, 1977).[4] But Barthes's twentieth-century understanding of modern Western culture's tendency to disparage the sentimental simultaneously affirms its transgressive status:

> Discréditée par l'opinion moderne, la sentimentalité de l'amour doit être assumée par le sujet amoureux comme une transgression forte, qui le laisse seul et exposé; par un renversement de valeurs, c'est donc cette sentimentalité qui fait aujourd'hui l'obscène de l'amour. (*Fragments*, p. 207)

[1] Featuring reader-submitted, real love stories, the column has spun off a book, *Modern Love: True Stories of Love, Loss, and Redemption*, ed. by Daniel Jones (New York: Broadway Books, 2007; repr. 2019); a 'miniature series' consisting of love stories of no more than 100 words; a weekly newsletter entitled *Love Letters*; a podcast; a 'Modern Love' college essay contest; a Facebook page; and a TV show (2019 and 2021).

[2] Writing about sentimentality in American popular culture, Lauren Berlant suggested as much when they pointed out that the 'hard-edged titles [of contemporary popular culture] conceal the tender fantasies of a better good life' (Lauren Berlant, *The Female Complaint: The Unfinished Business of Sentimentality in American Culture* (Durham, NC: Duke University Press, 2008), p. 1). Such fantasies, Berlant reminded us, perpetuate normative notions of ideal femininity by teaching women to remain committed to love despite it being 'the gift that keeps on taking' (ibid.).

[3] Linda Kauffman, *Discourses of Desire: Gender, Genre, and Epistolary Fictions* (Ithaca, NY: Cornell University Press, 1986), p. 316.

[4] Roland Barthes, *Fragments d'un discours amoureux* (Paris: Seuil, 1977); Roland Barthes, *A Lover's Discourse: Fragments*, trans. by Richard Howard (New York: Hill and Wang, 1978).

Modern Language Review, 119 (2024), 431–55, doi:10.1353/mlr.00001
© Modern Humanities Research Association 2024

Discredited by modern opinion, love's sentimentality must be assumed by the amorous subject as a powerful transgression which leaves him alone and exposed; by a reversal of values, then, it is this sentimentality which today constitutes love's obscenity. (*A Lover's Discourse*, p. 175)

Here, Barthes hints at sentimental love's subversive potential—which includes, crucially, a resistance to cultural derision that can ultimately free the amorous subject from the late twentieth-century form of repression Kauffman comments on. Two decades into the twenty-first century, the success of *Modern Love* may well confirm that subversive potential in acknowledging at least some aspects of the centuries-old power of sentimental love and its representations—albeit in a modern iteration in which the amorous subject concedes that, to use the current expression, 'it's complicated'.[5] This essay traces the development of one of its most unironic literary figurations—the myth of Portuguese Love[6]—and demonstrates its relevance for literary history by exploring its transcultural reach and its lasting presence in literature and culture. In doing so, it invokes what, following Barthes, can be termed Portuguese Love's transgressive value in order to underscore the potential of its continued affirmation to resist the 'renversement de valeurs' ('reversal of values') identified by Barthes, and thus undermine the related repression diagnosed by Kauffman. Ultimately, as we shall see, this continued affirmation also ensures its ability to triumph over patriarchal and nationalist ideological appropriations.[7]

Portuguese Love: Origin and Consolidation of the Myth

Still surviving today, the myth of Portuguese Love has a long history, and its literary influence is widespread. Generally transgressive—adulterous or otherwise forbidden, be it for reasons of class difference, or religious or familial prohibition—it is characterized by an overwhelming depth of passion that is typically represented as self-sustaining and fatalistic, centring female constancy and devotion. Above all, Portuguese Love has long fascinated readers

---

[5] Sentimental love's power to survive irony is implied in the ideological interstices between the 'obscenity' of unfettered feeling and its open derision. For a discussion of how the rise of the sentimental and the crisis of irony (as he characterizes it) currently manifest in American literary production see Christian Lorentzen, 'Like Rain on your Wedding Day: Between the Sentimental, the Gothic, and the Ironic', *Bookforum*, August 2021, pp. 23–24, 43; see also <https://www.bookforum.com/print/2802/between-the-sentimental-the-gothic-and-the-ironic-24490> [accessed 17 March 2024].

[6] The term was originally coined in seventeenth-century France as love 'à la portugaise'. I will use the English expression throughout.

[7] Barthes, *Fragments*, p. 175; *A Lover's Discourse*, p. 207. Barthes's injunction regarding love that 'il ne faut attendre que son affirmation' (*Fragments* p. 12: 'we must look for no more than its affirmation', *A Lover's Discourse*, p. 8) seems potentially fulfilled by *Modern Love*, which echoes Portuguese Love in its affirming impulse.

and writers alike by its sincerity. The concept and its sustained, unironic deployment of the sentimental arguably sparked from a medieval instance of extreme love made famous in Portuguese history and literature: the love of Prince Pedro and Inês de Castro, which is considered 'the Portuguese subject most widespread in Western culture'.[8]

Historical records show that Inês de Castro, a Galician lady-in-waiting to Pedro's second wife, was sent into exile as a result of the scandal of her affair with the prince.[9] Pedro brought Inês back to Portugal after his wife's death, but his father, concerned that her influence might jeopardize Portuguese independence—some maintained that she was a spy for Castile—ordered her killed in 1355. History and legend mixed to create the account of what followed: mad with grief, Pedro went to war against his father. Once king, he had Inês's murderers executed by having their hearts pulled out of their chests, ordered Inês's body exhumed, and crowned her queen in a ceremony in which her corpse sat on the throne as the entire court filed by and kissed her hand.[10]

Inês, the constancy of her love, and the violence of her death were immortalized by the fifteenth-century Portuguese poet Garcia de Resende (1470–1536) in 'Trovas à Morte de D. Inês de Castro' ('Song on the Death of Inês de Castro'), and her story became the symbol of tragic Portuguese Love.[11] Indeed, António Saraiva and Óscar Lopes point out the role of Resende's 'Trovas' in forging this symbol and in establishing a literary sensibility that continued for centuries. Importantly, they acknowledge that it created 'uma imagem convencional da índole portuguesa, caracterizada pelo sentimentalismo e pelo saudosismo' ('a conventional image of the Portuguese character characterized by sentimentality and nostalgia').[12] 'Trovas' appeared in Resende's 1516 compilation of late medieval and early Renaissance Portuguese poetry, the *Cancioneiro Geral*. Its indebtedness to other stories of transgressive medieval lovers (Lancelot and Guinevere, for example, or Paolo and Francesca) already suggests Portuguese Love's indebtedness to the early courtly love tradition—particularly the transgressive nature of the love, and the ennobling potential

---

[8] Maria Leonor Machado de Sousa, 'Inês de Castro in English Literature', *Journal of Anglo-Portuguese Studies*, 27 (2018), 71–98 (p. 72).

[9] Martin Nozick, 'The Inez de Castro Theme in European Literature', *Comparative Literature*, 3 (1951), 330–41 (p. 330). As Nozick states, the first Portuguese historical account of Inês de Castro is by the Portuguese historian Fernão Lopes (*c.* 1380–*c.* 1460) in Fernão Lopes, *Chrónica de El-Rei D. Pedro I, por Fernão Lopes* (Lisbon: Commercio de Portugal, 1895). Further references to Nozick's work are given after quotations in the text.

[10] Machado de Sousa, 'Inês de Castro', p. 73.

[11] Garcia de Resende, 'Trovas à Morte de D. Inês de Castro', *Projecto Vercial* <http://alfarrabio.di.uminho.pt/vercial/resende.htm#poesias> [accessed 15 May 2023]. Further references to this poem are to this edition and given after quotations in the text.

[12] António José Saraiva and Óscar Lopes, *História da Literatura Portuguesa* (Porto: Porto Editora, 1976), pp. 165–66. Here and throughout the essay, unless otherwise indicated, all translations are my own.

of the lovers' suffering.[13] But in making Inês the speaker of the poem, Resende follows a distinctly Galician–Portuguese strain of male-composed yet
female-voiced medieval love songs known as *cantigas de amigo* which fem-
inize the expression of the ideals of constancy, devotion, and sacrifice that
came to define Portuguese Love. Unlike their contemporaneous *cantigas de
amor* (male-authored and male-voiced, centring male subjectivity, and clearly
following the courtly love tradition of the Provençal troubadours), the male-
authored *cantigas de amigo* are female-voiced and specific to the medieval
Galician–Portuguese lyric.[14]

'Trovas' opens with a stanza dedicating the poem to ladies who might be
ready to accept an offer of love and service—'quem tomar tal servidor, | eu lhe
quero descobrir | o galardam do amor' (I. 3–5: 'whoever takes such a servant |
I wish to reveal to them | the rewards of love')—but immediately after centres
Inês's emotions. Addressing the audience directly, Inês narrates her dire fate
once she accepted Pedro's love, stressing her 'fervente | lealdade, fé, amor | ó
príncepe, [seu] senhor' (II. 7–10: 'fervent | loyalty, faith, and love | to the prince,
[her] lord'), and lamenting that her reward for so much love was death by the
sword: 'Dous cavaleiros irosos [. . .] com as espadas na mam | m'atravessam o
coraçam [. . .] | este é o galardam | que meus amores me deram' (xx. 1, 6–7, 9–
10: 'Two knights [. . .] holding their swords in ire | plunged them into my heart
[. . .] | this is the reward I received for all my love'). From the earliest moment

---

[13] Courtly love's historical authenticity vs. its status as a textual conceit has been extensively de-
bated, as has the sincerity vs. irony of its representations. That it is a conventional literary model of
refined love influenced by ideas of chivalry (including reverence for the sufferings of love, as well as the
idealization of, and service to, women) is generally undisputed, though. For thorough discussions, see
Simon Gaunt, *Troubadours and Irony* (Cambridge: Cambridge University Press, 1989); id., *Love and
Death in Medieval French and Occitan Courtly Literature: Martyrs to Love* (Oxford: Oxford Univer-
sity Press, 2006); *The Troubadours: An Introduction*, ed. by Simon Gaunt and Sarah Kay (Cambridge:
Cambridge University Press, 1999); Toril Moi, 'Desire in Language: Andreas Capellanus and the Con-
troversy of Courtly Love', in *Medieval Literature: Criticism, Ideology, and History*, ed. by David Aers
(New York: St Martin's Press, 1985), pp. 11–33; and Gregory B. Stone, *Death of the Troubadour: The
Late Medieval Resistance to the Renaissance* (Philadelphia: University of Pennsylvania Press, 1994).

[14] Arguably, by employing this generic element, Resende grafts onto Portuguese Love the inherent
ideological ambiguity in male-authored women's voices who speak a disempowering feminine constancy, devotion, and sacrifice. For if the use of the female voice in male-authored texts has often been
interpreted as potentially feminist, it has also often been seen as ideological appropriation. Indeed,
only the *trobairitzi*, the rare women troubadours of the Occitan tradition, have left any examples of
medieval female-authored and female-voiced love songs that are, in themselves, a challenge to the
norms of male courtly love poetry. See Ana Paula Ferreira, 'Telling Woman What She Wants: The
Cantigas d'amigo as Strategies of Containment', *Portuguese Studies*, 9 (1933), 23–38, for an overview
of the debates about the female voice of the Middle Ages, including the *cantigas de amigo* and the
songs of the *trobairitzi*. See Gaunt and Kay, *The Troubadours*, for further discussion of the *trobairitzi*.
See C. P. Bagley, 'Cantigas de Amigo e Cantigas de Amor', *Bulletin of Hispanic Studies*, 43 (1966),
241–52, as well as Rip Cohen and Stephen Parkinson, 'The Medieval Galician–Portuguese Lyric', in *A
Companion to Portuguese Literature*, ed. by Cláudia Pazos Alonso and T. F. Earle (Martlesham: Boy-
dell and Brewer, 2009), pp. 25–44, on differences between medieval Portuguese lyric poetry and its
counterparts elsewhere in Europe.

of its formation, then, the trope of Portuguese Love denotes female sacrifice and even death—an element which will become particularly conspicuous in its nineteenth-century literary figurations.

The love of Pedro and Inês became famous beyond Portuguese borders: there is evidence that French chroniclers mentioned it in 1586, and that translations of those chronicles into English were made in 1612.[15] Importantly, Luís de Camões, Portugal's most celebrated poet, included their tragic love story in his 1572 epic *The Lusiads*. As the poem was translated in subsequent centuries, it further disseminated this particularly Portuguese idea of extreme love.[16] By the seventeenth century, versions of the story diffused across European literature had further shaped the literary trope of Portuguese Love. For example, in 1688 Aphra Behn published *Agnes de Castro; or, The Force of Generous Love*, a translation of the novel *Agnes de Castro* by Mlle Barbier de Brillac, published in Amsterdam in 1680.[17]

But the text that most widely disseminated and, indeed, crystallized this notion was the French epistolary work *Lettres portugaises* (*Letters of a Portuguese Nun*, 1669). The critical history of the letters, marked by debates about their authenticity, is aptly summarized in different studies.[18] Here, it suffices to stress that initially they were accepted as real, but by the middle of the twentieth century scholarly consensus was that the letters were too exquisitely crafted to be the real outpourings of a broken-hearted nun, and were instead fictional, written by the man who had claimed to edit them—Gabriel de Lavergne, viscount of Guilleragues. The all-consuming love that Mariane, the Portuguese nun, expresses in her five letters to her lover—a French officer whom she met during Portugal's war of independence against Spain, and who abandoned her without explanation—became famous once the letters appeared in France in 1669. Discussed in every fashionable salon, they were held as a model for the expression of sincere, passionate love—so much so that to receive or to send 'une portugaise' ('a true Portuguese') referred to a letter that conveyed the most ardent love. Writing to her daughter about a suitor's letter in July 1671, for example, Mme de Sévigné stresses: 'si je le faisois réponse sur le même ton, ce

[15] Machado de Sousa, 'Inês de Castro', p. 74.

[16] There are at least eighteen different English translations of the poem, the first that is known being Sir Richard Fanshawe's in 1655. See Landeg White, 'Introduction', in *The Collected Lyric Poems of Luís de Camões*, trans. by Landeg White (Princeton: Princeton University Press, 2008), pp. 1–21 (p. 1). See also Iolanda Ramos and Isabel Lousada, 'Traduções de *Os Lusíadas* em Inglaterra', in *Camões em Inglaterra*, ed. by Maria Leonor Sousa (Lisbon: Ministério da Educação, 1992), pp. 7–63.

[17] Nozick, p. 339; Machado de Sousa, p. 76. Nozick provides a detailed account of the dissemination of the story of Inês de Castro in European literature, paying attention to how it was adapted and changed. More narrowly, Machado de Sousa details the theme in English literature.

[18] See especially F. Deloffre and J. Rougeot, 'L'Énigme des *Lettres portugaises*', in *Lettres portugaises, Valentins et autres œuvres* (Paris: Garnier, 1962), pp. v–xxiii (pp. v–xvii); Kauffman, pp. 92–93; and Anna Klobucka, *The Portuguese Nun: Formation of a National Myth* (Lewisburg, PA: Bucknell University Press, 2000), pp. 11–14.

seroit une portugaise' ('if I wrote back in the same tone, it would be a true Portuguese').[19]

The success of the *Portuguese Letters*, as they are commonly referred to, is partly explained by the preoccupation, at the time, with the appropriate expression of love both in literature and in high society.[20] As Jean-Michel Pelous discusses in his study of the representation of love in the early modern period,[21] a distinction was made between three main types: *amour tendre*, a 'pure, submissive ideal of love'[22] typified by the novels of Mlle de Scudéry; *amour galant*, a more libertine type famously depicted in Choderlos de Laclos's epistolary novel *Les Liaisons dangereuses* (1782); and *amour précieux*, a form of love that 'attempted to reconcile the previously divergent tendencies of puri-fying devotion and carefree self-indulgence' of the other two.[23]

A fascinating visual rendition of this coded discourse of love is the map of *amour précieux* known as the *Carte du Tendre* (*Map of the Tender*), which depicts and labels the different potential paths to love through a topography resembling the female reproductive system (Figure 1).[24] This famous allegori-cal map was created by Madelaine de Scudéry and later incorporated into the first volume of her ten-volume romance *Clélie* (1654–61). According to Franz Reitinger, the *Carte du Tendre* was 'the most successful example of an alle-gorical map ever printed [and was] conceived as a social game between 1653 and 1654'.[25] Joan DeJean describes it as a 'course in gallantry, giving men the woman's perspective on both the ways to win her heart [. . .] and the ways to lose it'.[26] As part of the social game, men seeking a romantic (if platonic) re-lationship would make personal copies of the map—presumably in order to learn how to play properly.[27]

In establishing the centrality of a woman's feelings and expectations, the *Carte du Tendre* and the *amour précieux* it codifies have been read as a poten-

---

[19] Cited in Kauffman, p. 95.

[20] The discourse of love was highly codified in early modern France, a practice with possible roots in troubadour love poetry, where the representation of feeling was not individualized, but rather conventionalized—expressed in what Gregory B. Stone terms a 'relatively universal [literary] dialect' (Stone, p. 15).

[21] Jean-Michel Pelous, *Amour Précieux, Amour Galant, 1654-75: essai sur la représentation de l'amour dans la littérature et la société mondaine* (Paris: Klincksieck, 1980).

[22] James Gaines, 'Review of *Amour Précieux, Amour Galant, 1654-75: essai sur la représentation de l'amour dans la littérature et la société mondaine* by Jean-Michel Pelous', *French Review*, 54 (1981), 734-35 (p. 734).

[23] Ibid.

[24] The illustrations may be viewed in full colour and in greater detail in the online version of this article, available at https://muse.jhu.edu/journal/822.

[25] Franz Reitinger, 'Mapping Relationships: Allegory, Gender, and the Cartographic Image in Eighteenth-Century France and England', *Imagomundi*, 51 (1999), 106–30 (p. 109).

[26] Joan DeJean, *Tender Geographies: Women and the Origins of the Novel in France* (New York: Columbia University Press, 1991), p. 57.

[27] Jeffrey Peters, *Mapping Discord: Allegorical Cartography in Early-Modern French Writing* (Ne-wark: University of Delaware Press, 2004), pp. 90–93.

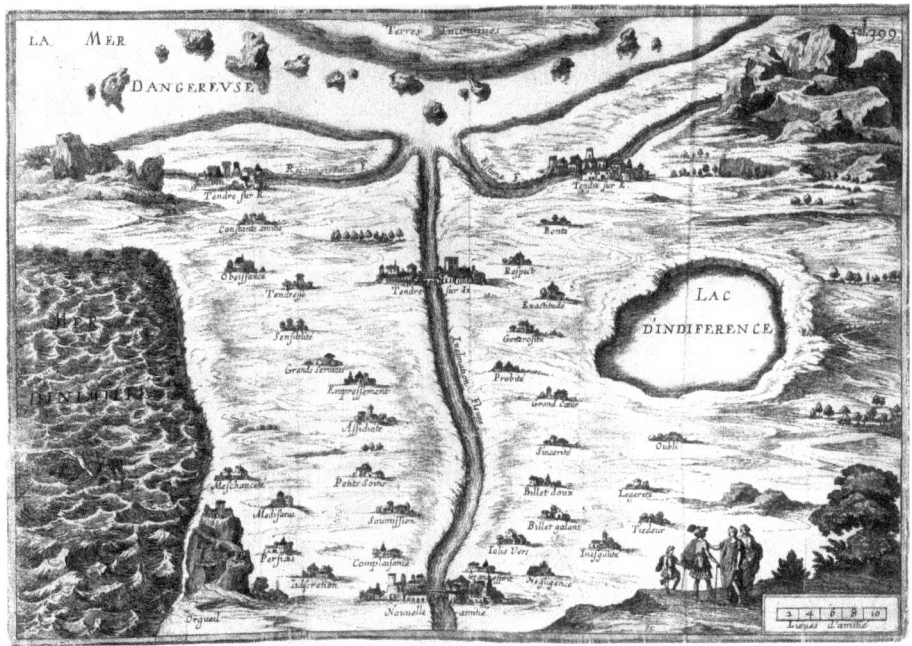

FIG. 1. Carte du Tendre
<https://commons.wikimedia.org/wiki/File:Carte_du_tendre.jpg>
Reproduced by permission

tially feminist turn that underscored the social power of the *salonnières*.[28] But from its original emphasis on refinement of thought, speech, and sentiments, *préciosité* was eventually pushed too far into affectation; thus, when the *Lettres portugaises* were published ten years later, their impact was due partly to the perceived authenticity of feeling they demonstrated. As Pelous maintains, the dazzling success of the *Lettres portugaises* allowed 'la societé mondaine de prendre conscience de tout ce que sa propre image de l'amour peut avoir d'insuffisant' ('French society to become aware of what its own image of love was lacking').[29]

Systematically and unequivocally, the *Lettres portugaises* affirm the superiority of Portuguese Love, typified by Mariane's feelings, over the *amour galant*, exemplified by her lover's. In her third letter, the nun states this discrepancy explicitly:

Vous n'avez regardé ma passion que comme une victoire, et votre cœur n'en a jamais été profondément touché. N'êtes-vous pas bien malheureux, et n'avez-vous pas bien

[28] See DeJean p. 89; Pamela Cheek, *Sexual Antipodes: Enlightenment, Globalization, and the Placing of Sex* (Stanford: Stanford University Press, 2003), p. 45.

[29] Jean-Michel Pelous, 'Une héroïne romanesque entre le naturel et la rhétorique: le langage des passions dans les *Lettres portugaises*', in *Le Roman au XVIIe siècle* (=*Revue d'Histoire Littéraire de la France*, 3–4 (May–August 1977)), pp. 554–63 (p. 296).

peu de délicatesse de n'avoir su profiter qu'en cette manière de mes emportements? Et comment est-il possible qu'avec tant d'amour je n'aie pu vous rendre tout à fait heureux? Je regrette pour l'amour de vous seulement les plaisirs infinis que vous avez perdus. [. . .] Si vous les connaissiez, vous trouveriez sans doute qu'ils sont plus sensibles que celui de m'avoir abusée, et vous auriez éprouvé qu'on est beaucoup plus heureux [. . .] quand on aime violemment que lorsqu'on est aimé.[30]

You have looked on my passion as a victory, and your heart was never profoundly touched by it. You must be quite unfortunate and lack delicacy of feeling to be unable to enjoy my affection except in this manner! And how is it possible that with so much love, I have been unable to make you happy? I regret, for your sake, the infinite pleasures you have missed. [. . .] If you knew them, no doubt you would realize they are much greater than the pleasure of conquering me, and you would have understood that one is much happier [. . .] when one loves violently, than when one is loved.

All the sentiments the nun expresses here became synonymous with Portuguese Love, but none more so than the greater importance of loving over being loved. And if, in courtly love, the male protagonist also values loving over being loved, in Portuguese Love the experience is feminized, and the woman is changed from object to agent in loving.[31] Indeed, the wish to keep her passion alive regardless of her lover's feelings becomes Mariane's main motivation for continuing the correspondence. Early in letter 4 she asks, 'et enfin, pourquoi ne m'avez-vous point écrit?' (p. 82: 'and after all why haven't you written?'). Six pages later, she closes the letter by admitting: 'J'écris plus pour moi que pour vous, je ne cherche qu'à me soulager' (p. 88: 'I write more for myself than for you; I simply attempt to comfort myself'). And in her last letter she confesses: 'J'ai éprouvé que vous m'étiez moins cher que ma passion' (p. 90: 'I felt that you were less dear to me than my passion').

Mariane's devotion to her passion and the letters that register it have come to emblematize Portuguese Love. Klobucka offers the most comprehensive discussion of the systematic fabrication of the myth of the Portuguese Nun, arguing that Portuguese scholars shaped Mariane into 'not merely [. . .] a fully formed mythical figure, but also [. . .] a nationally representative epitome

---

[30] Gabriel-Joseph de Lavergne de Guilleragues, *Lettres portugaises*, in *Lettres Portugaises, Lettres d'une Péruvienne et autres romans d'amour par lettres*, ed. by Bernard Bray and Isabelle Landy-Houillon (Paris: Flammarion, 1983), pp. 57–98 (p. 79). Further references to this edition are given after quotations in the text.

[31] For an analysis of *Lettres portugaises* that explores the force of a reading of the text that interprets the nun's 'active desire' as a feminist statement see Peggy Kamuf, *Fictions of Feminine Desire: Disclosures of Heloise* (Lincoln: University of Nebraska Press, 1982), pp. 44–66. Unlike Kauffman's, Kamuf's reading does not engage with Barthes's *Fragments*, but her emphasis on the nun's writing as cure evokes Barthes's section 'Aimer l'Amour' ('To Love Love'), where he writes: 'Bouffée de langage au cours de laquelle le sujet en vient à annuler l'objet aimé sous le volume de l'amour lui-même' (*Fragments*, p. 39: 'Explosion of language during which the subject manages to annul the loved object under the volume of love itself', *A Lover's Discourse*, p. 31). See also Manuela Mourão, *Altered Habits: Reconsidering the Nun in Fiction* (Gainesville: University Press of Florida, 2002), pp. 4–10.

of femininity and, by a uniquely Portuguese extension, of national identity in general' (p. 16). But while Mariane crystallized and came to embody the concept of Portuguese Love scrutinized here, the myth is not limited to her figure and, as we have seen, precedes it. The myth has become part of Portuguese literature and culture and has also influenced writers outside Portugal to affirm ideal love.[32]

British Refractions: Felicia Hemans and Elizabeth Barrett Browning

By the nineteenth century, facilitated in part by Romanticism's fascination with extreme feelings, Portuguese Love was inspiring multiple writers. In Britain, two of the century's most-read women poets, Felicia Hemans (1793–1835) and Elizabeth Barrett Browning (1806–61), engaged with this trope in works marked by their appreciable knowledge of Portuguese literature, and refracted both through their personal experiences and through their specific poetic projects: Hemans experimented with the interplay between form and content to contain excessive feeling, and Barrett Browning used a female speaker to revise the courtly tradition of love poetry while reaching for the trope of Portuguese Love to suggest its potential to expand the meaning of the personal.

Felicia Hemans's interest in Portuguese literature is clear from her study of Camões, whose tragic romantic life she was aware of, and whose work she had read in the original Portuguese and then translated: first, twenty of his love sonnets, which appeared in the 1818 volume *Translations of Camoens and Other Poets*; then, a section of the epic *The Lusiads*, which appeared posthumously in 1840. 'The Coronation of Inez de Castro' (1828), collected in her *Songs of the Affections, with Other Poems* (1830), further signals her interest in Camões and the myth he helped solidify in the section of his epic dedicated to the medieval lovers.[33]

'The Coronation of Inez de Castro' captures the extreme, often tragic, nature

[32] For a thorough account of the literary influence of the *Lettres portugaises* see François Jost, 'L'Évolution d'un genre: le roman epistolaire dans les lettres occidentales', in *Essais de littérature comparée* (Fribourg: Éditions Universitaires, 1968), pp. 89–180. See also Kauffman, who notes that 'from Rousseau to Rilke, critics have imitated the *Portuguese Letters*' (p. 19). She stresses the generic connecting thread between different types of amorous discourse—from authentic love letters (such as Charlotte Brontë's letters to Monsieur Héger) to poetic or fictional iterations (such as Ovid's *Heroides* and Richardson's *Clarissa*) (p. 315).

[33] Felicia Hemans, *Translations from Camoens, and Other Poets, with Original Poetry* (Oxford: J. Parker; London: J. Murray, 1818); Felicia Hemans, 'Appearance of the Spirit of the Cape to Vasco da Gama (Translated from the Fifth Book of the Lusiad of Camoens)', in *The Sceptic; A Tale of the Secret Tribunal; The Siege of Valencia; and Other Poems* (Edinburgh and London: William Blackwood, 1840), pp. 123–36; Felicia Hemans, 'The Coronation of Inez de Castro', in *Songs of the Affections, with Other Poems* (Edinburgh: William Blackwood; London: T. Cadell, 1830), pp. 30–35. See Ramos and Lousada on English translations of *The Lusiads*. Hemans's translations of Camões constitute a significant contribution to the dissemination of his work in Britain (Nozick

of Portuguese Love with its focus on Pedro's extravagant gesture: crowning Inês's exhumed corpse in a ceremony attended by the whole court. But Hemans's representation of this ultra-Romantic iteration of Portuguese Love is inflected by what Jason Rudy calls her 'aesthetic of restraint'.[34] Hemans's tendency to avoid excessive feeling and favour intellectual distance via highly structured verses had early been recognizable in her work (Rudy, pp. 548–51), but especially so in her 1828 volume *Records of Woman; with Other Poems*, where, Rudy maintains, 'every poem seems designed to interrogate passion' (p. 552). While not part of *Records of Woman*, 'The Coronation of Inez de Castro' was first published in the *Monthly Magazine* in the same year and demonstrates an analogous attempt at aesthetic restraint.[35]

A narrative poem in twelve octaves, each with six alternating rhymes (except in the first and third lines, which are unrhymed), 'The Coronation of Inez de Castro' juxtaposes this formal structure with a Gothic setting of excess suited to its subject. A series of contrasts in each of the first six stanzas establishes tension by emphasizing a number of clashing sensorial impressions: in stanza I, royal music and the tolling of funeral bells; in stanza II, the loud sound of many hurrying feet becoming gradually muffled by dread at the scene; in stanza III, an exhumed corpse sitting on a throne surrounded by radiant drapery that creates a 'gorgeous gloom'; in stanza IV, glittering jewels and brilliant lights highlighting the stillness of Inês's breast and pulse, and her 'stone-like rest'. All these contrasts culminate in the shiver of horror in stanzas V and VI: as the actual coronation is performed and the court files by the dead queen ''midst the hush profound' (v. 7) to kiss her hand, each person experiences the Gothic climax of a 'faint cold shuddering' (VI. 1).

Then, starting with stanza VII, Hemans modulates this Gothic intensity with two rhetorical questions that invite abstract, intellectual reflection on death's effect on the living:

> Death, Death! Canst *thou* be lovely
> Unto the eye of Life?

p. 340, n. 64), which suggests that during the Romantic period, educated British readers had some knowledge of his life and work—and through it, some notion of Portuguese Love. Hemans's 'The Coronation of Inez de Castro' would have been read within that context.

[34] Jason Rudy, 'Hemans' Passion', *Studies in Romanticism*, 45 (2006), 543–62. Rudy discusses how late Romantic and Victorian reviewers praised Hemans's reserve and control of emotion. He analyses the formal strategies she deploys to contain passion, and to develop an 'aesthetic of restraint' (p. 546). As he argues, this aesthetic 'arrive[d] just in time to relieve public exhaustion with Romantic overflow, Byronic cavorting, and gothic sensibility' (p. 546), and positioned Hemans well to appeal to the reviewers and readers of the time (p. 544). Further references to this essay are given after quotations in the text.

[35] Felicia Hemans, 'The Coronation of Inez de Castro', *Monthly Magazine*, 23 (1828), 513–15. Further references to the poem are to this edition and are given after quotations in the text.

> Is not each pulse of the quick high breast
>   With thy cold mien a strife?
>
> (VII. 1–4)

Even as they retain the Gothic mood, these lines invite rational consideration of the living's fear of, and reluctance to accept, death—suggesting that
Hemans is testing the principle she noted in a letter of 14 May 1823: 'there can
be no real grandeur [in poetry] unless *mind* is made the ruling power, and
its ascendancy asserted, even amidst the wildest storm of passion' (quoted in
Rudy, p. 549).

Accordingly, in the remaining five stanzas Hemans's emphasis is less on
Pedro's actual emotions as he watches the ceremony, and more on his attempt
to control them:

> And beside her stood in silence
>   One with a brow as pale,
> And white lips rigidly compress'd,
>   Lest the strong heart should fail.
>
> (VIII. 1–4)

Struggling to remain composed, Pedro looks everywhere but on Inês's dead
body, for 'It was not for him to bear' (IX. 8). As he leads the procession that
follows the corpse back to the tomb, his self-control lends a dignity and pathos
to his suffering that no Gothic excess could supplant:

> And tearlessly and firmly,
>   King Pedro led the train,—
> But his face was wrapt in his folding robe,
>   When they lower'd the dust again.
>
> (XII. 1–4)

Hemans's restrained treatment of the story of Pedro and Inês stands out
among its many depictions in Western European literature. Tracing in some
detail how different writers chose to emphasize different elements of the
story, Nozick notes that it 'has not received its full due' because 'its romantic,
idealistic qualities, and the pity, admiration, and horror it arouses call for epic
treatment' (p. 330). He pronounces Hemans's poem 'too nineteenth-century
for our taste' (p. 340), though granting it has 'a certain heavy beauty' (p. 340)
due to her choice of 'the macabre chapter of Ines [*sic*] coronation' (p. 340). The
'heavy beauty' in Hemans's 'macabre' choice, I would argue, precisely results
from her aesthetic experiment with tempering the tension of extreme emotion
with reason and self-control. The representation of Pedro's contained grief
pushed to the limit by the coronation of the exhumed body of his murdered
lover is a far more affecting depiction of an alliance of love and death than
the one evoked in the epigraph Hemans chose for her poem. Excerpted from

Mme de Staël's *De l'Allemagne*, the lines discussing Goethe's poem 'The Bride of Corinth' read: 'Tableau où l'Amour fait alliance avec la tombe; union redoutable de la mort avec la vie' ('Tableau where love makes an alliance with the grave; dreadful union of death with life').[36] By invoking Goethe's poem and its macabre coupling of love and death, Hemans evokes the ultra-Romantic quality which the story of Pedro and Inês lends to the notion of Portuguese Love; however, her own poem avoids Goethe's Gothic excess, and by its concluding lines—'Who call'd thee strong as Death, O Love? | *Mightier* thou wast and art!' (XII. 7–8)—love's triumph over the horror of death affirms the emotional intensity of Portuguese Love even as it modulates its Gothic aesthetic.

Like Hemans, Elizabeth Barrett Browning's first evocation of Portuguese Love was partly inspired by her knowledge of Camões, whose work sparked her interest in Portuguese literature.[37] On 17 November 1831 she wrote the first draft of the poem entitled 'Catarina to Camoens', which alludes to an episode of the Portuguese poet's tragic love life: the death of the woman he loved while he was exiled in India.[38] The poem was first published in *Graham's Magazine* in October 1843 after Barrett Browning revised it, and then again in her *Poems* (1844) after further revisions. That, as Neri stresses, it 'occupied EBB's imagination from the age of 25 till age 38',[39] and that it was one of Barrett Browning's 'most loved and often cited poems in the nineteenth century',[40] confirms the compelling nature of the trope for the author and her readership alike; it also confirms its continued dissemination in nineteenth-century British literature. Written before Barrett Browning and Robert Browning had met,[41] the poem became a favourite of his, and he often

[36] In Goethe's poem, the consummation of the couple's love happens after the death of the bride, whose ghost (or her animated corpse) joins him so that their union can happen.

[37] See Barbara Neri, 'A Lineage of Love: The Literary Bloodlines of Elizabeth Barrett Browning's *Sonnets from the Portuguese*', *Studies in Browning and his Circle*, 23 (2000), 50–69; Barbara Neri, 'Sonnet 1 and Sonnet 2 of Elizabeth Barrett Browning's *Sonnets from the Portuguese*: Setting the Stage for Divine Reunification', *Studies in Browning and his Circle*, 26 (2005), 41–53; and Barbara Neri, '"Cobridme de flores": (Un)Covering Flowers of Portuguese and Spanish Poets in *Sonnets from the Portuguese*', *Victorian Poetry*, 44 (2006), 571–83, for evidence of the influence of Camões and Portuguese literature in Barrett Browning's work.

[38] Elizabeth Barrett Browning, 'Catarina to Camoens', in *Sonnets from the Portuguese and Other Poems* (Garden City, NY: Doubleday, [n.d.]), pp. 285–90. Further references to the poem are to this edition and given after quotations in the text.

[39] Neri, 'Lineage', p. 52.

[40] Headnote to 'Catarina to Camoens', in Elizabeth Barrett Browning, *Elizabeth Barrett Browning: Selected Poems*, ed. by Marjory Stone and Beverly Taylor (Peterborough, Ontario: Broadview Press, 2009), p. 166.

[41] As is well known, after having corresponded with Robert Browning for a few months, Elizabeth Barrett, eminent poet and an invalid at 39, finally allowed him to visit her. In what remains one of the most famous love stories in nineteenth-century British literature, they fell in love and, because of her father's prohibition, eloped and moved to Italy. For biographical information, see Rebecca Stott, '"How do I Love Thee?": Love and Marriage', in *Elizabeth Barrett Browning*, ed. by Simon Avery and Rebecca Stott (New York: Longman, 2003), pp. 134–55; Julia

echoed it in his letters to her.[42] It also inspired both his nickname for her—'my little Portuguese'—and, somewhat obliquely, the title of the *Sonnets from the Portuguese* (1850).

The speaker of 'Catarina to Camoens' is Catarina de Ataide, a lady of the Portuguese court, whose beautiful eyes Camões praised in his poetry. In her analysis of the poem, Neri foregrounds the potential parallel between Catarina as Camões's muse, and Laura as Petrarch's and Beatrice as Dante's.[43] But more important for this argument is the poem's more explicit evocation of Portuguese Love: as with Mariane in the *Portuguese Letters*, in 'Catarina to Camoens' it is the woman who addresses the lover and laments his absence:

> On the door you will not enter,
> I have gazed too long: adieu!
> Hope withdraws her peradventure;
> Death is near me,—and not you!
> Come, O lover,
> Close and cover
> These poor eyes you called, I ween,
> 'Sweetest eyes were ever seen!'
> (I. 1–8, p. 285)

The refrain—'Sweetest eyes were ever seen!'—ends each of the nineteen stanzas with only occasional slight variations. It reads as a soothing utterance through which, stanza after stanza, Catarina reassures herself that he still loves her. By the end, the wish she utters encapsulates the selfless devotion that marks Portuguese Love:

> Should he ever be a suitor
> Unto sweeter eyes than mine,
> Sunshine gild them,
> Angels shield them,
> Whatsoever eyes terrene
> *Be* the sweetest HIS have seen.
> (XIX. 3–8, p. 290)

For not only has she accepted that she will not see him again, but she also wishes him future happiness in the love of someone else whose eyes will then become 'the sweetest HIS have seen' (XIX. 8, p. 290). The loftiness of the sentiment, emphasized by the invocation of the protection of angels, elevates her love to a climax of selflessness characteristic of Portuguese Love.

Markus, *Dared and Done: The Marriage of Elizabeth Barrett Browning and Robert Browning* (New York: Knopf, 1995); and *The Letters of Robert Browning and Elizabeth Barret Browning, 1845–1846*, ed. by Elvan Kintner, 2 vols (Cambridge, MA: Belknap and Harvard University Press, 1969).

[42] For example, in the letter of 18 October 1845 Browning alludes to the poem when he writes: 'Blessed eyes my eyes have been...' (Kintner, I, 241; Stone and Taylor, p. 167).

[43] Neri, 'Lineage', p. 57.

If in 'Catarina to Camoens' Barrett Browning already gestures to the trope of Portuguese Love, in the *Sonnets*, written for Robert Browning during the courtship period, and in the love letters, she fully embraces it, not only by foregrounding aspects of her personal experience that echo the trope, but also by reversing the tradition of courtly love poetry in choosing a female speaker for the entire sonnet sequence.[44] Indeed, in 'clear[ing] space in order to articulate the desiring female subject',[45] Barrett Browning distinctly evokes the Portuguese nun's affirmation of her desire. Originally, she had not intended to publish the sonnets; however, once Browning persuaded her to do so, she chose the title partly in the hope of hiding their personal nature by vaguely insinuating they were translations from Portuguese poetry. But because they are, in fact, autobiographical, there is a long tradition of reading them as an authentic record of the poet's emotions.[46] Other interpretations, however, have challenged such biographical readings by calling attention to Barrett Browning's sophisticated engagement with the sonnet tradition, as well as her artistic construction of the poems' authenticity.[47] Yet, I would argue, the construction of this effect precisely underscores Barrett Browning's deliberate choice to have the *Sonnets* 'continually announce that they authen-

---

[44] Critics have repeatedly acknowledged the importance of Barrett Browning's choice of a female speaker for the *Sonnets*. See Natalie M Houston, 'Affecting Authenticity: *Sonnets from the Portuguese* and *Modern Love*', *Studies in the Literary Imagination*, 35.2 (2002), 99–121 (p. 106); Tricia Lootens, *Lost Saints: Silence, Gender, and Victorian Canonization* (Charlottesville: University Press of Virginia, 1996), p. 119; and Dorothy Mermin, 'The Female Poet and the Embarrassed Reader: Elizabeth Barrett Browning's *Sonnets from the Portuguese*', *ELH*, 48 (1981), 351–67 (p. 351). Still, she was not the first woman poet who articulated 'romantic desire in a woman's voice' (Lootens, p. 119). Sappho immediately comes to mind as a precursor, the more so as she is the only woman poet mentioned by Barrett Browning in 'A Vision of Poets' (Lootens, p. 122). So do the *trobairitzi* (already mentioned), and so does Lady Mary Wroth, with her sequence of love sonnets *Pamphilia to Amphilanthus* (1621). But there is also the intriguing likelihood that a little-known female Portuguese poet and nun influenced her choice. Neri mentions Sister Maria do Ceo [*sic*] (1658–1753) as a potential influence after discovering her poem 'Cobridme de flores' ('Cover me with flowers') in Barrett Browning's 1832 reading notebook. Neri characterizes this 1741 'lyric from [a] longer work [. . .] consisting of prose and about twenty poems [as] a kind of moral tale about love from and about the perspective of a female pilgrim' ('Cobridme', p. 573).

[45] Houston, p. 106.

[46] See Elizabeth Barrett Browning and Robert Browning, *Sonnets from the Portuguese, Illuminated by the Brownings' Love Letters*, ed. by Julia Markus and William Peterson (New York: Harper Collins, 1996), for suggestive juxtapositions between poems and letters that foreground biographical elements in the poems.

[47] Houston, for example, discusses Victorian readers' perception of the authenticity of feelings in the *Sonnets* and its impact in obscuring the artistic construction of that authenticity (p. 109). In turn, Neri argues that they were far more than personal explorations of love: 'the "low ground" of her personal life is the source of the higher truths she would have us find in the *Sonnets*' ('Sonnets 1 and 2', p. 49). Neri has also argued that the collection's title is 'an attempt [. . .] to direct EBB's audience towards other levels of meaning and influence beyond the personal' which, Neri stresses, can be understood only if we read the *Sonnets* in the light of Barrett Browning's knowledge of Camões, Petrarch, and Dante, the classical lineage of her love poetry ('Lineage of Love', p. 50).

tically represent real emotions'[48]—which they often do without diminishing their artistry—and thus places them within the discourse of authenticity of feelings that, as we have seen, the *Lettres portugaises* made so central to Portuguese Love.

Looking at Barrett Browning's treatment, in both the couple's personal letters and her *Sonnets*, of her initial conviction that their love was impossible highlights how the trope of Portuguese Love surfaces in both and further contributes to the performance of authenticity that critics have noted. The letter that Robert Browning wrote to her on 23 May 1845 declaring his love after they first met has not survived because she asked that he never mention it again, stating in her answer later the same day:

You have said some intemperate things... fancies,—which you will not say over again, nor unsay, but *forget at once, & forever, having said at all,*—and which (so) will die out between you and me alone, like a misprint between you and the printer.... Now, if there should be one word of answer attempted to this,—or of reference; I must not.. I WILL not see you again—& you will justify me later in your heart..[49]

In his answer, Browning requested that she return his offending letter, 'the printer's error' (p. 77), and then burnt it.

Her initial hesitation is also treated in several sonnets, particularly sonnet 32, where she alludes to the moment Browning professed his love:

The first time the sun rose on thine oath
To love me, I looked forward to the moon
To slacken all those bonds which seemed too soon
And quickly tied to make a lasting troth.
Quick-loving hearts, I thought, may quickly loathe;
And, looking on myself, I seemed not one
For such a man's love![50]

The speaker worries that a love professed so quickly will not last, especially since she does not believe herself worthy of it. The sonnet's turn, however, resolves her doubts:

I did not wrong myself so, but I placed
A wrong on *thee*. For perfect strains may float
'Neath master-hands, from instruments defaced,—
And great souls, at one stroke, may do and doat.[51]

Through the conceit of the master singer who needs no perfect instrument

[48] Houston, pp. 108–9.
[49] Kintner, I, 72. Further references to this edition of the letters are given after quotations in the text.
[50] Barrett Browning, *Sonnets*, p. 394. 1–7.
[51] Barrett Browning, *Sonnets*, p. 394. 11–14.

to play perfect music, Barrett Browning artistically overcomes, even as she invokes, the impossible love element of Portuguese Love.

The already transgressive nature of their relationship was made more so by the necessity of eloping, given that her father had forbidden all his children to marry. Together with the origin of Browning's pet name for her and the title of her sonnet collection (including the influence of Camões's life and work on both), this transgressive element further anchors their relationship in the concept of Portuguese Love. If we add to this evidence Barrett Browning's allusions to the French tradition of *amour précieux*—which, as we have seen, Portuguese Love redefined for its own version of ideal love—it is hard to doubt that she was knowingly evoking the tradition being traced here. One such significant allusion can be found in her letter of 18 December 1845 to Browning: 'On point of the general affections, I have in thought applied to myself the words of Mme. de Staël... *"jamais je n'ai pas été aimée comme j'aime"* [I have never been loved as I love].' And she continues: 'The capacity of loving is the largest of my powers I think' (Kintner, I, 325).

Interestingly, this letter was written over two days, while she waited for Browning's uncharacteristically late reply to her previous letter, and it continued in a tone reminiscent of that of Mariane's letters: 'I am disappointed to-night—I expected a letter which does not come—& I felt sure of having a letter to-night.. unreasonably sure perhaps, which means doubly sure' (Kintner, I, 325). And two pages later: 'How I go on writing!—and you, who do not write at all!' (ibid., p. 327). Besides its oblique allusion to the early modern French code of love, then, this letter also evokes the poignant trope of the self-conscious letter-writer established in the *Lettres portugaises*: like Mariane, Barrett Browning self-consciously writes on as she waits in vain for a reply.

Earlier, in a letter of 12 November 1845, she had already gestured towards a crucial notion also established in the *Lettres portugaises*: love for love's sake. Referring to Browning's letter of 23 October 1845, in which he had told her 'I love you because I love you' (Kintner, I, 345), Barrett Browning writes:

The first moment in which I seemed to admit to myself in a flash of lightning the possibility of your affection for me being more than dream-work, the first moment was that when you intimated... that you cared for me not for a reason, but because you cared for me. (Kintner, I, 265)

Reportedly, this conviction had been with her long: as a young woman, she had argued with her sisters—in words that evoke the Portuguese nun's—that 'real love is love that has no cause at all for it, and the more wholly unreasonable, the better. It is love itself that counts and not the object of it.'[52] And

[52] Quoted in Frances Winwar, *The Immortal Lovers: Elizabeth Barrett Browning and Robert Browning* (New York: Harper and Row, 1950), pp. 49–50. Cf. Mariane: 'que ne me laissiez-vous ma passion?' (Guillerages, *Lettres portugaises*, p. 90: 'why did you not leave me my passion?').

in sonnet 14 she reiterates the belief that love should not be grounded in reason(s): 'If thou must love me, let it be for nought | Except for love's sake only'.[53] When it comes to love, the speaker continues, reasons other than love itself are superfluous and may even be detrimental; love must be its own reason for being: 'But love me for love's sake, that evermore | Thou may'st love on, through love's eternity.'[54] Echoing the words of the letter, the sonnet's female speaker echoes Barrett Browning—and both echo this key aspect of Portuguese Love.

The sincerity of Elizabeth Barrett Browning's treatment of love in the sonnets and letters to her husband and the fascinating ways in which her life and her love poems rework elements of the trope of Portuguese Love suggest that she deliberately embraced the ideal quality of the emotion to affirm the possibility of ideal love despite the oppressive pressures of the nineteenth-century ideologies of gender, love, and marriage that she denounced most famously in *Aurora Leigh* (1856), her epic poem about a woman artist. And her critique of the ideological construction of notions of female love as detrimental to women also surfaces in some of her ballads, in what Stott terms her 'ethics of love'.[55] Thus, the affirmation of ideal, authentic love in the sonnets and letters strongly suggests that the poet intuits the potential of Portuguese Love to resist and even transcend the culture's ideological deployment of the sentimental to raise selfless women. Certainly, as Neri suggests, it is important to 'bring all of our knowledge and more to our reading of her *Sonnets from the Portuguese* [. . . and] trace their roots back and forward in time to an ancient and ongoing discourse on Love'.[56] But as is clear from this analysis, the widely acknowledged personal nature of the poems—which some critics believe makes them sentimental and embarrassing[57]—expands in a different direction when we acknowledge their place in the context of the equally sophisticated, transgressive, and feminized literary tradition of Portuguese Love. In this context, the movement from the personal to the universal that Neri sees at work in the *Sonnets* lends them a subversive quality: they can be read as resisting the derision of the sentimental that has marked much of the critical attention they have historically received—and, by extension, as affirming Portuguese Love's triumph in the liminal space between sincere feeling and its ideological distortions.

---

[53] Barrett Browning, *Sonnets*, p. 386. 1–2.
[54] Ibid., p. 386. 13–14.
[55] Stott, 'How do I Love Thee?', pp. 134–55.
[56] Neri, 'Cobridme de flores', p. 58.
[57] See Mermin, esp. pp. 351–53 and 355–57; Lootens, esp. p. 120; and Houston, esp. p. 105, for discussions and critiques of this critical approach to the *Sonnets*.

Portuguese Refractions: Almeida Garrett and Camilo Castelo Branco

Given their international success, the *Sonnets from the Portuguese* arguably constitute one of the nineteenth century's most influential vehicles for the dissemination of the myth of Portuguese Love and its potential as a counter-discourse of genuine feeling. In Portugal, at the time, the two best-known works inflected by the concept offer iterations that foreground instead the myth's potentially 'deforming' effects (especially because their male authors endorse patriarchal notions of ideal femininity).[58] The two novels—the formally innovative *Viagens na Minha Terra* (*Travels in my Homeland*, 1846) by Almeida Garrett, and the ultra-Romantic *Amor de Perdição* (*Doomed Love*, 1862) by Camilo Castelo Branco—became the two most iconic love stories in nineteenth-century Portuguese literature.[59] The writers approach the myth of Portuguese Love in different ways: Garrett systematically complicates it through the use of irony, while Castelo Branco explicitly embraces it by sounding a note of sincerity. Crucially, though, while both novels perform an ideological distortion as they exalt female devotion and constancy, they also ultimately affirm ideal love through their assertion of the intensity of the Portuguese national love temperament.

Unlike Castelo Branco, who, as a second-generation Portuguese Romantic, openly embraces intensity of emotion, Garrett consistently uses the first-person narrator recounting his travels and commenting ironically on the shortcomings of Portuguese society to undercut the Romantic intensity of the framed narrative of the love story.[60] Nevertheless, Garrett does juxtapose

[58] In *Mythologies*, Barthes uses the term 'deform' to refer to ideological distortion. See Roland Barthes, *Mythologies*, trans. by Annette Lavers (New York: Hill and Wang, 1972), p. 122.

[59] Almeida Garrett, *Viagens na Minha Terra* (Lisbon: Editores Reunidos, 1994); Camilo Castelo Branco, *Amor de Perdição* (Lisbon: Vercial, 2017). In nineteenth-century Portugal, the popularity of Portuguese Love was reignited by the appearance of the first Portuguese translations of the *Lettres portugaises*—Filinto Elísio, *Cartas Portuguesas*, in *Obras*, vol. x (Paris: A. Bobée, 1819); José Maria de Sousa Botelho, *Cartas Portuguesas* (Paris: Firmin Didot, 1825)—and by the ensuing debates about the identity of the Portuguese nun (Klobucka, pp. 12–14); as a result, the myth was echoed in many other works of different degrees of literary interest.

[60] Castelo Branco's irony shows instead in the Preface to the fifth edition of the novel (*Amor de Perdição*, Quinta edição prefaciada e revista pelo autor (Porto e Braga: Livraria Moré, 1879)). Written several years after the novel was first published, when Realism was the dominant literary movement, the Preface satirizes the rejection of the sentimental that accompanied the new literary taste: 'O *Amor de Perdição*, visto à luz eléctrica do criticismo moderno, é um romance romântico, declamatório, com [. . .] ideias celeradas que chegam a tocar no desaforo do sentimentalismo' (p. 15: 'Seen in the electric light of modern criticism, *Amor de Perdição* is a romantic and declamatory novel with [. . .] appalling ideas that nearly reach an insulting sentimentalism'), writes Castelo Branco, mock-regretting having come of age as a writer before the hegemony of Realism. 'Faz-me tristeza pensar eu que floreci nesta futilidade da novela quando as dores da alma podiam ser descritas sem grande desaire da gramática e da decência' (p. 16: 'It makes me sad to think I flourished in this futility of the genre when the soul's pains could be described without much failure of grammar or decency'), he adds, predicting that if, through metempsychosis, he could return to life in the twenty-first century, he might be delighted 'de ver outra vez as lágrimas em

the differences between the English and Portuguese national love temperaments to underscore the Portuguese superior depth of feeling—especially in
a passage in which Carlos, the protagonist, explains the English concept of
flirting:

> *To flirt* é um verbo inocente que se conjuga ali entre os dois sexos, e [. . .] não obriga a
> nada, não tem consequências, começa-se, acaba-se, interrompe-se, adia-se, continua-se
> ou descontinua-se à vontade e sem comprometimento. [. . .] Para quem nasceu naquilo,
> não é perigoso, para mim degenerou, breve, aquela plácida sensação em mais profundo
> sentimento. (pp. 327–28)

> *To flirt* is an innocent verb conjugated there between the sexes, and it [. . .] demands
> nothing, has no consequences, it starts, it ends, it is interrupted, postponed, continued
> or discontinued at ease and without commitment. [. . .] To those born to it, it poses no
> danger, but to me, that placid sensation soon became deep feeling.

Suffused with irony, the passage nonetheless affirms the superiority of Portuguese Love as it pronounces the English custom of 'flirting' inconsequential
to Carlos's English friends, but not to him. Yet, if capable of deep feeling, Carlos is incapable of constancy. This essential characteristic of Portuguese Love
is rather modelled by the female protagonists: Joaninha in *Viagens* and Teresa
Albuquerque in *Amor de Perdição*. The lives of both women (who are barely
sixteen years old) are represented as entirely circumscribed by, and devoted
to, their love for Carlos and Simão Botelho, respectively. In keeping with the
excess of feeling typical of many Romantic works, Joaninha and Teresa die
because their love ultimately proves impossible.

Further highlighting the intensity of Portuguese Love are the contrasting
representations of the two women who rival the protagonists for the love of
the heroes: Georgina, an upper-class English woman, in *Viagens*; and Mariana,
a lower-class Portuguese woman, in *Amor de Perdição*. In *Viagens*, Georgina,
whom Carlos loved before falling in love with his cousin Joaninha, nurses him
after he is wounded while fighting in the Portuguese civil war but renounces
him once she learns of his new romantic attachment. While Georgina's renunciation is represented as painful, her noble determination not to stand in
Joaninha's way is shored up by her contained, controlled English character:
she retires from the world to a convent she founded with her fortune. By
contrast, in *Amor de Perdição*, Mariana loves Simão without hope. She nurses
him after he is wounded in a fight during the attempt to kidnap Teresa from
the convent in which she had been imprisoned, and when he is sent into exile
for killing Teresa's cousin in that fight, Mariana accompanies him aboard
the ship. Her selfless devotion is represented as noble, and when—partly due

---

moda [. . .] e esta 5ª edição do *Amor de Perdição* quase esgotada' (p. 16: 'to find tears back in
fashion [. . .] and this fifth edition of *Amor de Perdição* nearly sold out').

to the grief of leaving Teresa behind—Simão does not recover and dies, she jumps overboard embracing his corpse.

In both novels, the myth of Portuguese Love 'deforms', to use Barthes's term, the patriarchal, oppressive nature of female constancy and devotion: repeatedly, these qualities are elevated and represented as the natural corollary of female love, naturalizing for women ideals of selflessness and sacrifice for a lover who offers little or nothing in return. In *Amor de Perdição*, this ideological distortion is mitigated by the intensity of Simão's love for Teresa: he, too, dies at least in part due to an excess of feeling. But in *Viagens*, the tragic end met by Joaninha—who 'enlouqueceu e morreu' (Garrett, p. 354: 'went mad and then died')—so appallingly contrasts with the turn taken by Carlos's life—'engordou, enriqueceu e é barão [. . .] e vai ser deputado qualquer dia' (ibid.: 'he got fat, got rich and is a baron [. . .] soon to become a member of parliament')—that the myth of Portuguese Love, always strongly feminized, is in this novel entirely so, and easily reads as patriarchal distortion.

The contrast between the conflicting workings of the myth in these novels and its more straightforwardly sincere function in Elizabeth Barrett Browning's *Sonnets from the Portuguese* draws attention to the ambiguity that myth always carries.[61] But it also confronts us with the imperative of going beyond traditional demystifying readings and acknowledging that myths can develop 'a symbolic vitality all their own' (Klobucka, p. 20). This essay has shown that, by the nineteenth century, this was the case with Portuguese Love. In Britain, Elizabeth Barrett Browning certainly intuited the myth's broader, sincere aspiration and, as we saw, reached for it repeatedly in her more personal writings. In Portugal, in *Viagens na Minha Terra* and *Amor de Perdição*, while the myth undeniably performs its narrower ideological function of promoting oppressive patriarchal notions of ideal femininity, it also suggestively reaches beyond it, as demonstrated by the enduring allure of the novels' iconic lovers.

Facilitated by a long process of dissemination in the culture, and shored up by repeated literary iterations that precede these novels, the myth's potential to transcend the narrower limits of its ideological function surfaces clearly. Eduardo Lourenço helps us further understand this potential by making a connection between Portuguese Love and *saudade*—a word which the Portuguese claim to be untranslatable because it refers to an emotion believed to be singularly Portuguese (a combination of nostalgia and longing). Although Lourenço asserts that *saudade* refers to a universal experience, he believes that 'before it became the myth which [. . .] shapes it into a hagiographic-patriotic role, *saudade* was nothing more than the expression of the excess

---

[61] The ideological implications of the myth's distorting effects, as well as readings that reject the way it disempowers the feminine by bolstering patriarchal ideologies of gender and sex, have already been explored by feminist readings of the *Portuguese Letters*. See e.g. Kamuf and Kauffman, and also Barreno and others, further explored below.

of love towards everything that deserves to be loved'.[62] In other words, to explain the singularly Portuguese emotion of *saudade*, Lourenço reaches for a combination of myth, patriotism, and excess of love, which, as we have seen, are also part of the combination that makes up the concept of Portuguese Love discussed here.

The Triumph of Portuguese Love

Anchored in a brooding and fatalistic national character that historically embraced and cultivated a depth of passion that defied social norms, Portuguese Love found fertile ground to thrive in Portuguese culture and became a myth.[63] Admittedly, there have also been challenges to it—most notably in the text *As Três Marias: Novas Cartas Portuguesas* (*The Three Marias: New Portuguese Letters*).[64] A feminist critique mounted by three Portuguese women writers known as the three Marias—Maria Isabel Barreno, Maria Teresa Horta, Maria Velho da Costa—and first published in 1974 (the same year as the revolution that overthrew the Portuguese fascist regime, and a year before the country began the process of granting independence to its African colonies), this collection of poems, short fictional narratives, and letters denounced the patriarchal structures of Portuguese society and its oppressive political regime. As the title indicates, the writers chose to evoke the myth of Portuguese Love by engaging with its best-known emblems—the Portuguese nun and her letters—in order to denounce how the text's exaltation of female love and devotion deformed the oppressive nature of the ideals of love it fostered. In dramatizing a multiplicity of voices, conflating different genres, and engaging intertextually with literary tradition (by, for example, pointedly including love letters from women left behind to their men fighting in the colonial wars), the authors systematically uncover the far-reaching scope of the myth's distorting potential. Aptly, as a gesture of defiance against an oppressive political regime shored up by nationalist and patriarchal ideologies that reinforced women's docility, their work complicates the figure of the Portuguese nun rather than attempting a recuperative reading of her affirmation of her desire. The writers

[62] Eduardo Lourenço, 'Tempo Português', in *Portugal como Destino Seguido de Mitologia da Saudade* (Lisbon: Gradiva, 1999), pp. 87–94 (p. 91).
[63] See Klobucka's discussion of the analogous process of mythification of the Portuguese Nun, including the nationalist impulse behind it (pp. 19–22). See also Boaventura de Sousa Santos, 'Onze Teses por Ocasião de Mais uma Descoberta de Portugal', *Luso-Brazilian Review*, 29 (1992), 97–113, whom she cites, for a critique of the 'mythic excess' of interpretations of Portuguese society and culture (pp. 97–98). Sousa Santos's critique can be read, at least in part, as a response to Lourenço's sustained analysis of the Portuguese character in Eduardo Lourenço, *O Labirinto da Saudade: Psicanálise Mítica do Destino Português* (Lisbon: Dom Quixote, 1978); and in *Portugal como Destino Seguido de Mitologia da Saudade*.
[64] Maria Isabel Barreno and others, *As Três Marias: Novas Cartas Portuguesas* (Columbia, LA: Readers International, 1994).

became an international cause célèbre when their work was censored and removed from circulation, and they were accused of 'abuse of the freedom of the press' and 'outrage to public decency'.[65]

Still, the mythification of the Portuguese love temperament has persisted. Nurtured and celebrated as the culture continues to claim it as a defining characteristic, it offers the Portuguese a special identity repeatedly rehearsed in a variety of literary and other cultural texts that reaffirm its allure. In 1994, for example, 'Love in Portugal', an exhibition at the Portuguese National Library focusing on 'some amorous couples of particular significance in the Portuguese tradition',[66] was introduced by Machado de Sousa in an opening address entitled *...como é diferente o amor em Portugal!* (*...how different is love in Portugal!*) that demonstrated yet again the cultural impact of this mythic inheritance.[67]

Even more recently, *The Triumph of Portuguese Love* (2004) by Portuguese poet, essayist, and fiction writer Mário Cláudio confirms that the myth remains a recurrent cultural focus in the country and continues to strike a chord.[68] Cláudio's short historical fictions revisit Pedro and Inês, Camões, Mariane, and several other famous lovers in the pantheon of Portuguese Love, at once reaffirming and perpetuating their centrality to Portuguese identity.[69] Suggestively, in her introduction to the book, poet Agustina Bessa-Luís foregrounds the work's evocation of the loftiest attributes of Portuguese Love—the self-exaltation, the sublimity of aspiration, and even the spiritual dimension

[65] Helen R. Lane, 'Translator's Preface', *The Three Marias: New Portuguese Letters* (New York: Doubleday, 1975), pp. 7–130 (p. 7). For further information, including a concise discussion of the critical reception of *New Portuguese Letters* and its importance as a feminist intervention, see Kauffman, pp. 307–11.

[66] Cited in Klobucka, p. 94.

[67] The title of the exhibition's opening address is a quotation from the 1902 play *A Ceia dos Cardeais* (*The Supper of the Cardinals*) by Júlio Dantas. As Klobucka points out, the exhibition included both historical and fictitious couples who were considered emblems of Portuguese Love (e.g. Pedro and Inês, as well as Carlos and Joaninha, discussed above) and who, therefore, belonged in the 'gallery of nationally celebrated lovers' (Klobucka, p. 94).

[68] Mário Cláudio, *O Triunfo do Amor Português* (Lisbon: Circulo de Leitores, 2004).

[69] The title *The Triumph of Portuguese Love* ironically evokes the work of Rocha Martins, who, between c. 1910 and c. 1930, published dozens of popular historical novels in a series entitled *Coleção História* (*Collection History*) with two subsets, including one entitled *Os Grandes Amores de Portugal* (*Portugal's Great Loves*). The novels *Soror Mariana* (i.e. the Portuguese nun), *O Sangue de Inês de Castro* (*The Blood of Inês de Castro*), *Pecados de Paixão* (*Sins of Passion*), *A paixão de Camilo* (*Camilo's Passion*), etc., demonstrate how widespread the notion of Portuguese Love remained at the time, and how its mythification was intertwined with the nationalist fervor that shored up the Estado Novo (New State), the fascist regime developing during that period. Yet, as Fredric Jameson, among others, has stressed, the subjects of ideology need not necessarily submit to ideological adherence, and may rather allow their proto-political impulses to be rechannelled (Fredric Jameson, *The Political Unconscious: Narrative as a Socially Symbolic Act* (Ithaca, NY: Cornell University Press, 1981), p. 287). The sincerity of sentiment retained in the iterations of Portuguese Love explored here, I would argue, confirms this conviction.

of ideal love whose derision Barthes lamented in *Fragments*.[70] Importantly, if such derision may be suspected in *The Triumph of Portuguese Love*, if the stories do not necessarily pre-empt an ironic reading, they nonetheless perform a persistent affirmation of the myth by a return to the same couples, and a mesmerizing repetition of the same love stories: in short, a reiteration of the potentially transgressive power of a sincere, idealized, transcultural amorous tradition. In the tale 'A Severa e o Conde de Marialva' ('Severa and the Count of Marialva'), for example, the heroine is characterized as one 'que amara mais, muito mais, do que o que fora amada' ('who had loved more, much more, than she had been loved').[71] In echoing the words of Mme de Staël, earlier echoed by Elizabeth Barrett Browning, this story adds another link to the transcultural chain of Portuguese Love and confirms Barthes's insight regarding the power of sincere love to resist derision and, ultimately, to free the amorous subject from the detriments of the repression of the sentimental that Kauffman exposed.

Paradoxically, it is the Portuguese people's latent nostalgia for the country's long-gone 'heroic' aspirations—nostalgia that the myth was once invoked to stoke—that suggests that we read it now as a symbolic affirmation of an idealized identity. Indeed, Portuguese Love was once appropriated by a nationalist discourse that unabashedly peddled nostalgia for the country's 'glorious past' as ideological compensation for its inglorious present. A people who have long felt irrelevant to History, having remained for centuries at the periphery of Europe, and who have not yet reckoned with their role in the Atlantic slave trade or with being the last Western colonial power, the Portuguese may be clinging to the myth that they love more and better as their last bastion of national pride.[72] The names of Pedro and Inês, Camões, Mariane, and Severa will continue to resonate in the culture because Portuguese Love's hold on the collective imagination, sustained through the centuries by repeated iterations, now functions symbolically to unify the collective Portuguese identity as that of a people who are exceptional because they feel exceptionally. As we saw, the allure of this idealized amorous identity was felt strongly enough in other cultures to be appropriated or emulated in numerous texts well beyond national borders.

[70] Agustina Bessa-Luís, 'Introdução', in Cláudio, *O Triunfo do Amor Português*, pp. 11–20 (pp. 12–14).

[71] Mário Cláudio, 'A Severa e o Conde de Marialva', in *O Triunfo do Amor Português*, pp. 175–93 (p. 192).

[72] See Sousa Santos; and Klobucka (esp. pp. 20–58) for a discussion of Portugal's semi-peripheral position in Western Europe and its impact on Portugal's imperial identity. See also Margarida Calafate Ribeiro, 'Empire, Colonial Wars and Post-Colonialism in the Portuguese Contemporary Imagination', *Portuguese Studies*, 18 (2002), 132–214, a study of twentieth-century Portuguese literary representations of different perspectives of the country's five centuries of empire. Following Sousa Santos, she argues that for Portugal, imagining itself at the centre remains connected to its position as a former empire (p. 134) and, indeed, 'represents a longing for [its] old empires' (p. 136).

FIG. 2. 'More Love Letters, Please!', sticker produced by 'Positive Sticker Activism' <https://spaceutopian.com/>: postbox, Lisbon, May 2023. Photograph by Julie Sorge Way, reproduced by permission

Today, Portuguese Love and its potential for resisting irony persist. So does its transcultural reach, which signals its success in overcoming the prohibition of socially unsanctioned emotions noted by Barthes in his claim that 'l'histoire d'amour [est] asservie à l'opinion générale qui déprécie toute force excessive et veut que le sujet réduise lui-même le grand ruissellement imaginaire [. . .] à une crise douloureuse, morbide, dont il faut guérir' (*Fragments* p. 11: 'the love story [is] subjugated to the [. . .] general opinion which disparages any excessive force and wants the subject to reduce the great imaginary current [. . .] to a painful, morbid crisis of which he must be cured', *A Lover's Discourse* p. 7). Eruptions of resistance to this cure, I have been arguing, can be read as traces of Portuguese Love or, to borrow Barthes's subtle insight, as 'le lieu, si exigu soit-il, d'une affirmation' (*Fragments* p. 5: 'the site, however exiguous, of an affirmation', *A Lover's Discourse*, p. 1). A perfect example of such resistance is a sticker that could be seen affixed to a postbox in Lisbon in the spring of 2023. It reads 'MORE LOVE LETTERS, PLEASE!' (Figure 2).

Anchored, then, by Barthes's insight, my conviction that the myth 'reso-nates a universal value'[73] seems justified—not in the sense that Portuguese Love represents a transhistorical or transcultural concept of ideal love, but rather that even as the notion of ideal love has evolved and changed at dif-ferent times in different cultures, Portuguese Love has remained recognizable as ideal because it affirms the power of a counter-discourse of genuine feeling discussed above. And even though in Portugal the myth once had strong implications of nationalism, the long history of its appropriations outside Portuguese literature also more widely affirms the power of the sentimental and its representations in contemporary culture. If so, the *New York Times*'s 'Modern Love' may well constitute its most recent, continuing affirmation. Emulating Portuguese Love's freeing potential, 'Modern Love' seems to echo its sincerity and assert its symbolic power, even while acknowledging the ten-sion between unfettered feeling and its open derision that Barthes so poetically explored—a double gesture which recognizes that, indeed, 'it's complicated'.

OLD DOMINION UNIVERSITY   MANUELA MOURÃO

[73] Jameson, p. 288.

THE NATION ON TRIAL:
TENGIZ ABULADZE'S *REPENTANCE* (1987)
AND CHRISTIAN FROSCH'S *MURER* (2018)

This article compares two films, both of which thematize historical events which were, for a long time, absent from the screen. In his taboo-breaking *Repentance* (USSR, 1987),[1] Georgian director Tengiz Abuladze (1924–1994) reflects on the Stalinist purges of the 1930s from the vantage point of the glasnost era. The film presents an allegorical and surrealist show trial of Ketevan Barateli, who repeatedly digs up the corpse of despotic mayor Var-lam Aravidze, thereby seeking to avenge her parents, whom he persecuted and murdered. Aravidze's corpse stands for the repressed past, which Bara-teli refuses to leave buried, instead performatively bringing this past to light, prompting a long-overdue process of repentance and reckoning with Stalinism in her Georgian town. This also resonated beyond the screen. The historical drama *Murer* (Austria, 2018),[2] directed by Christian Frosch (1966–), recon-structs the 1963 trial and acquittal in Austria of 'the Butcher of Vilnius', Nazi war criminal Franz Murer (sentenced to twenty-five years' hard labour under Soviet jurisdiction in 1948, but released in 1955 under the Austrian State Treaty). From a contemporary vantage point, the film presents Murer's trial as a missed opportunity for post-war Austria to face up to its Nazi past, due to the vested political and geopolitical interests of the Cold War, as well as hangovers from the Nazi era. Drawing on scholarship related to the courtroom film genre as well as on Shoshana Felman's ground-breaking 2002 work *The Juridical Unconscious*, which foregrounds 'the interaction of law and trauma in the twentieth century',[3] I will show how both Abuladze's and Frosch's films, through their courtroom scenes, put the nation on trial and seek to confront their audiences with hitherto repressed aspects of their countries' historical legacies.

Both *Repentance* and *Murer* can be termed landmark films, which drew significant interest from home and international audiences as well as critical acclaim at the time of their release. Abuladze's *Repentance* won the Special Jury Prize at the 1987 Cannes international film festival. Meanwhile, in the Soviet Union, following preview screenings, the film was described in su-perlative terms by the Soviet literary critic and essayist Vladimir Lakshin as

---

[1] *Monanieba/Pokayaniye/Repentance*, dir. by Tengiz Abuladze (Georgia-Film Studio, 1987) [Rus-cico DVD, OCLC No. 1152844023; ASIN No. B001AQ0T1S]. Henceforth, timestamps from this film appear in parentheses in the text.

[2] *Murer*, dir. by Christian Frosch (Filmladen, 2018) [Filmladen DVD No. X07270172-8; EAN 9120026072971]. Henceforth, timestamps from this film appear in parentheses in the text.

[3] Shoshana Felman, *The Juridical Unconscious: Trials and Traumas in the Twentieth Century* (Cambridge, MA: Harvard University Press, 2002), p. 3.

Modern Language Review, 119 (2024), 456–75, doi:10.1353/mlr.00002
© Modern Humanities Research Association 2024

'a significant milestone for Soviet cinema and for cinema everywhere' and as 'a spiritual earthquake'.[4] Abuladze, a long-established film-maker by that point, began working on the script for *Repentance*, the third film of his trilogy on Georgian history,[5] in 1981 and finished the script in 1982. The film was shot over five months and completed in December 1984, whereupon it was shown only once on Soviet Georgian television, thanks to the efforts of Eduard Shevardnadze, then leader of Soviet Georgia, who supported Abuladze's project.[6] The film was then shelved, Abuladze reportedly keeping the only copy of it under his bed because he was so scared that it might be confiscated.[7] Following the coming to power of Mikhail Gorbachev in 1985 and the advent of glasnost (openness) and perestroika (reform) in the late Soviet period, the film could finally be released in the Soviet Union in January 1987. Glasnost extended to discussion of the era of Stalinist purges in the Soviet Union (1937–38), which *Repentance* focuses on—a period marked by mass arrests, executions, and deportations of any dissenting voices, leading to the deaths of an estimated 950,000–1.2 million people, though some historians put the figure far higher.[8] *Repentance* was met with packed domestic cinema audiences and critical acclaim, and has been described by Woll and Youngblood as 'the movie that came to symbolize the glasnost era for Soviet citizens'.[9] In its thematization of the long-repressed Stalinist past *Repentance* is, to this day, hailed as one of a handful of the most significant films of the glasnost era, and in 2021 it was screened in the 'Cannes Classics' section at the Cannes film festival.[10]

Murer: Anatomie eines Prozesses (*Murer: Anatomy of a Trial*), Frosch's fifth fiction feature and most successful film to date, premiered at the Diagonale Film Festival on 13 March 2018 in Graz, and won the festival's foremost prize (Großer Spielfilm-Preis). The film also went on to win the Special Jury Prize at the 2018 Viennale, as well as Best Feature Film at the Austrian Film

[4] Vladimir Lakshin, 'Neproshchaiushchaia pamiat'' ('Unforgiving Memory'), *Moskovskie novosti*, 30 November 1986, as cited in Josephine Woll and Denise J. Youngblood, *Repentance* (London and New York: I. B. Tauris, 2001), p. 93.

[5] The first two parts of the trilogy, *The Prayer* and *The Wishing Tree*, were released in 1968 and 1977 respectively.

[6] Woll and Youngblood, pp. 90–91.

[7] Richard Taylor, 'Obituary: Tengiz Abuladze', *The Independent*, 10 March 1994 <https://www.independent.co.uk/news/people/obituary-tengiz-abuladze-1428146.html> [accessed 8 February 2024].

[8] For a discussion of the various figures estimated by historians, based on NKVD statistics and Gulag deaths, see Michael Ellman, 'Soviet Repression Statistics: Some Comments', *Europe–Asia Studies*, 54 (2002), 1151–72 (p. 1155).

[9] Woll and Youngblood, p. 2.

[10] '"Repentance" at the 2021 Cannes Film Festival', *Georgian Journal*, 29 June 2021 <https://georgianjournal.ge/culture/37174-repentance-at-the-2021-cannes-film-festival.html> [accessed 8 February 2024].

Awards in 2019.[11] The Austrian writer Robert Menasse described *Murer* as the Austrian version of Robert Mulligan's 1962 film adaptation of Harper Lee's *To Kill a Mockingbird*, which is regarded as a key work in the trial film genre.[12] Frosch's film, through its subtitle, alludes to a further landmark film of the trial film genre, Austrian émigré Otto Preminger's *Anatomy of a Murder* (1959). However, in Frosch's film it is not the crime, or multiple crimes, that are dissected in the courtroom, but the justice process itself, and specifically the justice process in post-war Austria. Following the Second World War, Austria fashioned an image of itself as having been 'the first victim of Hitlerite aggression' that had to be liberated from German domination, as the Moscow Declaration issued by the Allies in 1943 terms it,[13] rather than having played a central role, as 'Nazis made in Austria', in the crimes of the Third Reich.[14] The 'first victim' myth would only begin to be unravelled during the course of the so-called Waldheim Affair (1986–88)—the controversy surrounding former United Nations General Secretary Kurt Waldheim's successful campaign for the Austrian presidency, during which it emerged that he had lied about his military record and knowledge of war crimes.

The trial film genre, which typically centres on a criminal trial by jury, is almost as old as cinema itself, providing a stage upon which past personal and collective traumas can be confronted, and 'offer[ing] filmmakers a chance to dramatize and personalize divisive issues, such as racial tensions'.[15] Trial films offer potential for high drama, as 'there are always plenty of conflicts between lawyers, lawyers and witnesses, lawyers and clients, or lawyers and judges'.[16] Trial by jury, which has been a constituent feature of criminal law cases in the 'Anglo-American trial tradition',[17] also provides dramatic suspense; part of the fascination that trial films provide resides in the jury delivering its climactic verdict. Due to the dominance of Hollywood, studies

---

[11] See 'Murer — Anatomie eines Prozesses/Murer—Anatomy of a Trial, Christian Frosch', *Austrian Films* <https://www.austrianfilms.com/film/murer_anatomie_eines_prozesses> [accessed 8 February 2024].

[12] *Murer*, DVD sleeve.

[13] 'The Moscow Declaration; October 1943. Joint Four-Nation Declaration', *The Avalon Project: Documents in Law, History and Diplomacy, Yale Lillian Goldmann Law Library* <http://avalon.law.yale.edu/wwii/moscow.asp> [accessed 8 February 2024].

[14] 'Nazis Made in Austria' is the title used in Germany and Austria for the documentary *Le Nazisme, une aventure autrichienne*, dir. by Barbara Necek (Cinétévé and ARTE France, 2022). The documentary focuses on the pivotal role of Austrians at all levels of the Nazi war machine and administration.

[15] Paul Bergman and Michael Asimow, *Reel Justice: The Courtroom Goes to the Movies* (Kansas: Andrews McMeel, 2006), p. xix.

[16] Ibid.

[17] Austin Sarat, Jessica Silbey, and Martha Merrill Umphrey, 'The Pleasures and Possibilities of Trial Films', in *Trial Films on Trial: Law, Justice, and Popular Culture*, ed. by Sarat, Silbey, and Umphrey (Tuscaloosa: University of Alabama Press, 2019), pp. 1–16 (p. 2).

on the trial film typically deal with American films.[18] However, the defini-
tions and cornerstones of the trial film are easily transferable to every cultural
context as attested by a number of recent survey articles, situated within the
interdisciplinary field of 'law and film'.[19]

Other key features of the genre have been highlighted by scholars: 'trials
are by their very nature public performances that bring past events to life
in the courtroom', which especially lends them to the cinematic medium.[20]
Moreover, the effect of trial films, including their tendency to put the spectator
in the position of juror, and to include the events and atmosphere surrounding a trial, may be that 'judgment of a defendant is transmuted into judgment
of a people or time or culture'.[21] This is precisely what we observe in the case
of the two films under consideration in this article, both of which present
missed opportunities for adequately confronting the past and the legacy of
totalitarianism, in the Soviet Union under glasnost and in post-war Austria.

Murer may be categorized as one of a number of recent German-language
trial films that look back on the paltry efforts to bring Nazi criminals to justice
in the early decades of the post-war era. Notable examples include *Hannah
Arendt* (dir. by Margarethe von Trotta, 2012), focusing on the trial of Adolf
Eichmann in Jerusalem in 1961; *Der Staat gegen Fritz Bauer* (dir. by Lars
Kraume, 2015), which concerns the Frankfurt Auschwitz trials (1963–65) and
prosecutor Fritz Bauer's key role in instigating these; and *Im Labyrinth des
Schweigens* (Giulio Ricciarelli, 2014), which also features the Frankfurt Auschwitz trials, albeit more tangentially. *Schächten* (dir. by Thomas Roth, 2022)
briefly depicts the Austrian trial and acquittal of Mauthausen camp guard Jo-
hann Gogl, which serves as a catalyst for the film's protagonist—a Holocaust
survivor—to take justice into his own hands. However, *Murer* remains unique
in the Austrian context in its sustained concentration on a trial and its failure
to bring a Nazi war criminal to justice in post-war Austria.

In the late Soviet context (in which *Repentance* arose) and in the post-Soviet
era, a number of films focused their attention on the Stalinist show trials. The
last year of the Soviet Union saw the release of *Bukharin—Enemy of the People*

[18] Cases in point include Bergman and Asimow's *Reel Justice*; Sarat, Silbey and Umphrey's
Trial Films on Trial; David Alan Black, *Law in Film: Resonance and Representation* (Urbana and
Chicago: University of Illinois Press, 1999); Steve Greenfield, Guy Osborn, and Peter Robson, *Film
and the Law: The Cinema of Justice*, 2nd edn (Oxford and Portland, OR: Bloomsbury, 2010); Stefan
Machura and Peter Robson, *Law and Film: Representing Law in Movies* (Malden, MA: Blackwell,
2001).
[19] See e.g. Dorian Sabo and Josip Berdica's survey of law and film in Croatia: 'Law and Film:
An Essay on Legal Culture', *In Medias Res: Časopis Filozofije Medija*, 10 (2001), 3205–18. Giacomo
Calorio and Giorgio Fabio Colombo offer an analysis of the Japanese context: 'Inside a Frame,
behind a Glass: A Preliminary Inquiry on Law and Film in Japan', *Law and Humanities*, 14 (2000),
83–112.
[20] Sarat, Silbey, and Umphrey, 'The Pleasures and Possibilities of Trial Films', p. 2.
[21] Ibid., p. 6.

(*Vrag naroda—Bukharin*, dir. by Leonid Maryagin, 1991), a fictionalization of the life and trial of the Bolshevik revolutionary Nikolai Bukharin, executed in the Great Purge of 1938. *Defence Counsel Sedov* (*Zashitnik Sedov*, dir. by Evgeniy Tsymbal, 1988) is another late Soviet film that returns the viewer to the era of Stalinist purges, focusing on the efforts of an idealistic young lawyer to save agronomists put on trial. Many late Soviet and post-Soviet films also deal with Stalinist purges and trials, albeit in a peripheral way: examples include *My Friend Ivan Lapshin* (*Moy drug Ivan Lapshin*, dir. by Aleksei German, 1985) and *Burnt by the Sun* (*Utomlyonnye solntsem*, dir. by Nikita Mikhalkov, 1994). However, as I will show in the following discussion, Abuladze's *Repentance* (1987) remains unique in both late Soviet and post-Soviet cinematic output in putting on trial Stalinism *itself*, rather than merely *representing* Stalinist show trials (as in the case of Maryagin's *Bukharin— Enemy of the People*). While several critics acknowledge the significance of the trial on which *Repentance* is centred,[22] there is no sustained analysis of *Repentance* as a trial film. This article provides that analysis.

In her 2002 study *The Juridical Unconscious*, Shoshana Felman analyses key trials of the twentieth century—primarily, the trial of Adolf Eichmann in Jerusalem in 1961 and the trial of O. J. Simpson in 1994–95, as well as the Nuremberg Trials of 1945–46. Felman views these landmark trials as transcending the status of mere legal disputes, such that they are transformed into 'veritable theaters of justice', which 'staged paroxistic spectacles both of the drama of the law and of the drama of culture'.[23] With reference to Nuremberg specifically, Felman traces how the tribunal '(through the trial of the Nazi leaders as representatives of the historical regime and the historical phenomenon of Nazism) for the first time called history itself into a court of justice'.[24] The Eichmann trial in turn was 'a trial of collective crime (and of an archetypal perpetrator of that crime)',[25] whereby it was not only the individual who is put on trial—in this case a key orchestrator of the Holocaust, Adolf Eichmann—but the Nazi regime that he stood for, where, as he repeatedly stressed, he 'did his *duty*' and 'obeyed *orders*'.[26] Felman analyses how the Eichmann trial set a precedent:

[22] See Woll and Youngblood, who note that Keti's words in court are 'a story that transforms her trial for grave robbery into a trial of something much more serious: the trial of Varlam Aravidze for his crimes against humanity' (p. 8). See also Julie Christensen, who argues that 'Varlam's funeral and the trial that follows serve as the structural framework for the film', with Keti Barateli's trial being a 'cinematic pre-enactment of the Last Judgment' ('Tengiz Abuladze's *Repentance* and the Georgian Nationalist Cause', *Slavic Review*, 50 (1991), 163–75 (pp. 166 and 167)).

[23] Felman, *The Juridical Unconscious*, p. 4.
[24] Ibid., p. 11.
[25] Ibid., p. 6.
[26] Hannah Arendt, *Eichmann in Jerusalem: A Report on the Banality of Evil* (London and New York: Penguin, 2006), p. 135 (emphases original).

[I]t was also a conscious and deliberate attempt to transform an incoherent mass of private traumas (the secret, hidden, silenced individual traumas of the survivors) into one collective, national, and public trauma, and thus to give a public stage to a collection of individual abuses and private traumas, to render public and politically transform into public, abuses that were lived as private and hidden away by the individual traumatized subjects, who had become, in their own self-perception, 'the bearers of the silence.'[27]

We see the same processes of individual testimonies coalescing into a collective narrative in both *Murer* and *Repentance*. Both films similarly focus on crimes that extend far beyond individual injustices meted out by individuals, instead putting historical events, involving countless victims, centre stage. The collective witness statements of the Jewish victims presented in *Murer* (which makes diegetic reference to the Eichmann trial) add up to an overwhelming moral indictment of an Austrian Holocaust perpetrator. Keti Barateli's recollections of her parents' persecution during the Stalinist era, recounted in *Repentance*, similarly encompass many more victims than her own family. In contrast to the international scope of the Nuremberg and Eichmann trials that Felman analyses, and in spite of the transnational nature of the testimonies in *Murer* in particular, I argue that both *Repentance* and *Murer* place the focus firmly on the national and put the nation in whose name these historical injustices took place on trial. Those assembled in court are shown to form a microcosm of the nation in both films: the respective trials prompt a fraught confrontation with the historical past in the courtroom, which becomes symptomatic of a wider national reckoning.

Reckonings with the Past

Repentance presents a reckoning with the Stalinist past in a small Georgian town in the 1980s. The film opens with a scene depicting a woman preparing a cake, while a friend visiting her home is shown reading in a newspaper that the town's despotic former mayor, Varlam Aravidze, has died. On the night following the funeral, the corpse of the deceased mayor turns up in the garden of his son Abel's house. To comic effect, the corpse is reburied, only to reappear again and again—three times in total. A woman, Ketevan (Keti) Barateli (played by the same actor, Zeinab Botsvadze, as the cake-maker in the opening and closing sequences of the film), is eventually arrested and accused of digging up the corpse. She defends herself by stating that Varlam does not deserve to be buried on account of his crimes, which included the imprisonment and death of her parents. She is put on trial, and the story of Varlam's reign of terror during the 1930s, which consisted of brutal suppression of any

[27] Felman, *The Juridical Unconscious*, p. 7.

dissent against his regime, is told in flashbacks from the courtroom. During the trial Varlam's son, Abel, denies any wrongdoing on the part of his
father, and the family's lawyer tries to have Ketevan declared insane, which,
the viewer must surmise (for it is left ambiguous), they eventually succeed
in doing. Varlam's grandson Tornike is, however, shocked by the revelations
about the crimes of his grandfather and commits suicide. At the end of the
film we are returned to the frame narrative of the cake-maker, which adds yet
more instability and uncertainty to the surreal narrative.[28] This instability is
symptomatic of a glasnost-era film, which was certainly pushing the boundaries with regard to its treatment of the legacy of Stalinism, but doing so in a
cautious way through its use of symbolism. This is achieved, not least, through
the figure of Varlam Aravidze, who in his appearance, predilections, and heri-
tage may be viewed as a composite of several twentieth-century dictators and
despots.[29] Moreover, in Georgian 'Aravidze' means 'no man' or, by extension,
'everyman', as Julie Christensen highlights.[30] Given the setting and language
of the film, it is ultimately the Stalinist allusions that predominate, however.
Aravidze is a Stalinist figure, if not Stalin himself; his indirect posthumous
trial thereby represents a 'trial of collective crime', here that of Stalinism, as
well as 'of an archetypal perpetrator of that crime' in Felman's terms.[31]

   Murer also presents the audience with Felman's 'archetypal perpetrator' of
collective crime, here the crimes of National Socialism. As Tobias Ebbrecht-
Hartmann notes, the film's broader focus on the nation of post-war Austria,
beyond the titular protagonist, is also made clear by the poster for *Murer*,
which shows a dark silhouette of Murer against a background coloured in
red and white, the colours of the Austrian national flag.[32] In his view this is
symptomatic of the 'blurring' of the protagonist, such that Murer is reduced
to a 'typical case symbolizing the Austrian struggle of coming to terms with
its past'.[33] *Murer* presents a fictionalization of the trial of Franz Murer in
Graz in 1963. Nicknamed 'the Butcher of Vilnius', the SS officer, in his role
as deputy to *Gebietskommissar* (Area Commissioner) Hans Christian Hingst,

---

[28] Woll and Youngblood discuss the surrealist and symbolic elements of the film at length in
their study on *Repentance*, in a chapter entitled 'Signs and Symbols: *Repentance*'s Stylistic Devices',
pp. 75–87. However, surprisingly, they do not suggest that surrealism and symbolism are ways
in which Abuladze, in the fledgling glasnost era, offers a cautious rather than overt critique of
Stalinism.

[29] See Woll and Youngblood, pp. 76, 101, and especially p. 80, where they write: 'Varlam, garbed
like Mussolini, belting out an aria while Nino and Sandro are up to their necks in dirt, certainly
makes one of the movie's more obvious points about the links between Stalinism and fascism.' See
also Christensen, 'Tengiz Abuladze's *Repentance*', p. 168.

[30] Christensen, 'Tengiz Abuladze's *Repentance*', p. 166.

[31] Felman, *The Juridical Unconscious*, p. 6.

[32] Tobias Ebbrecht-Hartmann, 'Blind Spots, in the Present: The National Socialist Past in Recent
Austrian Films', *zeitgeschichte*, 46 (2019), 535–56 (p. 541).

[33] Ibid., p. 541.

was responsible for creating and presiding over the Vilna ghetto (located in Vilnius, Lithuania) between 1941 and 1943. Vilnius had been home to over 80,000 Jews before the war, whereas after the war only around 600 remained in the city once known as the 'Jerusalem of the North',[34] a sobriquet reputedly given to it by Napoleon in 1812.[35] *Murer* restages the former SS officer's trial in post-war Austria, a country which had regained its sovereignty less than a decade previously in 1955, and presents it as a gross miscarriage of justice. Despite overwhelming evidence of Murer's brutality and inhuman treatment of the Vilna ghetto population, underlined through the testimonies of surviving Jewish victims over the course of the ten-day trial in Graz, Murer was acquitted owing to a combination of party-political interests, resistance to perceived outside interference in Austrian internal affairs, and a desire to draw a line under Austria's wartime past.

Director Christian Frosch has referred to the trial, which drew worldwide attention, as having been deliberately forgotten about in post-war Austria, and has said that the aim of his film was to bring it to the surface and restore it to public consciousness in the present day,[36] an endeavour which has certainly been successful if one looks at the contemporary media reception of the film.[37] Ebbrecht-Hartmann specifically notes the significance of Frosch's film opening the Diagonale in Graz in March 2018, a significant memorial year in Austria,[38] marking eighty years since the *Anschluss*, as well as a hundred years since the end of the First World War and the foundation of the First Republic of Austria. The memorial year 2018 also coincided with the far-right Austrian Freedom Party once again entering the government as a coalition partner of the conservative Austrian People's Party. Thereby, according to Ebbrecht-Hartmann, '*Murer* turned the [Diagonale] festival into an alternative commemoration event that interconnected the Austrian National Socialist past with a post-war apologetic period of silencing and the present political situation'.[39]

Indeed, the motif of metaphorically dredging up a difficult past, something that may be observed in films and literature dealing with traumatic pasts in

[34] Abram Suzkever, as cited in Christoph Schiessl, *Alleged Nazi Collaborators in the United States after World War II* (Lanham, MD: Lexington, 2016), p. 47.

[35] Richard A. Freund, *The Archaeology of the Holocaust: Vilna, Rhodes and Escape Tunnels* (Lanham, MD: Rowman & Littlefield, 2019), p. 155.

[36] Frosch in 'Interview: Regisseur und Autor Christian Frosch', *Murer* DVD (00:06:16–00:06:33). Henceforth referred to as 'Frosch DVD Interview' followed by timestamps.

[37] Jakub Gortat traces the reception of *Murer* in the Austrian press, highlighting the fact that the cultural weekly *Falter* had Murer's face across its front page: Gortat, 'Excavating the Nazi Past in Austrian Contemporary Film: *Murer: Anatomy of a Trial* (2018) and *The Testament* (2017)', *Holocaust Studies*, 28 (2022), 506–29 (p. 523, n. 65).

[38] Ebbrecht-Hartmann, 'Blind Spots, in the Present', p. 554.

[39] Ibid., pp. 554–55.

multiple cultural contexts,[40] is a key one for both *Murer* and *Repentance*. In the latter, this is vividly conveyed through Keti Barateli's repetitive action of digging up Varlam Aravidze's corpse. She motivates her actions in court with the explanation that '(b)urying him means forgiving him, shutting our eyes to everything he had perpetrated' (1:44:46–1:44:51), and vows to 'dig him up three hundred times, not just three!' (26:37–26:40). Although Barateli's actions are not motivated in religious terms, culturally Georgia is a strongly Orthodox Christian nation (it was the second country on the European continent, after Armenia, to adopt Christianity).[41] Therefore the idea that someone should not be allowed to be buried in consecrated ground to rest in peace would resonate strongly with Georgian audiences. There are also more explicit Christian references throughout the film's flashback sequences set in the 1930s, where we see the town church being blown up (evoking the destruction of Moscow's Cathedral of Christ the Saviour on 5 December 1931) in a montage which also features the execution of Keti's father, Sandro Barateli. Here, Sandro is shown suspended, clinging to a rope over a well in a subterranean chamber, and wearing a loin cloth, evoking Christ's crucifixion. Moreover, *Repentance* notably concludes with an elderly woman enigmatically asking the cake-maker whether a street, which turns out to be 'Varlam Street' (named after the despotic leader), leads to a church (which stands more broadly in this context for intellectual and spiritual enlightenment). When told that it does not, she declares 'Varlam Street' useless. The film's title also evokes the Christian concept of repenting and atoning for one's sins. It is this repentance that Keti tries to prompt in the Aravidze family and in the assembled townspeople, who stand for Soviet society at large, attending the trial.

Murer is also concerned with the unearthing of a past that is deliberately being kept hidden, albeit in the different context of post-war Austria. This unearthing happens in a less literal sense than in *Repentance*, yet the very first shot of the film shows an archive wheel being turned, followed by a close-up of a file on Murer. As indicated above, this focus on archives is significant,[42] although it should be noted that it returns diegetically only in

[40] A notable example in the Austrian context is that of the ongoing search for a grave site in Rechnitz, Burgenland, where approximately 200 forced Hungarian Jewish slave labourers are assumed to have been buried. The repeated attempts to dig up the past in Rechnitz have been thematized in Margareta Heinrich and Eduard Erne's documentary film *Totschweigen* (1994), Elfriede Jelinek's play *Rechnitz: Der Würgeengel* (2008), and, most recently, Eva Menasse's novel *Dunkelblum* (2021). In the Spanish context, the issue of the excavation of the bodies of those persecuted by Francoist forces during the Spanish Civil War has been a notable feature in both documentaries, e.g. Almudena Carracedo and Robert Bahar's *El silencio de otros* (2018), and fiction films, e.g. Pedro Almodóvar's *Madres paralelas* (2021).

[41] Hubertus Jahn, 'Introduction', in *Identities and Representations in Georgia from the 19th Century to the Present*, ed. by Hubertus Jahn (Berlin and Boston: De Gruyter, 2021), pp. 1–8 (p. 2).

[42] See Ebbrecht-Hartmann, 'Blind Spots, in the Present', pp. 535–56, and Gortat, 'Excavating the Nazi Past', pp. 506–29.

the closing sequence of the film, which is composed of still photographs from the collection *Jerusalem of Lithuania*.[43] For the most part, the meta-phorical unearthing of the past takes place in the space of the courtroom, as witnesses, speaking Yiddish, Hebrew, English, and German, detail Murer's crimes in Vilnius, which included arbitrary punishments and shootings of the ghetto's Jewish population. In this manner, 'the court provides a stage for the expression of the persecuted' in Felman's terms.[44] While *Repentance* operates with metaphors of an (un)buried despot's corpse, *Murer* operates with less spectacular tropes, yet the trial setting provides the perfect forum for the resurfacing of an undead Nazi past, hidden in plain sight. It is this very past which, as we are shown, made the achieving of justice impossible in the Austria of 1963, in stark contrast to the conviction of Eichmann in Jerusalem just over a year earlier. *Murer* explicitly does not represent a 'legal process of translation of thousands of private, secret traumas into one collective, public, and communally acknowledged one', as Felman describes in the case of the Eichmann trial.[45] Or, more precisely, among the Murer trial witnesses there is indeed this process of collectivizing of individual traumas into what *should* be an overwhelming indictment of the former 'Butcher of Vilnius'. Yet, the Jewish witnesses were not 'communally acknowledged' in the historic Murer trial, their testimony not 'heard' by the vast majority of those assembled in the courtroom. Gortat writes that, akin to the Eichmann trial, 'Murer's trial also functioned as an oral history project, albeit its reception was totally different, because the survivor testimony was not welcome', and explains this by the fact that, while the Eichmann trial was covered widely by most of the world's media, this was not the case in Austria.[46] In his historical drama film Frosch further makes the lack of acknowledgement of the victims clear through the inclusion of subtle details, such as the antisemitic *Stürmer*-style caricatures of the Jewish witnesses drawn by a journalist,[47] inaudible jokes exchanged by the audience in the gallery, and the defending lawyer's presentation of Murer as a victim and scapegoat. As an audience of 'spectator–jurors',[48] we are invited to pass judgement on the clear injustices perpetrated in and around the film's courtroom. While the actions of the court audience are imagined for the purposes of Frosch's screenplay—which is not to say that these behaviours

---

[43] Cited in *Murer*'s end credits. A montage of photographs from the collection is also included as extra material on the *Murer* DVD.

[44] Felman, *The Juridical Unconscious*, p. 12.

[45] Ibid., p. 124.

[46] Gortat, 'Excavating the Nazi Past', p. 510.

[47] Frosch uses the phrase 'Stürmer-artige Karikatur' ('Stürmer-like caricature') in the screenplay for *Murer*. See Frosch, '*Murer: Anatomie eines Prozesses*, Fassung 7.1, 26.03.2017', p. 33 <http://www.drehbuchforum.at/files/drehbuch_murer_shooting_script_.pdf> [accessed 8 February 2024].

[48] Sarat, Silbey, and Umphrey, 'The Pleasures and Possibilities of Trial Films', p. 6.

are not highly plausible in the context of post-war Austria—the defending lawyer's words are drawn from actual summary records of the trial.[49]

While miscarriages of justice are not unusual in the classic Hollywood trial film, those which emerge in *Repentance* and *Murer* surpass the individual defendant and become symptomatic of the continuing lack of confrontation of past national crimes, even as these are ostensibly being cross-examined in the courtroom. Keti Barateli's trial in *Repentance* is presided over by three individuals, evoking an NKVD troika of the 1930s in the Soviet Union, whereby three officials from the secret police would act as judge and jury in a sped-up 'judicial' process whose outcome was a foregone conclusion, usually resulting in the imprisonment or execution of the accused. While there is, additionally, a pro-forma 'counsellor for the defence' (26:56) and prosecutor in Keti Barateli's trial, it is clear that it is the trio of officials who really hold sway in this judicial process. Indeed, the resonance with miscarriages of justice during the Great Terror is further underlined through Keti's words: 'The trial has already taken place, and the verdict has been passed!' (26:10–26:14). The trial takes on an absurd character as Barateli is led into the courtroom by two medieval knights, dressed in armour that covers their faces and carrying spears. These figures, who also reappear in various contexts in the film's flashback sequences, are especially incongruous when juxtaposed with one of the seated 'troika' members playing with a Rubik's cube, which places the film firmly in the 1980s (when it was made). Taken together, the contemporary and anachronistic elements of the mise-en-scène highlight the faceless and regressive authoritarianism, lack of interest, and sheer absence of humanity displayed by the judicial system in hearing the defendant's case. Elsewhere, the film narrative evokes the figure of Lady Justice, whereby a woman with her eyes blindfolded, and holding a sword and scales, silently presides over the interrogation of Sandro Barateli's former teacher, Mikhail Korisheli, falsely arraigned on trumped-up charges (to which he has probably 'confessed' under torture) as the leader of a secret organization numbering two thousand people which was planning to dig a tunnel from Bombay (Mumbai) to London. The presence of an embodied Lady Justice here is, of course, deeply ironic, her blindfold symbolizing, not blind justice, but rather the turning of a blind eye to the injustices perpetrated in the Great Terror. Subsequently we encounter Lady Justice, this time dressed in expensive furs with the blindfold pulled up to her forehead, enjoying the sight of Barateli's execution. Far from being blind and objective, justice's embodiment is depicted as corrupt and publicly complicit in its own miscarriage. Bergman and Asimow have described how

---

[49] As Frosch explains in the *Murer* DVD interview, the trial proceedings were not recorded verbatim but rather as a rough summary of the statements, which Frosch then imaginatively transposed into monologues for his screenplay and film, while trying to stick as closely as possible to the original sources: 'Frosch DVD Interview' (00:01:38–00:02:32).

'courtroom movies frequently attack the justice system as hopelessly corrupt and suggest that it can be manipulated by those who know which strings to pull', adding that 'evil political systems [. . .] can also pollute justice'.[50] We see this operating on both levels of the film diegesis in *Repentance*: in the miscarriages of justice evident in its flashback sequences depicting the era of Stalinism, as well as in the a priori biased trial that we see unfolding in the film's contemporary frame.

Corruption is also prevalent in *Murer*. From the outset the viewer is frequently made aware that a fair, impartial trial of the eponymous defendant is impossible, primarily because of the context in which the trial is taking place in the courtroom, namely Austrian domestic politics in the post-war era, as well as Austria's embeddedness within the wider geopolitics of Cold War Europe. A marked example of this is a conversation conducted in a corridor of the court, where the *Bauernbundpräsident* (Farmers' Association President) Josef Wallner warns Austrian Socialist Party (SPÖ) Justice Minister Christian Broda to rein in an SPÖ-loyal journalist reporting on Murer's membership of the conservative Austrian People's Party ÖVP, otherwise threatening to expose the 'braune Vergangenheit' ('Nazi past': 1:06:13) of Otto Rösch, the then State Secretary in the Ministry of Defence. As the *Bauernbundpräsident* laconically states: 'Es gibt Dinge in der Vergangenheit, die lässt man besser dort, besonders wenn man im Glashaus sitzt' ('There are things in the past that are better left there, especially when one lives in a glasshouse': 1:06:35– 1:06:41). The contingencies of Realpolitik in the first decades after the war in Austria are depicted as prevailing over any willingness to confront its Nazi past. This is made all the more evident in another backroom conversation between the SPÖ-leaning journalist Karl Nowak and Christian Broda, when Broda emphasizes the importance of the Austrian Socialists winning elections and aligning with other socialist governments in Cold War Europe: 'dazu müssen leider möglichst viele von den Ex-Nazis ihr Kreuzerl bei uns machen' ('and for that we unfortunately need as many of the former Nazis as possible to vote for us': 1:22:20–1:22:24). Moreover, in conversations between witness Jacob and journalists Rosa Segev and Nowak, as well as between the journalist Nowak and politician Broda, the viewer learns that the judge presiding over the trial, Judge Peyer, is a former Nazi who joined the party in 1938 (the year of the *Anschluss*), and even in the last year of the war was sentencing Wehrmacht deserters to death (1:21:06; 1:16:27). The narrative foregrounding of these fictionalized conversations, based on historical facts, underlines the impossibility of justice being served in the Murer trial, an impossibility that is made all the more evident with the benefit of hindsight, as the film, released

---

[50] Bergman and Asimow, *Reel Justice*, p. 117.

in 2018, looks back on this 1963 trial and on post-war Austria from a vantage point of more than five decades.

Jurors, as a representative cross-section of society, form another key aspect of the traditional criminal trial case, yet they are usually relatively absent on screen. As Gwyneth Hambley comments: 'In most courtroom dramas, the jury is just another audience, sitting quietly in the corner of the courtroom.'[51] There are notable exceptions to this—Sidney Lumet's *12 Angry Men* (1957), for example, is entirely focused on deliberations in a jury room. In *Repentance*, as previously discussed, there is no jury that can be described as such, beyond the 'troika' of individuals we see presiding over the court. In *Murer*, however, there are instances of fictionalized conversations between members of the jury beyond the courtroom, which serve to further underline the lack of fairness and impartiality in Murer's trial. One juror, Julius Kloiber, is shown to have his own personal crisis of conscience in the course of the trial, owing to his sense of guilt at his inaction while serving as a Nazi soldier during the perpetration of Wehrmacht crimes. He is spoken to by a fellow jury member, the school headmaster Friedrich, at the instigation of former SS-Standartenführer and Werwolf commander Richard Hochreiner (played by Heinz Trixner).[52] Friedrich insinuates that Kloiber himself was not pursued as a former Nazi as part of the denazification processes of 1948, and he argues further that it is now incumbent on Kloiber to acquit Murer: 'Findest du nicht, dass du jetzt was schuldig bist?' ('Don't you think you owe us something?': 1:41:11–1:41:14). As a result of this conversation, Kloiber withdraws from the jury and is not replaced. This, in turn, plays a decisive role in Murer's subsequent acquittal as it leads to an equal number of jurors voting for and against him, which, according to the Austrian legal code at the time, constituted a 'not guilty' verdict. For the film audience as 'spectator–juror', placed in the position of 'judging both the defendant and the law',[53] the miscarriage of justice perpetrated through the intimidation of a jury member (a criminal offence in all jurisdictions) serves as a heavy indictment of post-war Austrian society, which in *Murer* is presented as being more concerned to acquit a Nazi perpetrator than to ensure a fair and just trial.

[51] Gwyneth E. Hambley, 'The Image of the Jury in Popular Culture', *Legal Reference Services*, 12 (1992), 171–216 (p. 173), in Greenfield, Osborn, and Robson, *Film and the Law*, p. 160.

[52] Hochreiner, who by the early 1960s was a councillor for the Freiheitliche Partei (Freedom Party of Austria) in St Michael, Salzburg, was himself convicted on 27 June 1962 at the Graz Regional Court of killing nine Jewish slave labourers following the end of the war, and was sentenced to seven years in jail. However, this verdict was overturned by a jury on 6 March 1963, just a few months, therefore, before Murer's trial. See Manfred Wieninger, *Aasplatz: Eine Unschuldsvermutung* (Salzburg: Residenz, 2018), pp. 9–10.

[53] Sarat, Silbey, and Umphrey, 'The Pleasures and Possibilities of Trial Films', p. 3.

'Following Orders' in Service of a 'Great Cause'

Repeatedly, *Murer* portrays the defence of having only followed orders and thereby the denial of personal culpability or responsibility; here Frosch sticks closely to the original statements made during the course of Murer's Graz trial.[54] The 'following orders' defence is one that we see Murer personally deploying, with a deliberate appeal to the jury, who he anticipates share the experience of having served in the Wehrmacht: 'Damals war Krieg, wir mussten gehorchen. Alle, die gedient haben, wissen, wovon ich spreche' ('It was wartime then, we had to obey. Everyone who's served, knows what I'm talking about': 1:03:36–1:03:43). The film script makes this appeal to the jury explicit with the stage direction 'Murer blickt Verständnis suchend zur Geschworenenbank. Der einarmige Mesner nickt' ('Murer looks to the jury bench in search of understanding. The one-armed sacristan nods').[55] Meanwhile, the defence lawyer Böck asserts in his summing up: 'Franz Murer, einem steirischen Bauernsohn, hat das Schicksal übel mitgespielt' ('Fate played a dirty trick on Franz Murer, a Styrian farmer's son': 1:47:19–1:47:32). As the above discussion suggests, the defence is at pains throughout the trial to 'reverse victim and offender', in the DARVO strategy elucidated by Jennifer J. Freyd.[56] Murer is presented as a passive victim of fate, with Böck explicitly connecting him to the Austrian nation and mobilizing the 'Austrian victim' myth in a bid to absolve him of blame: 'Österreich war das erste Opfer Hitlers!' ('Austria was Hitler's first victim!': 1:50:52–1:50:54). The presentation of the defendant as a victim continues: 'Franz Murer sitzt hier als Sündenbock, als Objekt der Rache von ausländischen Interessen' ('Franz Murer sits here as a scapegoat, as an object of revenge for foreign interests': 1:50:56–1:51:04). The 'foreign interests' are a reference to the Jewish witnesses, who are defamed by the defence, accused of lying and of being steered by outside forces in a supposed conspiracy against Murer. A similar antisemitic campaign against 'foreign' interference from the Ostküste (East Coast) would later be infamously mobilized in Kurt Waldheim's 1986 presidential election campaign.[57] The parallels between the case of Murer and that of Waldheim more than twenty years later have been highlighted by Frosch himself as forming part of a pattern

---

[54] As Frosch comments regarding the summary statements of the defence lawyer: 'Although it sounds absolutely incredible, his closing statement is almost word for word factually correct': in Christian Frosch, 'If an event is never described, it's as though it never took place: Interview with Karin Schiefer', *Austrian Films*, February 2018 <https://www.austrianfilms.com/Interview/christian_frosch/murer_EN> [accessed 8 February 2024].

[55] Frosch, '*Murer — Anatomie eines Prozesses*, Fassung 7.1, 26.03.2017', p. 53.

[56] Jennifer J. Freyd, 'Violations of Power, Adaptive Blindness, and Betrayal Trauma Theory', *Feminism & Psychology*, 7 (1997), 22–32.

[57] Steven Beller, *A Concise History of Austria* (Cambridge: Cambridge University Press, 2006), p. 288.

of a national sweeping of the Austrian Nazi past under the carpet in the post-war era.[58]

Similarly, in the intergenerational conflict in the Aravidze family accompanying the trial of Ketevan Barateli, Varlam Aravidze too is presented by his son Abel as having been a victim of fate and of having acted out of necessity. When challenged by his own son Tornike (Varlam's grandson), Abel refers to the period of his father's reign of terror as 'a very complicated time', which is 'difficult to explain' to his son's generation (1:50:07–1:50:09). He asserts: 'I don't mean to say that we [the regime] made no mistakes. But what is the life of one man when the happiness of millions is at stake?' (1:50:49–1:50:56). Abel's weak defence of his father to Tornike culminates in a *reductio ad absurdum*: 'Your grandfather never killed anyone with his own hands!' (1:52:06–1:52:08). The overall tenor of Abel's argument is that 'the ends justify the means', something that we also see voiced in *Repentance* by Yelena Korisheli in the 1930s narrative strand, who acknowledges that 'of course, the arrest of Sandro [Barateli] and Mikhail [Korisheli] is a mistake' (1:30:24–1:30:26), but admonishes Nino, Sandro's wife, not to forget that 'we're serving a great cause' (1:31:06–1:31:08), and that 'since the scale of the events is so grand, big mistakes are inevitable. It may even happen that innocent people are victimized' (1:31:16–1:31:23).

These sentiments recall Stalin's infamous 'Dizzy with Success' ('Golovokruzheniye ot uspekhov') article, published in *Pravda* on 2 March 1930, detailing how the Soviet Union had '*overfulfilled* the five-year plan of collectivization by more than 100 per cent'.[59] The article, published at a time of mass repressions against so-called *kulaks* (landowners),[60] only obliquely alludes to these in the context of the 'head-spinning successes' of the five-year plan, blaming regional officials for 'forc[ing] the pace of collectivization',[61] and calling for a more measured pace to ensure that it was properly embedded. Yet Yelena, a fervent believer in the ideals of communism, proclaims that Beethoven's 'Ode to Joy', which extols the idea of the brotherhood of man,

[58] 'Da dachte ich: "Wow — das haben wir doch bei Waldheim auch gehabt"' ('And I thought: "Wow, that's what we had with Waldheim as well"'): Frosch, as cited in Dominik Kamalzadeh, 'Regisseur Christian Frosch: "Wenn die Justiz nicht funktionieren soll"', *Der Standard*, 13 March 2018 <https://www.derstandard.at/story/2000075933753/regisseur-christian-frosch-wenn-die-justiz-nicht-funktionieren-soll> [accessed 8 February 2024].

[59] A translation of the article may be accessed here: J. V. Stalin, 'Dizzy with Success: Concerning Questions of the Collective-Farm Movement' (1930), *Marxists Internet Archive* <https://www.marxists.org/reference/archive/stalin/works/1930/03/02.htm> [accessed 8 February 2024] (emphasis original).

[60] Approximately 1.8 million *kulaks* were deported, primarily to Siberia, between 1928 and 1932. For more on this see Martin McCauley, *The Rise and Fall of the Soviet Union* (London and New York: Routledge, 2014), p. 141.

[61] Sheila Fitzpatrick, *Stalin's Peasants: Resistance and Survival in the Russian Village after Collectivization* (Oxford and New York: Oxford University Press, 1994), p. 62.

'will surely sound all over the world very soon' (1:31:27–1:31:29). Yelena—who is herself later arbitrarily arrested—is then shown diegetically singing the words of the 'Ode to Joy' before, in one of the most outstanding examples of montage in the film, her singing transmutes into a non-diegetic orchestral recording, which segues to the scene of Sandro's execution, symbolizing the effects of despotism and persecution, with Lady Justice, as discussed earlier, looking on approvingly. Both the defence of blindly following orders in *Murer* and that of the necessity for individual lives to be sacrificed in the service of an idealized greater good in *Repentance* are presented as attempts at self-exoneration and self-exculpation which serve to sideline the experience of the real victims.

The Verdict

The writer Robert Menasse has described *Murer* as 'Ein Gerichtssaalkrimi, in dem sich der Freispruch für einen Mann als Urteil über eine Nation herausstellt' ('A courtroom thriller in which one man's acquittal emerges as a judgement upon a nation').[62] The verdict is the recognizable final part of the criminal trial and of the trial film, which typically progresses from opening statements, evidence and cross-examination, to the trial's conclusion.[63] In both *Murer* and *Repentance*, it is not only the individual defendant, however, but the entire nation that receives the verdict of the court. In *Murer* the withdrawal of Kloiber from the jury leads to the acquittal of Murer on all charges, a verdict that is met with jubilation in the courtroom by his supporters, and despondency from the witnesses who testified against him. We also see a montage of individuals (Simon Wiesenthal, Christian Broda, former juror Kloiber and his grandmother) and groups (members of the Bauernbund) listening to a diegetic radio broadcast of the verdict in homes, pubs, and offices, which conveys the sense that all key sections of society have a stake in the judicial decision. To return to Menasse's assessment of *Murer* as the Austrian version of *To Kill a Mockingbird*,[64] in both film narratives the objectively wrong verdict in the trial serves as a judgement upon the respective societies depicted, rather than merely upon an individual. In *To Kill a Mockingbird*, where an African American man is wrongly convicted of rape, the 'spectator–juror' views this as a reflection of racism and discrimination in the United States (both in the American South of the 1930s, where the narrative is set, and in the Civil Rights era of 1960s America, when Mulligan's film adaptation of Harper Lee's 1960 novel was made). Similarly, the depiction of Murer's

[62] *Murer* DVD sleeve.
[63] Sarat, Silbey, and Umphrey, 'The Pleasures and Possibilities of Trial Films', p. 3.
[64] *Murer* DVD sleeve.

acquittal in Frosch's film serves as a verdict upon post-war Austria, and its inability to confront the Nazi past and bring perpetrators to justice.

From the jubilant scenes in the courtroom in *Murer* there is a cut to a (fictionalized) conversation in the washroom between defence lawyer Böck and prosecutor Schuhmann. When Böck expresses surprise that Schuhmann made several errors in his statements, including focusing on just a couple of key witnesses, Schuhmann retorts 'Ich tue meine Pflicht [. . .] wir sind nicht immer Herr unserer Entscheidungen' ('I do my duty [. . .] we are not always masters of our decisions': 2:00:12–2:00:20). Böck's question as to whether Schuhmann's actions were due to an instruction from Vienna is met with tacit assent (2:00:36). *Murer* presents a cynical portrait of the post-war Austrian justice system, where there is no room for heroic lawyer figures akin to Atticus Finch in *To Kill a Mockingbird*,[65] the justice system being instead subservient to political interests. Böck recognizes that he has been unknowingly used— in contrast to Schuhmann's cynical complicity—as a pawn of party-political interests, and that Murer's acquittal was a foregone conclusion. In possession of this knowledge, Böck in turn bitterly tells Murer's wife, who comes to his office to thank him for his efforts, that 'Ich habe nur meine Pflicht erfüllt' ('I only did my duty': 2:04:23–2:04:26).

In face of a justice system manipulated behind the scenes and lawyers controlled like marionettes in the political consensus of 1960s Austria, the idea of justice being served can only be a wishful fantasy, as is made clear through the sequence which immediately follows the conversation between Böck and Elisabeth Murer. In blurred focus and with a non-diegetic dissonant soundtrack, we see Rosa Segev stabbing Murer in the neck as he exits the courthouse and is almost mobbed by jubilant supporters handing him flowers. The stabbed Murer falls to the ground as he opens the door to his car, and there is then a cut to a shell-shocked Rosa still sitting in the courtroom, while the subsequent shot shows Murer getting safely into his car to cheers from the assembled crowd. This temporary break in continuity reveals Rosa's reverie of justice being meted out to Murer as nothing more than a wish-fulfilment dream (*Wunschtraum*) in Freud's conception.[66] We see Murer safely reach his home, where he is welcomed by his extended family, while the closing intertitles inform us that, despite further efforts from Wiesenthal, all judicial cases against Murer were formally suspended in 1974 and he died peacefully in 1994, at the age of eighty-two. In contrast to the paradigmatic nature of

[65] Atticus Finch was named the greatest film hero of all time by the American Film Institute in 2003. For a discussion of this, see Michael Asimow and Shannon Mader, *Law and Popular Culture: A Course Book* (New York: Peter Lang, 2004), pp. 41–44.

[66] Freud believed wish fulfilment to be central to every dream: 'also daß es keine anderen als Wunschträume geben kann' ('so that there can be no dreams other than wishful dreams': Sigmund Freud, *Die Traumdeutung*, in *Sigmund Freud: Studienausgabe*, ed. by Alexander Mitscherlich and others, vol. II (Frankfurt a.M.: Fischer, 1969), p. 151.

the Eichmann trial, where Arendt's maxim 'justice must not only be done but must be seen to be done' was realized,[67] justice is neither done nor seen to be done in *Murer*, which reconstructs a missed opportunity for Austria to come to terms with its National Socialist past. While I agree with Jakub Gortat that Rosa Segev's fantasy 'attempt[s] to provide a sense of catharsis by showing a belated act of justice', I disagree with his view that 'by offering solace through wishful thinking, Frosch [is] able to preserve the memory of the excavated past'.[68] Certainly, Frosch's film about the Murer trial is an act of preservation of this shameful chapter in Austrian post-war history, but Rosa Segev's wishful reverie offers little solace to the viewer, only a continuing sense of injustice.

Abuladze's *Repentance* also presents us with a miscarriage of justice. Unlike *Murer*, the film diegesis of *Repentance* does not incorporate the pronouncement of a verdict. Instead, we see the prosecutor repeatedly return to the question of Barateli's sanity. Definitive establishment of Barateli's insanity would lead to her being institutionalized—this is indeed what Barateli herself anticipates in a conversation with Tornike in her prison cell—but also to the case being dismissed, ultimately benefiting the Aravidze family. The actual verdict reached in *Repentance* is not definitively communicated to us; like so much else in the film, it is left open. This puts the focus, to an even greater extent than in *Murer*, on events surrounding the anticipated verdict. These include the aforementioned conversation between Barateli and Tornike Aravidze; the assembled friends of the Aravidze family celebrating the expected verdict in their home; and, most significantly, the continuing intergenerational conflict between Abel and Tornike regarding Varlam's legacy, a confrontation that culminates in Tornike's suicide using the rifle gifted to him by his grandfather. Upon discovering his son's dead body, we see Abel curse himself and his father. The next shot shows us Abel digging up Varlam Aravidze's body himself before throwing it over a cliff. This is almost certainly a wishful reverie on the part of Abel, akin to Rosa Segev's revenge fantasy in *Murer*, yet it tellingly fulfils Keti Barateli's wish, spoken in court, that Aravidze's body be dug up by his own family (1:44:17–1:44:21). Certainly, Barateli's repeated disinterring of Aravidze's body and subsequent trial prompt the wider confrontation with a buried past that she has been seeking. The fact that this confrontation takes such ferocious and violent forms, as Tornike's suicide tragically highlights, is symptomatic of the zeal with which this past has been previously repressed.

Moreover, while Aravidze's descendants remain powerful in the town and in the courtroom, Barateli is also shown to have supporters, who laugh

---

[67] Hannah Arendt, *Eichmann in Jerusalem: A Report on the Banality of Evil* (New York: Penguin, 1963), p. 277, as cited in Felman, *The Juridical Unconscious*, p. 162.
[68] Gortat, 'Excavating the Nazi Past', pp. 507 and 524.

approvingly as she exits the courtroom, vowing that she will 'dig him [Ara-vidze] up anyway' (2:10:13–2:10:15). Thus, *Repentance* presents the legacy of Aravidze—and the Stalinist legacy that he stands for—as contested at this point of the glasnost era. Ultimately, however, justice is not served; Barateli's fate hangs in suspension, just like the legacy of Stalinism at the time of *Repentance*'s release. No decisive verdict is passed that would absolve Barateli from blame and, by extension, posthumously condemn Aravidze. Addition-ally, the sequence where Abel seemingly throws his father's body over a cliff is followed by a return to the frame narrative of the film, that of the cake-maker who advises a female passer-by asking for directions. This lends the whole preceding narrative a surreal instability, potentially suggesting that it was all a reverie on the part of the cake-maker (who, as previously noted, is played by the same actor as Ketevan Barateli). At this point in the late Soviet Union, a definitive 'not guilty' verdict for Ketevan Barateli would clearly have been a step too far. The film thus articulates a subtle critique of the legacy of Stalinism, its surreal elements allowing Abuladze to voice criticism but not in a flatly condemnatory manner.

Both *Murer* and *Repentance* have unsatisfying endings—*Murer* in the clear miscarriage of justice evidenced by the eponymous figure's acquittal, and *Repentance* in the suspended verdict and surreal frame narrative, which call the very idea of victims of Stalinism achieving justice into question. The audience as jurors, in the formulation of Sarat, Silbey, and Umphrey,[69] are placed in the position of drawing their own conclusions from the overwhelming evidence presented to them—the undeniable guilt of Varlam Aravidze as archetypal Stalinist perpetrator, that of Franz Murer as archetypal Nazi perpetrator, and the clear innocence of those individuals such as Ketevan Barateli and the witnesses in the Murer trial, who find themselves and their testimony being defamed in the courtroom.

As this comparative analysis has shown, Abuladze's and Frosch's films, through their courtroom scenes, put their respective nations on trial and seek to confront their audiences with hitherto repressed aspects of their countries' historical legacies. Whether the focus of the trial is on an archetypal Stalinist perpetrator, as in the case of *Repentance*, or a Nazi perpetrator, as in the case of *Murer*, both films present the courtroom as the setting where the historical past is rendered present. In the miscarriages of justice that follow, from the de-faming of victims to the self-exculpatory strategies employed by the defence, the missed opportunities for confronting the past become manifest. From the vantage point of Austria in the 2010s, Frosch presents the failure to convict a Nazi war criminal in 1960s Austria as symptomatic of a deeply problematic

---

[69] 'The Pleasures and Possibilities of Trial Films', p. 3.

post-war silencing of the wartime past, aided and abetted by party-political interests. Meanwhile, Abuladze's *Repentance*, made in 1984 and cautiously anticipating the glasnost era, presents an equivocal ending to the fictional trial of a Soviet individual seeking justice in the 1980s for her family and, by extension, the nation victimized by Stalinism. Neither film leaves the viewer as juror in any doubt as to who the perpetrators are or what crimes they committed, but the trials that Abuladze's and Frosch's films stage go far beyond this. The inadequate verdicts and deeply problematic confrontations that the attendant court audiences, as microcosms of the respective nations, have with the overwhelming evidence presented to them hold up a mirror to their respective audiences, in the hope of facilitating a wider conversation about the long-repressed national past. These discussions are as much needed in Soviet successor states and in the state of Austria today as they were in the time settings of the films. The international Memorial foundation, founded in Moscow in 1989 to document the crimes of Stalinism, remains liquidated since 2021,[70] while the spectre of a far-right coalition government in Austria, with a party that has repeatedly come under fire for historical amnesia and neo-Nazi rhetoric, remains present during every election campaign.[71] A profound and wide-ranging *repentance* for the crimes of Stalinism remains an unfulfilled desideratum in Russia, Georgia, and many other Soviet successor states. Meanwhile, Austria's confrontation with its Nazi past, though it has certainly made significant progress since the time of the Waldheim Affair, remains an ongoing project marked by insufficiencies, especially in the country's regions.[72] The uncompleted process of true repentance for and acknowledgement of traumatic historical legacies sadly renders Abuladze's and Frosch's films timeless.

UNIVERSITY OF ABERDEEN   KATYA KRYLOVA

[70] Robyn Dixon, 'Russian Court Abolishes Country's Most Prominent Human Rights Group, Memorial', *Washington Post*, 28 December 2021 <https://www.washingtonpost.com/world/2021/12/28/russia-rights-memorial-liquidated/> [accessed 8 February 2024].

[71] While the last coalition of the far-right Austrian Freedom Party and conservative Austrian People's Party was short-lived (2018–19), due to the so-called Ibiza scandal, the Austrian Freedom Party has consistently continued to win votes in regional elections, making the prospect of a renewed conservative/far-right coalition in the 2024 Austrian legislative election a distinct possibility. See Liam Hoare, 'Austria is sleepwalking toward a far-right victory', *Politico*, 7 February 2024 <https://www.politico.eu/article/austria-sleepwalking-far-right-victory-european-election-freedom-party-fpo-nazis-herbert-kickl/> [accessed 12 April 2024].

[72] For an analysis of the contrast between Austrian memory culture at the central and regional level, using the example of the legacy of Austrian Wehrmacht deserters, see Katya Krylova, '"Unsere mutigen Feiglinge": Remembrance of Austrian Wehrmacht Deserters in Hanna Sukare's *Schwedenreiter*', *Journal of Austrian Studies*, 55.3 (2022), 77–109.

'THE CONTENTS O'TH' STORY': THE DIANA AND ACTAEON MYTH IN SHAKESPEARE'S *CYMBELINE*

That *Cymbeline* 'probably exceeds any other Shakespearian play in its fecundity of classical, and especially mythological, reference' has long been established.[1] This drama stands out as a perfect example of reception—that is, of the way classical texts were read or, better, reread in the Renaissance. As such, it also has a lot to reveal about early modern reading practices. What is particularly worth noting about Shakespeare's use of Ovid late in his career is that, as Colin Burrow puts it, in the romances 'references to his [Ovid's] works tend to be oblique or even metaphorical'.[2] This is especially true for *Cymbeline*. As I argue, the Diana and Actaeon myth from Book III of Ovid's *Metamorphoses* connects in subtle and unexpected ways several motifs that are at the core of the play: from sexual exposure and illicit viewing to matters of reading, writing, and publishing. I also contend that references to this myth, which are even more pervasive than has been noted so far, contribute to reinforcing the imagery of birth and of reunion that is so central in the final part of the drama.[3]

Cymbeline certainly deserves special consideration also in the light of the peculiar position it occupies in the 1623 Folio. Not only is it placed at the very end of the collection, but it is also listed among the tragedies, an editorial choice which has generated much critical commentary over the years. Recent scholarship, however, has emphasized the 'valedictory' character of this late romance, pointing out that it functions as the appropriate conclusion of the Folio, just as *The Tempest* has long been recognized as its perfect opening.[4]

An earlier version of this essay was presented at the Annual Graduate Conference of the Italian Association of Shakespearean and Early Modern Studies at the British Institute of Florence (April 2023). Professor Michael Stapleton generously read earlier drafts, and I am grateful for his comments. I am also deeply indebted to the anonymous referees of *Modern Language Review* for their insightful suggestions.

The title is from William Shakespeare, *Cymbeline*, ed. by Valerie Wayne, The Arden Shakespeare (London and New York: Bloomsbury, 2017), II. 2. 27. Further references to act, scene, and line numbers are to this edition, and are given parenthetically in the text.

[1] G. Wilson Knight, *The Crown of Life* (Oxford: Oxford University Press, 1947), p. 183.

[2] Colin Burrow, 'Shakespeare', in *The Oxford History of Classical Reception in English Literature*, ed. by David Hopkins and Charles Martindale, 5 vols (Oxford: Oxford University Press, 2012–19), II, 599–605 (p. 604).

[3] For a more general study of the Actaeon myth in Shakespeare and Marlowe, see François Laroque, 'Ovidian V[o]ices in Marlowe and Shakespeare: The Actaeon Variations', in *Shakespeare's Ovid: 'The Metamorphoses' in the Plays and Poems*, ed. by A. B. Taylor (Cambridge: Cambridge University Press, 2000), pp. 165–77.

[4] In her introduction to *Cymbeline*, Wayne explains that '[w]hen the compilers of the First Folio of 1623 positioned *Cymbeline* last in the collection of Shakespeare's plays, among the tragedies, they launched an ongoing problem of its generic classification' (*Cymbeline*, ed. by Wayne, p. 1). Jonathan Bate first pointed out the play's appropriateness as the Folio's final play. As he writes, *Cymbeline*'s 'stylistic experimentation almost serves as an ironic epilogue to the Folio's tripartite

Modern Language Review, 119 (2024), 476–94, doi:10.1353/mlr.00003
© Modern Humanities Research Association 2024

In the words of Valerie Wayne, *Cymbeline*'s recapitulations and references to the dramatist's earlier production serve as 'a peroration for the entire volume [sc. the First Folio]'.[5]

The drama's sustained emphasis on matters related to writing, reading, and publishing, as well as the 'writerly language'[6] of some passages, highlights even more clearly that this play is a particularly suitable choice to conclude the collection. In *Cymbeline*, characters read different sorts of texts and are, in their turn, 'read' as texts. To cite just one instance, when King Cymbeline is given news of the queen's death in the final act, he associates women's inscrutability with matters of interpretation and reading and exclaims 'Who is't can read a woman?' (v. 5. 48), thereby also reiterating the body–text analogy that recurs throughout. Even the king's final lines, 'Publish we this peace | To all our subjects' (v. 5. 477–78), with their heightened insistence on issues of publishing, emphasize the retrospective character of this romance, which consciously looks back at Shakespeare's dramatic works as well as the narrative poems.

In order to shed light upon the dramatist's peculiar use of the Diana and Actaeon narrative in *Cymbeline*, and upon the way the underlying presence of this myth heightens the play's engagement with matters of disclosure and publication, it is worth focusing on a work that presents similar concerns: *The Rape of Lucrece*. Several connections between Collatine and Posthumus, as well as between Lucrece and Innogen, suggest how Shakespeare reworked in a renewed way the same narrative material which he drew upon in the 1590s and how he managed to adapt it to specific issues which became particularly relevant late in his career.

From 'Lucrece' to 'Cymbeline'

Given the play's recapitulatory character, it is significant that *Cymbeline*'s concluding lines echo Shakespeare's *The Rape of Lucrece*, patterned upon the version of the narrative which the dramatist read both in Ovid's *Fasti* and in Livy's *History of Rome*. This foundation myth recounts the expulsion of the tyrannical kings from Rome and the establishment of the republic, an event notoriously consequent upon Tarquin's rape of the chaste Lucrece.

division into comedies, histories, and tragedies' (William Shakespeare, *Complete Works*, ed. by Jonathan Bate and Eric Rasmussen (Basingstoke: Macmillan, 2007), p. 2240). On *Cymbeline* as a retrospective and valedictory drama, see Valerie Wayne, 'The First Folio's Arrangement and its Finale', *Shakespeare Quarterly*, 66 (2015), 389–408.

[5] Wayne, 'The First Folio's Arrangement', p. 391.

[6] I borrow this expression from Colin Burrow's introduction to *The Rape of Lucrece*, in which he highlights the poem's peculiar emphasis upon issues of reading and writing. See William Shakespeare, *The Complete Sonnets and Poems*, ed. by Colin Burrow (Oxford: Oxford University Press, 2002), pp. 40–73 (p. 64).

Shakespeare's narrative poem was first published in 1594 and then reissued for a fifth time in 1607, a few years before the composition of *Cymbeline*, which was very likely written between March and November of 1610.[7] King Cymbeline's explicit use of the verb 'Publish' (v. 5. 477) at the end of the drama inevitably calls to mind the 'publishing' of Lucrece's dead body at the end of *The Rape of Lucrece* and induces us to reflect upon the thematic affinities between the two works. In Shakespeare's poem, the term 'publish' is employed in the final stanza, when Tarquin's 'foul offence' against Lucrece is 'publish[ed]', i.e. 'made public', by 'show[ing]' the woman's 'bleeding body thorough Rome':

> They did conclude to bear dead Lucrece thence,
> To show her bleeding body thorough Rome,
> And so to publish Tarquin's foul offence.
>   (*Lucrece*, ll. 1850–52)[8]

These lines, which clearly emphasize the relation between 'showing' and 'publishing', are the culmination of a narrative that highlights how 'publication is bound up with illicit seeing, erotic display, and sexual guilt'.[9] Before looking at how these same matters have a central relevance in *Cymbeline*, it is important to note that what distinguishes Shakespeare's version of the Lucrece story from its Latin sources, and also from the numerous retellings of the narrative, is the fact that Tarquin's impetus does not seem to be aroused by the sight of Lucrece: instead, the tyrant's lustful desire is kindled by Collatine's rhetorical display of his wife or, in other words, by his verbal description of Lucrece, which eventually results in display.[10] The reader might recall that in Ovid's *Fasti* it is the sight and then the recollection of the woman's image that inflames Tarquin's passion:

> Her lilie skin, her gold-deluding tresses,
> Her native splendour slighting art him pleases.
> Her voice, her stainlesse modesty h' admires:
> And hope's decay still strengthens his desires.[11]

---

[7] See *Cymbeline*, ed. by Wayne, p. 30.

[8] All quotations from *The Rape of Lucrece* are taken from Shakespeare, *Sonnets and Poems*, ed. by Burrow; line numbers are given parenthetically within the text.

[9] Wendy Wall, *The Imprint of Gender: Authorship and Publication in the English Renaissance* (Ithaca, NY, and London: Cornell University Press, 1993), pp. 214–15.

[10] This is also confirmed by Burrow, who, in his introduction to *The Rape of Lucrece*, maintains that 'in the poem Tarquin does not seem to have visited Lucrece's house before the rape' (*Sonnets and Poems*, p. 47). See also Nancy J. Vickers, 'This Heraldry in Lucrece's Face', *Poetics Today*, 6 (1985), 171–84 (pp. 174–75).

[11] John Gower, *Ovids festivals, or, Romane Calendar Translated into English Verse Equinumerally* (Cambridge: Printed by Roger Daniel, 1640), Book II, pp. 43–44. Where there are reliable signature marks or page numbers in early modern sources, I will use them; otherwise, I will refer to chapter titles or chapter numbers. Original spelling and punctuation have been retained.

A few words later, when the tyrant returns to his tent at Ardea, we read that '[h]is mazing fansie on her picture roves'.[12] Even in William Painter's second novel from *The Palace of Pleasure*, which retells the story of how '*Sextus Tarquinius* rauisheth *Lucrece*' and which is one of Shakespeare's possible sources,[13] it is when seeing Lucrece 'not as the other before named, spendyng the time in idleness, but late in the night occupied and busie' that 'Sextus Tarquinius [. . .] was attached and incensed with a libidinous desire'.[14] In Shakespeare's *Lucrece*, instead, Tarquin's desire is inflamed before he actually visits the woman's house. Significantly enough, the passage in which the tyrant meets Lucrece is omitted in Shakespeare's poem.[15] And indeed, there is no need for Tarquin to see Lucrece since her husband Collatine has already turned her into a 'published' text: as the narrator points out, Collatine '*set[s] forth* that which is so singular' (l. 32), or 'private', and thus he becomes 'the *publisher* | Of that rich jewel he should keep unknown | From thievish ears, because it is his own' (ll. 33–35, my emphasis).[16] Given that to 'set forth' means 'to express in words' (*OED*, s.v. 'set, v.1', §6.a), 'to display' (ibid., §10), and also 'to publish (a literary work)' (ibid., §5), the last of these being attested by the *Oxford English Dictionary* from the early sixteenth century, by distancing himself from the Ovidian narrative and its adaptations, Shakespeare highlights the power of verbal description and of language, while at the same time he ties together issues of disclosure and publication. As has been rightly observed, '[i]n *Lucrece*, Shakespeare offers a commentary on the pervasive verbal associations and tropes that publishers and writers used in introducing printed works to the public'.[17] As we shall see, in *Cymbeline* the dramatist explores these same issues, which acquire even greater significance if read through the lens of the Diana and Actaeon myth.

In order to understand the parallels between the two works, it is worth focusing on that moment inside the so-called wager scene in *Cymbeline* (I. 4)

---

[12] Ibid., p. 44.

[13] As for Shakespeare's main sources for the Lucrece story, see Burrow's introduction to *The Rape of Lucrece* in *Sonnets and Poems*, p. 45, and Colin Burrow, *Shakespeare and Classical Antiquity* (Oxford: Oxford University Press, 2013), pp. 116–17.

[14] William Painter, *The Palace of Pleasure Beautified, Adorned and Well Furnished, with Pleasaunt Histories and Excellent Nouelles, Selected out of Diuers Good and Commendable Authors* (London: Printed by John Kingston and Henry Denham for Richard Tottell and William Iones, 1566), vol. I, fol. 5^r–v.

[15] See Amy Greenstadt, '"Read it in me": The Author's Will in Lucrece', *Shakespeare Quarterly*, 57 (2006), 45–70 (p. 52).

[16] As Vickers has put it, in Shakespeare's poem, '[r]ape is the price Lucrece pays for having been described' ('This Heraldry in Lucrece's Face', p. 176). Naomi Yavneh likewise observes that 'the woman [Lucretia] is raped because her husband did such a good job of describing her' ('The Ambiguity of Beauty: Tasso and Petrarch', in *Sexuality and Gender in Early Modern Europe: Institutions, Texts, Images*, ed. by James Grantham, 2nd edn (Cambridge: Cambridge University Press, 1995), pp. 133–57 (p. 139).

[17] Wall, *The Imprint of Gender*, p. 215.

when Posthumus brags about his wife Innogen with his comrades. As another Collatine, Posthumus makes the private public by expressing in words, and therefore *setting forth*, Innogen's chastity and virtues. The woman becomes, once again, a 'published' text. The connection with the classical story of Lucrece (or, better, with Shakespeare's own rereading of the narrative in *The Rape of Lucrece*) is clearly established in Act II. When the Italian villain Iachimo illicitly intrudes into Innogen's bedchamber, after wagering with Posthumus that he would be able to seduce the lady by deceit, he explicitly invokes the association with Tarquin:

> IACHIMO   Our Tarquin thus
> Did softly press the rushes ere he wakened
> The chastity he wounded.
>   (II. 2. 12–14)

However, the threatened rape is only metaphorical: just like Philomel's narrative, which is Innogen's bedtime reading material—as the audience will soon discover—the story of Lucrece remains folded in the pages of the untitled volume that is brought onstage and rape is averted.[18] In *Cymbeline*, as in Shakespeare's *Lucrece*, then, emphasis is placed upon the husband's verbal description of his wife. As a repentant Iachimo reveals near the end of the drama, when he 'utter[s] that | Which torments [him] to conceal' (v. 5. 141–42), Posthumus's display of Innogen is made through language:

> IACHIMO   he began
> His mistress' picture, which, *by his tongue being made*,
> And then a mind put in't, either our brags
> Were cracked of kitchen trulls or *his description*
> Proved us unspeaking sots.
>   (v. 5. 174–78, emphasis added)

Considering that 'tongue' in English has the meaning of 'language' and also of 'the power of description' (*OED*, s.v. 'tongue, n.', §II.4.a), just as the Latin term *lingua* is used for both 'tongue' and 'language',[19] the stress on Posthumus's verbal 'description' is most evident and related to the consequent inarticulacy provoked by his linguistic display. As we shall see, Posthumus's exposure of Innogen, modelled upon Collatine's 'publishing' of Lucrece, acquires special significance if considered in the light of the Diana and Actaeon myth, which functions as a connecting theme throughout.

---

[18] As Iachimo remarks in a celebrated passage, 'She [Innogen] hath been reading late | The tale of Tereus: here the leaf's turned down | Where Philomel gave up' (II. 2. 44–46). In her edition of Shakespeare's play, Wayne highlights that the remark is inaccurate, since Philomel never 'gave up' (*Cymbeline*, ed. by Wayne, p. 203, note to l. 46).

[19] See Burrow, *Shakespeare and Classical Antiquity*, p. 108.

'Unspeaking sots': The Diana and Actaeon Myth

Willing to expose the whole truth, in the final act of the play Iachimo enigmatically remarks that Posthumus's verbal 'description' (v. 5. 177), or rather public display, of Innogen turned them into 'unspeaking sots' (v. 5. 178). This heightens the importance of the Actaeon and Diana story if we consider that the narrative is related to the motif of inarticulacy and of linguistic injury. One is also reminded of another Ovidian legend that is central in *Cymbeline*, that of Philomela and Tereus. In this myth, 'the tongue becomes a thing, a dying snake', which makes this Ovidian story a 'tragedy of inarticulacy'.[20] In a way, the myth of Diana and Actaeon is a tragedy of inarticulacy too. The enraged goddess challenges the prying hunter to describe in words what he has seen: 'Now make thy vaunt among thy Mates, thou sawste Diana bare. | Tell if thou can: I giue thee leaue: tell hardily: doe not spare' (III. 227–28). However, Actaeon, who is eventually transformed into a stag, is not able to speak and is torn to death by his own dogs. As we read in Arthur Golding's popular translation of Ovid:

> Even from his owne folke is he faine (alas) to flee away.
> He strayned oftentymes to speake, and was about to say.
> I am Acteon: know your Lorde and Mayster, sirs, I pray.
> But use of wordes and speach did want to utter forth his minde.
>
> (III. 275–78)

It is thus appropriate that, just like Actaeon—so Iachimo suggests—the five male listeners lose a key feature of humanity, i.e. speech, and become inarticulate ('unspeaking') while participating in Posthumus's display of his wife as an object of male gaze and lust.[21] Analogously, the Ovidian hunter was unable to speak when his hounds tore him to pieces as a punishment for seeing Diana bathing naked.

The reference to the Diana and Actaeon narrative is made all the more explicit a few lines later, when Iachimo reports how Posthumus actually 'spake of her [Innogen] as Dian had hot dreams | And she alone were cold' (v. 5. 180–81). By displaying his wife as Diana, Posthumus allows his male audience to venture into a private, forbidden domain. 'There it begins' (v. 5. 179), Iachimo clearly explains. This illicit, though imaginary, access into Innogen's

---

[20] Ibid., pp. 108–09. Burrow refers to the following passage from Book VI of Ovid's *Metamorphoses*: 'And with a paire of pinsons fast did catch hir by the tung, | And with his sword did cut it off. The stumpe whereon it hung | Did patter still. The tip fell downe and quivering on the ground | As though that it had murmured it made a certaine sound. | And as an Adders tayle cut off doth skip a while: euen so | The tip of Philomelaas tongue did wriggle to and fro' (VI. 709–14). All quotations from Ovid's *Metamorphoses* are from the 1567 translation by Arthur Golding, ed. by John Frederick Nims (Philadelphia: Paul Dry Books, 2000). Further references are given parenthetically within the text.

[21] The five listeners who participate in the so-called wager scene (I. 4), set in Renaissance Rome, are Philario, Iachimo, a Frenchman, a Dutchman, and a Spaniard.

intimacy through words symbolically turns them into Actaeon-like intruders. It should be pointed out that in the Ovidian narrative Actaeon steps into Diana's sacred space inadvertently. Ovid himself highlights Actaeon's innocence and compares his own exiled condition to the undeserved chastisement of the Theban hero in a celebrated passage from *Tristia*: 'Thus poore *Actaeon* unawares once spy'd | *Diana* naked; yet a prey he dy'd.'[22] As recalled by Leonard Barkan, 'Ovid's stress upon Actaeon's victimized innocence is virtually unique in the myth's history, and all subsequent versions which dramatize the young man's crime and justify his punishment derive in part from the exegesis of non-Ovidian versions.'[23] In the *Metamorphoses*, Ovid acknowledges the fact that his narrative gave rise to diverging views regarding the hunter's destiny:

> Much muttring was upon this fact. Some thought there was extended
> A great deale more extremitie than neded. Some commended
> Dianas doing: saying that it was but worthely
> For safegarde of hir womanhod. Eche partie did applie
> Good reasons to defende their case.

(III. 305–09)

As might be expected, multiple renditions of the narrative, coming from medieval moralizations, Renaissance collections of novellas, such as William Painter's and George Pettie's, but also from the mythographic and emblematic traditions, influenced Shakespeare's writing.[24] In a recent essay, Bettina Boecker convincingly argues that the untitled volume which Innogen reads is not necessarily Ovid's original masterpiece but, most likely, a medieval or early modern reworking of it—or perhaps both.[25] Original narratives (both from classical antiquity and from the Italian tradition of novellas) were enriched and embellished with new details and were thus received in a reworked form by early modern readers. Although the Actaeon myth was submitted to several early modern interpretations, scholarship has shown that English poets of the sixteenth century were especially fascinated by that aspect of the episode which highlights precisely 'the act of seeing forbidden things and the

---

[22] John Gower, trans., *Ovids festivalls*, sig. A3ʳ. Gower included excerpts from Ovid's *Tristia* in his 1640 English edition of the *Fasti*.

[23] Leonard Barkan, 'Diana and Actaeon: The Myth as Synthesis', *English Literary Renaissance*, 10 (1980), 317–59 (p. 323).

[24] See Daniel Dornhofer and Susanne Scholz, 'The Hounds of Desire: Elizabethan Variations on Ovid's Actaeon Episode', in *Re-inventing Ovid's 'Metamorphoses': Pictorial and Literary Transformations in Various Media, 1400–1800*, ed. by Karl A. E. Enenkel and Jan L. de Jong (Leiden and Boston: Brill, 2021), pp. 377–99 (p. 386); see also Peggy Muñoz Simonds, *Myth, Emblem, and Music in Shakespeare's 'Cymbeline': An Iconographic Reconstruction* (Newark: University of Delaware Press, 1992), esp. pp. 101–08.

[25] Bettina Boecker, '"The Tale of Tereus" and the Story of Procne: Innogen's Bedside Reading', *Shakespeare* (2023) <http://dx.doi.dx.org/1080/17450918.2023.2214115>.

danger of talking about the sight, of passing on knowledge gained visually'.[26] *Cymbeline* testifies that Shakespeare was no exception.

The dramatist draws upon the contradicting readings deriving from the Actaeon story when both Posthumus and Iachimo become 'Actaeons' at different moments in the play. After listening to Iachimo's revelation and acknowledging his own guilt, Posthumus portrays himself as an Actaeon-like offender and pleads with the king to 'set | The dogs o' th' street to bay me: every villain | Be call'd Posthumus Leonatus' (v. 5. 222–23). Since 'bay' signifies 'To pursue with barking like a pack of hounds' (*OED*, s.v. 'bay, v.1', §5) and was 'most commonly applied to the deep voice of a large dog, as a hound or mastiff' (ibid., §1.a), Posthumus's lines recall the fate of the mythic hunter. Actaeon as a dismembered man, punished (rightly or unjustly) for encroaching on a strictly feminized domain, is therefore subtly related to the figure of Posthumus, whose linguistic display of Innogen is indeed the cause of Iachimo's transgressive viewing.[27] Even though it is the latter who wilfully plays the role of the Actaeon-voyeur in II. 2, by associating Posthumus with the punishment suffered by the Theban hunter (i.e. dismemberment), Shakespeare highlights his culpability. As Wall puts it, 'Diana dismembers Actaeon precisely because she does not want to be published',[28] which is exactly what Posthumus (just like his literary predecessor Collatine) does with his wife.

Although, once again, the allusion to the Ovidian myth turns out finally to be only metaphorical, since Posthumus is reformed rather than physically punished, he nonetheless suffers a symbolic process of dismemberment when Innogen wakes up near Cloten's headless corpse in IV. 2 and mistakes this mutilated body for her husband's:

> INNOGEN A headless man? The garments of Posthumus?
> I know the shape of 's leg; this is his hand,
> His foot Mercurial, his Martial thigh,
> The brawns of Hercules, but his Jovial face—
> Murder in heaven? How? 'Tis gone.
> (IV. 2. 307–11)[29]

In a sort of parody of the Ovidian narrative, in which Actaeon cries his name but is unable to prove his identity and is torn asunder by his dogs, Posthumus

---

[26] Dornhofer and Scholz, 'The Hounds of Desire', p. 386.

[27] Jonathan Bate argues that 'the prying gaze is the direct consequence of Posthumus's own proprietorial display of his wife's chastity [. . .]. In his way, he is an Actaeon too, which is why the play has to punish him' (*Shakespeare and Ovid* (Oxford: Clarendon Press, 1993), p. 219).

[28] Wall, *The Imprint of Gender*, p. 190.

[29] Charles and Michelle Martindale have pointed out the Ovidian nature of these lines, noting that this is a 'characteristic scene, which owes nothing directly to Ovid, but which Ovid might surely have applauded' (*Shakespeare and the Uses of Antiquity* (London and New York: Routledge, 1990), p. 56).

strongly lays claim to his identity the very moment he admits his Actaeon-like crime and evokes, not by chance, the image of the hounds that should punish him for having 'publicized' Innogen:

> POSTHUMUS   It is I
> That all th'abhorred things o'th' earth amend
> By being worse than they. I am Posthumus,
> That killed thy daughter—villain-like, I lie—
> [. . .]
> Spit and throw stones, cast mire upon me, set
> The dogs o'th' street to bay me. Every villain
> Be called Posthumus Leonatus.
>
> (v. 5. 215–18 and 222–24)

The themes of bodily dismemberment and of mistaken identity are at the core of the Actaeon narrative, given that the hunter's dogs mistake their master for their prey. Just like his mythological prototype, Posthumus suffers a loss of identity and even a symbolic death that bring about his transformation. This is certainly Ovidian if one thinks that, as Barkan explains, 'metamorphosis suggests the loss of one identity and the gaining of another'.[30] The last time we see Posthumus is in II. 5, when he declares his intention to curse women in the belief that his wife has been seduced by Iachimo: 'I'll write against them, | Detest them, curse them. [. . .] | The very devils cannot plague them better' (II. 5. 31–34).[31] After this misogynistic invective, he disappears for two acts and reappears only in v. 1, a device which allows for his role onstage to be doubled with Cloten's.[32] In the eyes of the audience, then, Posthumus is replaced by the animal-like figure who is associated with violence and with animalistic desire throughout the drama.[33] The play highlights the fact that Posthumus is disturbingly similar to his flawed alter ego, as when, for instance, he expresses the intention to dismember Innogen: 'O that I had her here to tear her limb-meal! | I will go there and do't i'th' court, before | Her father' (II. 4. 147–49). The husband's desire to assassinate and tear his wife to pieces echoes Cloten's plan to behead his rival and then rape the woman:

---

[30] Barkan, 'Diana and Actaeon', p. 335.

[31] On Posthumus's misogyny, invested with diabolic significance, see Michael L. Stapleton, *Harmful Eloquence: Ovid's 'Amores' from Antiquity to Shakespeare* (Ann Arbor: University of Michigan Press, 1996), p. 145.

[32] For a discussion of the similarity between Posthumus and Cloten, see *Cymbeline*, ed. by Wayne, pp. 86–90.

[33] Wayne remarks that 'Cloten's desire for genuine harm shows that he is more dangerous than a simple buffoon' (*Cymbeline*, ed. by Wayne, p. 160, note to ll. 32–33). As a matter of fact, this character's beastly attributes are highlighted throughout the play. In Act I, Innogen emphasizes her husband's excellence by comparing him to the king of birds, the eagle, and associating Cloten with a puttock, i.e. 'a bird of prey and a scavenger' (ibid., p. 155, note to ll. 140–41): 'O blessed that I might not! I chose an eagle | And did avoid a puttock' (I. 1. 140–41).

Posthumus, thy head, which now is growing upon thy shoulders, shall within this hour
be off, thy mistress enforced, thy garments cut to pieces before her face; and all this
done, spurn her home to her father, who may haply be a little angry for my so rough
usage. (IV. 1. 15–20)

The identification between the two reaches its climax in IV. 1, when Cloten
appears onstage in Posthumus's clothes just before he is savagely beheaded
during a hunting party. The hunting imagery that underlies the scene is
particularly worth noting since it points to the Actaeon story, just like the
metaphor of dismemberment. As Wayne notes, not only does the drama
double its misogyny, but 'it also doubles body parts, severing and reconsti-
tuting them'.[34] Cloten, who is compared to a bird of prey in Act I (I. 1. 141)
and who is more than once associated with greed and rapacity,[35] pursues his
double Posthumus to Milford Haven with the expressed intention to execute
him: 'Even there, thou villain Posthumus, will I kill thee. [. . .] With that suit
upon my back will I ravish her—first kill him, and in her eyes' (III. 5. 131–
32, 138–39). However, he eventually dies as prey at the hands of Guiderius
(IV. 2. 148–53), Cymbeline's abducted son and now a cave dweller in Wales.
As a matter of fact, despite Cloten's intention to behead Guiderius and display
his severed head 'on the gates of Lud's town' (IV. 2. 99), it is the latter who
manages to 'cut off one Cloten's head, | Son to the Queen' (IV. 2. 117–18):

> I have ta'en
> His head from him. I'll throw't into the creek
> Behind our rock, and let it to the sea
> And tell the fishes he's the Queen's son, Cloten.
> (IV. 2. 149–52)

The reference here is to Ovid's *Metamorphoses* and, more particularly,
to Orpheus's gruesome death at the hands of the Thracian women, or
Bacchantes.[36] As recounted in Book XI, the legendary musician undergoes
sparagmos, a Dionysian ritual that consisted in sacrificing a victim by tearing
it asunder. After the mutilation, Orpheus's head is thrown into the River
Hebrus, exactly the same fate experienced by Cloten.

Like Actaeon, Orpheus is torn to pieces. Shakespeare returns to, and insists
upon, the metaphor of tearing limbs apart, already evoked by Posthumus to
threaten Innogen (II. 4. 147). The association between the two myths goes
much further and places emphasis on the threat of dismemberment consequent upon illicit seeing. It would be recalled that Orpheus's death is the
ultimate result of forbidden gaze. In Book X of the *Metamorphoses*, the Thracian singer commits the fatal error of gazing upon his wife Eurydice, thus

[34] *Cymbeline*, ed. by Wayne, p. 89.
[35] Ibid., p. 155, note to ll. 140–41.
[36] Ibid., p. 293, note to ll. 150–52.

causing her to die twice. Unable to tolerate the pain, Orpheus eventually resolves to shun all women, a misogynistic turn which unites him to both Posthumus and Cloten. As we read in Ovid's text:

> And Orphye [. . .]
>
>   [. . .] did utterly eschew
> The womankynd. Yit many a one desyrous were too match
> With him, but he them with repulse did all alike dispatch.
>
>   (X. 87–90)

This leads to the Bacchantes lashing out at him in Book XI: 'Behold (sayes shee) behold yoon same is he that doth disdeine | Us women' (XI. 7–8).

Cloten's association with Orpheus is consistent with the fact that the Shakespearian villain is identified with both music and rape, therefore embodying 'the extremes of harmony and violence in the Orpheus story'.[37] In fact, as Erin Minear highlights, '[t]he parallel with the revolting Cloten is disturbing'.[38] This is clear in Act II, where, in a scene that functions as a grotesque parody of Iachimo's attempted rape, Cloten organizes an *aubade* (or song of the morning), traditionally sung by lovers to prolong the pleasures of the night, in order to 'penetrate' (II. 3. 13) and 'assail' (II. 3. 39) Innogen with music. Arguably, Cloten enacts that hostility against women which Posthumus only expresses in II. 5, and therefore he deserves to be torn apart: 'Could I find out | The woman's part in me—for there's no motion | That tends to vice in man but I affirm | It is the woman's part' (II. 5. 19–21).[39]

It does not take much to see that, as Posthumus's doppelgänger, Cloten is an Acteon, too. His being punished for his beastly lust recalls Geoffrey Whitney's emblematic rendition of the Ovidian episode. In the emblem entitled 'Voluptas aerumnosa' ('Passion is full of misery'), Actaeon is condemned for gazing upon Diana 'With greedie lookes'. Following the moral tradition, Whitney's emblem focuses precisely on 'beastliness'.[40] As the epigram makes clear, the metamorphosis and the consequent dismemberment represent the right chastisement reserved for those who are led by 'affections base' and 'things vnlawfull craue'. These 'Like brutishe beastes appeare vnto the viewe':

[37] Bate, *Shakespeare and Ovid*, p. 110.

[38] Erin Minear, 'Speaking the Song: Music, Language and Emotion in Shakespeare's *Cymbeline*', in *The Edinburgh Companion to Literature and Music*, ed. by Delia da Sousa Correa (Edinburgh: Edinburgh University Press, 2020), pp. 189–94 (p. 191).

[39] On this, see also *Cymbeline*, ed. by Wayne, p. 87.

[40] Agnès Boyer-Lafont, 'Actaeon' (2013), in *A Dictionary of Shakespeare's Classical Mythology* (2009–), ed. by Yves Peyré <http://www.shakmyth.org/myth/4/actaeon/some+secondary+sources> [accessed 14 March 2024]. Faustus, too, in Marlowe's drama, is punished for his unlawful desires. On the parallels between Whitney's interpretation and the use of the Actaeon myth in *Doctor Faustus*, see Agnès Boyer-Lafont, 'Le Corps nu de Diane ou les égarements du cœur et de l'esprit dans *Doctor Faustus* et *Edward II*', Anglophonia/Caliban, 13 (2003), 69–92 (pp. 75–76).

By which is ment, That those whoe do pursue
Theire fancies fonde, and thinges vnlawfull craue,
Like brutishe beastes appeare vnto the viewe,
And shall at lenghte, Actaeons guerdon haue:
  And as his houndes, soe theire affections base,
  Shall them deuowre, and all their deedes deface.[41]

Interestingly, Ovid himself explicitly pairs Actaeon with Orpheus when, commenting upon the latter's gory death, he evokes the image of a stag hunted down by dogs: 'As when a Stag by hungrye hownds as in a morning found, | The which forestall him round about and pull him to the ground' (xi. 27–28). The original Latin text actually reads 'structoque utrimque theatro | ceu matutina cervus periturus harena | praeda canum est' ('or in the amphitheatre | Upon the morning sand a pack of hounds | Round a doomed stag').[42] Ovid's text turns the mutilation into a public spectacle and, as has been noted, it highlights 'the spectators' public gaze in the amphitheater'.[43] That Shakespeare obliquely alludes to Orpheus's association with Actaeon in Ovid's text in order to draw attention to the consequences of transgressive viewing is entirely plausible. Moreover, in a play in which the act of seeing is more than once linked with danger and with actual death, it is certainly significant that Cloten's dismemberment, just like Orpheus's and Actaeon's, is ironically submitted to the onlookers' gaze.

In the role of Posthumus's parodic and evil double, Cloten is the only character in the play who suffers a real dismemberment, which paves the way towards the final reconciliation. In his introduction to the play, Martin Butler maintains that his death 'kills a part of Posthumus, without which reunion is impossible'.[44] When the latter reappears before the audience in v. 1, after his comic alter ego has died, he suddenly repents for the faults committed: 'Let me make men know | More valour in me than my habits show' (v. 1. 29–30). Clearly, Cloten's actual dismemberment permits Posthumus's return, which can be seen as another reinvention of the Actaeon story: instead of a physical metamorphosis and an actual death, Posthumus is allowed a moral transformation.

[41] Geoffrey Whitney, *A Choice of Emblemes, and Other Deuises* (Leiden: In the house of Christopher Plantyn, by Francis Raphelengius, 1586), p. 15. As John M. Steadman discusses in a still seminal essay, Shakespeare already engages with Whitney's interpretation of the myth in the depiction of Falstaff; see 'Falstaff as Actaeon: A Dramatic Emblem', *Shakespeare Quarterly*, 14 (1963), 231–44.

[42] Ovid, *Metamorphoses*, xi. 25–27, trans. by A. D. Melville (Oxford: Oxford University Press, 1986), p. 249.

[43] Thérèse Migraine-George, 'Specular Desires: Orpheus and Pygmalion as Aesthetic Paradigms in Petrarch's *Rime sparse*', *Comparative Literature Studies*, 36 (1999), 226–46 (p. 232).

[44] William Shakespeare, *Cymbeline*, ed. by Martin Butler, 2nd edn (Cambridge: Cambridge University Press, 2019), pp. 1–74 (p. 34).

'My circumstances': Actaeon Readers

Posthumus's linguistic exposure of Innogen during the wager scene is what triggers the intentional act of voyeurism that takes place in II. 2. In this scene, Iachimo consciously casts himself in the role of Actaeon (although the latter is never mentioned by name in the entire play). In doing so, Shakespeare highlights an aspect of the myth which, as has already been said, is not included in Ovid's version, that of intentional voyeurism. The underlying presence of the myth in II. 2 is reiterated by the villain's use of a sort language of intrusion, as when he remarks that 'The flame o'th' taper | Bows toward her and would under-peep her lids' (II. 2. 19–20). As Jonathan Bate has rightly observed, 'Iachimo and with him the audience stand in the position occupied by Actaeon'.[45] Significantly, the entire scene builds on the analogy between body and text and on the common trope of reading as voyeurism.[46] Iachimo points out that his 'design' is first of all 'To *note* the chamber' (II. 2. 23–24, emphasis added) and thus, as the stage direction makes clear, *He begins to write* (SD at 2. 2. 24).[47] A few lines later, he draws his attention to 'some natural *notes* about her [Innogen's] body' (II. 2. 28, emphasis added). As attested by the *Oxford English Dictionary*, the term 'note', which signifies 'to notice, observe' (*OED*, s.v. 'note, v.2', §II), also has the meaning of '[a]n explanatory or critical annotation or comment appended to a passage in a book, manuscript, etc.' (*OED*, s.v. 'note, n.2', §IV.14.a). The very presence of a book on the stage actually reinforces the connections between the acts of reading and of transgressive viewing, as well as the relation between body and text. In her seminal study on authorship and publication in the English Renaissance, Wendy Wall has shown that in the early modern period 'readers were asked [. . .] to imagine themselves as vicarious intruders'.[48] In other words, to be a reader meant to be an Actaeon entering a private and secret sphere. This was primarily due to the fact that the Renaissance era saw 'a decided shift towards the publication of plays alongside the publication of poetry'.[49] It is thus fairly common for published works of the period to employ the trope of voyeurism in their prefaces—those addresses that introduced the book to public viewing. This prefatorial material declared that, just like the goddess Diana, the book was being displayed to the world, thus further highlighting

---

[45] Bate, *Shakespeare and Ovid*, p. 217.

[46] On the trope of reading as voyeurism in the early modern period, see Wall, *The Imprint of Gender*.

[47] Wayne notes that 'some editorial SDs indicate that Iachimo writes in his "tables" or a notebook'. However, as she points out, 'no specific object is indicated' (*Cymbeline*, ed. by Wayne, p. 201, note to l. 24 (SD)).

[48] Wall, *The Imprint of Gender*, p. 214.

[49] Charlotte Scott, '"To Show... and so to Publish': Reading, Writing, and Performing in the Narrative Poems', in *The Oxford Handbook of Shakespeare's Poetry*, ed. by Jonathan Post (Oxford: Oxford University Press, 2013), pp. 377–95 (p. 379).

the relation between showing and publishing. A passage from the preface to George Pettie's *A Petite Pallace of Pettie his Pleasure* (1576) is worth quoting in this respect. The publisher reports the words of his friend Pettie:

> I haue set downe in writinge, and accordynge to your request, sent vnto you certaine of those Tragicall trifles, whiche you haue heard mee in sundrie companies at sundrye times report [. . .] I pray you only to vse them *to your owne priuate pleasure*, and not to impart them to other [. . .] I pray you in any wise let them bee *an obiect only for your owne eyes*.[50]

The printer includes a letter from Pettie as a preface to his unauthorized publication and therefore conceives the act of publishing as an act of 'voyeurism', which involves both secrecy (since the verses should have remained an object for his own eyes only) and 'pleasure'. In this perspective, readers themselves are turned into unintentional voyeurs, or into Actaeons gazing upon something that should have remained private, or unpublished.[51]

The much-quoted preface to Philip Sidney's unauthorized edition of *Astrophil and Stella* by Thomas Nashe explicitly equates writing and publishing with an act of violation of female privacy. As Nashe writes, although poetry

> be oftentimes imprisoned in Ladyes casks, [. . .] yet at length it breakes foorth in spight of his keepers, and vseth some priuate penne (in steed of a picklock) to procure his violent enlargement.[52]

Iachimo himself associates his act of illicit viewing and of reading with the idea of having 'picked the lock and ta'en | The treasure of her [Innogen's] honour' (II. 2. 41–42). The metaphor is reiterated by the buffoon Cloten in the scene that immediately follows, which functions as a comic parody of Actaeon's intrusion and of Iachimo's own voyeurism. In a retelling of the myth, Cloten imagines that he could bribe 'Diana's rangers' and 'buy admittance' into Innogen's bedroom, thus connecting once again the Ovidian myth with sexual exposure and with the issue of unlawful seeing:

> CLOTEN   I know her women are about her: what
>   If I do line one of their hands? 'Tis gold

---

[50] George Pettie, *A Petite Pallace of Pettie his Pleasure Contaynyng Many Pretie Hystories by Him Set Foorth in Comely Colours, and Most Delightfully Discoursed* (London: Printed by R. Watkins, 1576), sig. A3ʳ ('The Letter of G. P. to R. B. concerning this worke'), emphasis added. On this, see also Wall, *The Imprint of Gender*, pp. 174–75.

[51] In the epistle addressed 'To the gentle Gentlewomen Readers', the publisher admits to having 'transgresse[d] the boundes of faithfull friendship for hauinge with great earnestnesse obtained of my very freinde Master George Pettie the copie of certaine Histories' and for this reason, as he writes, he is 'sure [. . .] to incur his [Pettie's] displeasure, for that he willed me in any wise to keep them secret' (Pettie, *A Petite Palace*, sig. A2ʳ).

[52] Philip Sidney, *Syr P.S. His Astrophel and Stella. Wherein the Excellence of Sweete Poesie is Concluded* (London: Printed for Thomas Newman, 1591), sig. A3ʳ. On this preface, see Colin Burrow's introduction to *The Rape of Lucrece* in Shakespeare, *Sonnets and Poems*, pp. 65–66, and Wall, *The Imprint of Gender*, p. 214.

> Which buys admittance—oft it doth—yea, and makes
> Diana's rangers false themselves, yield up
> Their deer to th'stand o'th' stealer.
>
> (II. 3. 66–70)

The Actaeon myth activates, then, the motif of the voyeur-reader, which pervades the entire bedchamber scene (II. 2). As Wall remarks, '[w]hen voyeurism becomes a trope for reading, it makes the reader complicitous in the more insidious act of display involved in public writing'.[53] This is best seen in *Cymbeline* when Iachimo takes notes on Innogen's body and actively participates in the act of displaying her as a text. By adding marginal annotations to Innogen's body–text, Iachimo *reads* the lady's body like an annotator, thus also testifying to a practice that was widespread in the early modern age, when passages from classical texts were constantly rewritten and embellished with new details and were often included in commonplace books.[54] Shakespeare himself very likely used as one of his sources for the story of Lucrece an edition of Ovid's *Fasti* edited by Paolo Marsi, in which numerous marginal notes adorn the book, and he might have had this image in mind when describing Iachimo's own reading experience.[55]

Importantly, miscellany readers and readers of commonplace books, in particular, even had 'the privilege of participating in the text's creation',[56] a practice that is replicated in *Cymbeline* II. 2. The voyeur-reader Iachimo actually reveals what he calls 'the contents o'th' story' (II. 2. 27) only in a subsequent narration. This draws attention to the 'gap' between his act of voyeurism (and therefore of reading) and his description of the event. Clearly, this gap consists in rewriting, annotating the narrative with new circumstances. Reading like an annotator, as Burrow explains, means 'taking account of circumstance [...] and of stories which cling around the story',[57] thus also inviting the reader to consider the larger picture. When recounting to Posthumus his own version of the story, two scenes later, Iachimo comments thus:

---

[53] Wall, *The Imprint of Gender*, p. 211.

[54] I refer here to Colin Burrow's talk 'Sources: Visible and Invisible' given at the online International Colloquium 'Classical Receptions in Early Modern English Drama' organized by the Skenè Research Centre of the University of Verona (10–11 January 2023) and due to be published in the forthcoming Skenè publication edited by Silvia Bigliazzi and Tania Demetriou, *What is a Greek Source on the Early English Stage? Fifteen New Approaches* (provisional title).

[55] Critics generally agree that Shakespeare 'was consulting both narratives [Ovid's and Livy's] simultaneously via the commentary composed by Paulo Marsi (1440–84) which was appended to early editions of the *Fasti*' (John-Mark Philo, *An Ocean Untouched and Untried: The Tudor Translations of Livy* (Oxford: Oxford University Press, 2020), p. 95). As documented by Philo (p. 96), in the 1550 Basel edition Marsus's extensive commentary adorns the text and quotes extensive passages from Livy's *History of Rome*. However, as Philo points out, '[i]n terms of distinguishing the sources at work in *Lucrece* [...], matters are complicated by the fact that Ovid himself so frequently and self-consciously draws his narrative material from the historian [Livy]'.

[56] Wall, *The Imprint of Gender*, p. 102.

[57] Colin Burrow, 'Introduction' to *The Rape of Lucrece*, in *Sonnets and Poems*, p. 63.

IACHIMO   Sir, my circumstances,
                Being so near the truth as I will make them,
                Must first induce you to believe.
                                        (II. 4. 61–63)

The term 'circumstance' is particularly worth noting. Besides signifying 'details' and 'particulars', 'circumstance' also has the meaning of 'the surrounding
sense or context of a passage' (*OED*, s.v. 'circumstance, n.', §I.1.c). Iachimo
adds his own annotations, or 'circumstances', to the original narrative in
order to convince Posthumus of his wife's infidelity, and therefore he cites
those exemplary stories which—according to his own *reading*—will testify
to Innogen's betrayal. In particular, he cites those stories that cling around
the main narrative, such as the myth of 'Chaste Dian bathing' (II. 4. 82) and
the story of 'Proud Cleopatra when she met her Roman' (II. 4. 70), which he
regards as being somehow related (just as the stories of Lucrece and Philomel
are, both narratives being mentioned in the bedroom scene). The reference to
'Chaste Dian bathing' emphasizes, of course, Iachimo's role as Actaeon.[58] In
Iachimo's view, the story of Cleopatra can be cited alongside that of Diana
since both narratives position Innogen as an object of male desire. However,
Cleopatra, just like Diana, is also a woman who does not want to be 'published', as we learn from Shakespeare's recent play *Antony and Cleopatra*,
when the Egyptian queen comments thus: 'I shall see | Some squeaking Cleo-
patra boy my greatness | I'th' posture of a whore' (V. 2. 218–20).[59] These lines
are once again reminiscent of a passage from *The Rape of Lucrece*, when the
protagonist expresses the fear that she will be 'quoted' as an example of sin:

                Yea, the illiterate that know not how
                To cipher what is writ in learnèd books
                Will quote my loathsome trespass in my looks.
                                        (*Lucrece*, ll. 810–12)

---

[58] Bate points out that in II. 2 Shakespeare reinvents the Ovidian myth by highlighting the
'audience's complicity' in the illicit viewing (*Shakespeare and Ovid*, p. 219). Moving from Bate's
remark, J. K. Barret observes that 'we are reminded of our voyeurism by being retroactively
implicated as Actaeon at the same moment that we become Actaeon and watch the bathing Diana
appear mentally through Iachimo's description' ('The Crowd in Imogen's Bedroom: Allusion and
Ethics in *Cymbeline*', *Shakespeare Quarterly*, 66 (2015), 440–62 (pp. 452–53)).
[59] It is not a matter of chance that in the quoted passage from *Cymbeline* Shakespeare echoes
precisely the lines spoken by Enobarbus, when the latter describes the seductiveness of Cleopatra
and observes how even the air, 'but for vacancy', would have joined the spectators to *gaze on*
the highly desirable woman at Cydnus: 'The city cast | Her people out upon her, and Antony, |
Enthroned i'th' market-place, did sit alone, | Whistling to th'air, which, but for vacancy, | Had
gone to gaze on Cleopatra, too, | And made a gap in nature' (II. 2. 223–28). Line references from
Shakespeare's *Antony and Cleopatra* refer to William Shakespeare, *Antony and Cleopatra*, ed. by
John Wilders (London: Routledge, 1995; repr. Bloomsbury, 2021).

'Publish we this peace': Reconciliation and Rebirth

As I said in my introduction, all the embedded references to the myth of Diana
and Actaeon, along with the play's sustained emphasis on issues of displaying,
writing, and publishing, reinforce the birth imagery that is so central at the
end of this romance. A passage from the preface to Philip Sidney's *Apologie for
Poetry* (1595), penned by the editor Henry Olney, is especially worth quoting:

> help to support me poore Midwife, whose daring aduenture, hath deliuered from
> Obliuions wombe, this euer-to-be-admired wits miracle. [. . .] those who Prophet-like
> haue but heard presage of his coming, wil (if they wil doe wel) not onely defend, but
> praise mee, as the first publique bewrayer of Poesies *Musaeus*.[60]

Olney here styles himself as a 'poore Midwife' who 'hath deliuered from
Obliuions wombe, this euer-to-be-admired wits miracle'.[61] In addition to
presenting his publication as a public birth, Olney describes himself as 'the
first publique bewrayer', which casts his readers and buyers of the book as
Actaeons. The presence of the term 'bewrayer' in association with the idea of
childbirth actually constructs publishing as an act of 'reveal[ing], expos[ing],
and discover[ing] (unintentionally, and usually what it is intended to conceal)' (*OED*, s.v. 'bewray, v.', §6) and also as a new birth. In a seminal essay on
the influence of the Ovidian story of Philomel in *Cymbeline*, Ann Thompson
highlights the fact that the metaphor of birth (and of rebirth) is particularly
apt in the conclusion of a play that deals with rape, dismemberment, and
suffering bodies: 'Birth can be seen as precisely the comic conclusion to some
of these themes.'[62] I argue that this is also a suitable conclusion to a play that
reflects so extensively upon issues of writing, displaying, and publishing. As a
matter of fact, King Cymbeline's claim to maternity in Act v turns the final
reunion into a symbolic rebirth:

> CYMBELINE   O what am I?
> A mother to the birth of three? Ne'er mother
> Rejoiced deliverance more.
>
>   (v. 5. 368–70)

The term 'deliverance' is particularly significant in the light of its association
with both childbirth and displaying. To 'deliver' actually signifies 'to give
birth' (*OED*, s.v. 'deliver, v.1', §I.2.c), but also 'to present (a person or thing)
to the public' (ibid., §II.11.c). It is not coincidental that these sets of meanings

---

[60] Philip Sidney, *An Apologie for Poetry* (London: Printed [by James Roberts] for Henry Olney,
1595), 'To the Reader'.
[61] On the metaphor of writing as reproduction and on this preface in particular, see Wall, *The
Imprint of Gender*, pp. 181–82.
[62] Ann Thompson, 'Philomel in *Titus Andronicus* and *Cymbeline*', *Shakespeare Survey*, 31 (1979),
23–32 (p. 28).

reach their climax in the final emphasis upon the idea of publishing. As the king comments at the very end of the play:

> CYMBELINE   Publish we this peace
> To all our subjects. Set we forward. Let
> A Roman and a British ensign wave
> Friendly together.
>
> (V. 5. 477–80)

Reading and writing, which are associated with threatened rape, with violence, and with voyeurism throughout the play,[63] become in the end the means with which to announce a universal peace and a reunion. Unlike *The Rape of Lucrece*, where the act of publishing is a means by which to display a bleeding body (and therefore a dead body), in *Cymbeline* 'publishing' becomes restorative: it is a way to announce, or *deliver*, the birth of a reunified body, which is Cymbeline's reunited (and symbolically reborn) family, but also the play itself, which revives the past while creating something new. This also suggests an Ovidian preoccupation: authorial immortality through the transmission and survival of published texts, an idea which is well expressed in a celebrated passage from Ovid's *Tristia*, where the classical poet reflects upon the possibility of rebirth through writing:

> I others honour'd: others honoured
> Me with the best; and through the world I'm read.
> If then we Poets can the truth divine;
> Come death whenever, Dust, I am not thine.
> Whether by favour or desert I be
> Thus fam'd; kind Reader, thanks I give to thee.[64]

Cymbeline's ending, which stages the reconstitution of what has been torn asunder (in both real and metaphorical terms), acquires special relevance in the light of the several, oblique allusions to the Actaeon myth. While showing the threat of dismemberment consequent upon the act of displaying, the Ovidian episode also functioned as a common trope used by writers and printers to introduce their works to the public. The fact that 'Actaeon

---

[63] Reading is more than once associated with death in the play, as in the following lines spoken by Innogen which address Pisanio, Posthumus's servant: 'Speak, man: thy tongue | May take off some extremity, which to read | Would be even mortal to me' (III. 4. 16–18). Pisanio himself associates the act of reading with death when he observes that 'The paper | Hath cut her [Innogen's] throat already' (III. 4. 32–33). Not surprisingly, then, when Innogen believes that Pisanio has conspired with Cloten against Posthumus, she comments thus: 'To write and read be henceforth treacherous' (IV. 2. 315–16).

[64] Ovid, *Tristia*, IV 10, in Gower, *Ovids Festivalls*, sig. B4ᵛ. As Colin Burrow points out, 'Ovid's self-consciousness about how his texts will survive and how they will be reread in the light of new circumstances come to play a central part in his reception' ('Re-embodying Ovid: Renaissance Afterlives', in *The Cambridge Companion to Ovid*, ed. by Philip Hardie (Cambridge: Cambridge University Press, 2002), pp. 301–19 (p. 302)).

allegorized the practices of reading and writing in a culture suddenly conscious of the repercussions of public display'[65] brings me to offer one final
reflection: rather than being the product of 'casual preference or the con-
venience of the moment',[66] Heminges's and Condell's decision to place this
precise play at the close of the Folio derived, at least partly, from the drama's
consistent use of a language of showing and publishing, in its turn reinforced
by the underlying presence of the Actaeon narrative.

University of Udine   Martina Zamparo

[65] Wall, *The Imprint of Gender*, p. 230.

[66] W. W. Greg, *The Shakespeare First Folio: Its Bibliographical and Textual History* (Oxford:
Clarendon Press, 1955), pp. 80–81. On Greg's remark, see Wayne, 'The First Folio's Arrangement',
p. 393. Highlighting the appropriateness of *Cymbeline* as a valedictory play and refuting Greg's
hypothesis, Wayne writes that '[t]he First Folio had a major role in "shaping" the posthumous
reputation of Shakespeare. Concluding his collected plays with one that recapitulated those that
preceded it in the volume was consistent with furthering Shakespeare's literary and cultural
authority within print culture' (p. 405).

JAMES L. W. WEST ON F. SCOTT FITZGERALD: A REVIEW ARTICLE

Business Is Good: F. Scott Fitzgerald, Professional Writer. By James L. W. West III.
  University Park: Pennsylvania University Press. 2023. xiii+188 pp. £34.95.
  ISBN 978-0-271-09487-8.

In 2019 James L. W. West III completed his editorial work for the Cambridge
Edition of the Works of F. Scott Fitzgerald with the eighteenth volume in the
series, a variorum edition of *The Great Gatsby*.[1] He had taken over as general
editor from Matthew J. Bruccoli in 1994 after Bruccoli's publication of the first
two volumes, *The Great Gatsby* and *The Love of the Last Tycoon: A Western*.
From what must have been both awkward circumstances along with a mixture
of exciting opportunity and the realization of a forbidding amount of work
to come, West entered into a twenty-five-year project that holds a special
distinction in modern scholarly editing as a complete set of authoritative texts
for an American author published almost entirely under the direction of a
single general editor. The achievement is remarkable not only in its extent
and unified approach but also in its scholarly utility and, with paperback
issues allied to the standard cloth volumes, general accessibility. The volumes
are uncluttered reading texts, use a clear format for variants and explanatory
notes, and include well-selected illustrations. One will also find what might
be called an openness and warmth in reading West's volume introductions,
which, besides providing crucial background to each publication's history and
relevant biographical ties, also make astute critical judgements and explain
the choices made in textual editing and the book's content.

Now West has supplemented his immense service to Fitzgerald Studies with
Business Is Good: F. Scott Fitzgerald, Professional Writer. This volume from the
Pennsylvania State University Press is both a tribute to his scholarly career
and a welcome extension to that work, with insights into the editor's craft, revelations about the kinds of textual decision made for the Cambridge Edition,
and explorations of, especially, *The Great Gatsby*'s composition, publication
history, and legacy. The table of contents lists six new essays and five others
updated from earlier publications, notably from the *F. Scott Fitzgerald Review*
and the *Fitzgerald Newsletter*. The chapters combine into an integrated whole
based upon two key themes: Fitzgerald's work as a professional author, and
the intricacies of editing Fitzgerald's texts. The book's main title derives from
a decidedly well-travelled, paint-chipped metal paperweight that Fitzgerald
kept with him, the front side reading 'BUSINESS IS GOOD' and the back
'KEEP SMILING'. From another perspective, the good business involved in

---

[1] *The Great Gatsby: A Variorum Edition*, ed. by James L. W. West III (Cambridge: Cambridge
University Press, 2019).

Modern Language Review, 119 (2024), 495–501, doi:10.1353/mlr.00004
© Modern Humanities Research Association 2024

producing the Cambridge Edition through the collaborative efforts of West's team at Penn State, Cambridge University Press, and the Fitzgerald Trustees is illustrated in chapters that show the diligent archival efforts and editorial care that went into the volumes. And smiling? The book is seriously informative but also engaging and witty, even quite funny, as in the incisive chapter outlining the desecrations visited on the text of *Gatsby* in several post-copyright editions.

The first two chapters stem from careful detective work in the Princeton archives. 'The Last "Triangle" Performance' investigates a letter that Fitzgerald wrote on 7 December 1916, a date that would otherwise live in obscurity except for West's analysis of the context involving Fitzgerald's wide-ranging social sphere and the undergraduate's contribution as a lyricist for the Princeton Triangle Club's winter shows, especially the 1916–17 production *Safety First*. The inspection of the letter extends to biographical details about Fitzgerald's military preparedness training in college, the drafting of *The Romantic Egoist* manuscript during the war, and the sensational change in his fortunes following the publication of *This Side of Paradise*. The chapter asks what his ambition and talent might have led him to, had fate and circumstances been otherwise. Perhaps he might have followed the path of his contemporary Oscar Hammerstein II and pursued a career as a song lyricist, or (less likely) become a Tin Pan Alley songwriter. Chapter 2 follows the trail of a 1924 letter written by Fitzgerald in reply to an admirer, and from that source comes a comparative study of authorship at the high and low ends of the magazine publishing market of the twenties and thirties. Fitzgerald's lucrative position in writing stories for the 'slicks' such as the *Saturday Evening Post*, as well as publishing novels and short-story collections with Scribner's, opened up opportunities for subsidiary earnings from newspaper serials and book reprints, along with film and theatre rights. His admiring fan was less fortunate in that regard, for Moran Tudbury earned his living mainly as a formula writer for the pulp magazines. The gulf is illustrated by calculating Tudbury's rate at five cents per word for a pulp story versus Fitzgerald's twenty-eight cents per word for 'The Rich Boy'. In mixing high literature with monetary value, West concludes, Fitzgerald 'balanced on the tightrope between commerce and art—a precarious trick that, most of the time, he managed to perform quite well' (p. 31).

Money features again in the chapter on the 1926 theatre production of *The Great Gatsby*. This also serves as the introduction to the 2024 Cambridge University Press publication of the play script, a very welcome and fascinating text from sources in the Princeton archives.[2] West provides a crisp synopsis

---

[2] *The Great Gatsby: The 1926 Broadway Script by Owen Davis*, ed. by James L. W. West III and Anne Margaret Daniel (Cambridge: Cambridge University Press, 2024).

of the play, with its many deviations from the novel's plot and cast but ones that worked well on the stage. The Fitzgeralds were still in Europe in 1926 and did not see the stage play, but their reaction to its many liberties with the novel's text would have been tempered by a $6,866 profit from the box office earnings (about $103,000 today).

'The Ledger as Autobiography' offers valuable advice about how scholars can examine and best utilize Fitzgerald's business ledger (available online from the University of South Carolina's special collections database).[3] After outlining the biographical context of the document, West explains how Fitzgerald worked professionally to earn income through first writing original material and then, usually through his agent, Harold Ober, gaining further financial outlets via republications, performance rights, and translations. 'Fitzgerald seems to have been happiest when he was writing,' West observes, 'but the money he earned from his work did not necessarily bring satisfaction. When he had money in his pocket he wrote relatively little. He needed the pressure of debt to bring him to the writing table' (p. 84). A sound judgement drawn from the ledger, perhaps, but one might also cite as motivation at different periods in the author's career his burning ambition, professional pride, guilt at not fully using his talent, as well as a stubborn belief in that gift.

'Fitzgerald's Seven-Year Plan' riffs on the unearthing of a sheet of paper from the Fitzgerald collection at Princeton, found within a box of miscellaneous material about the creation of *Tender Is the Night*. The misfiled sheet, probably sketched by Fitzgerald in late 1938 or early 1939, divides his life into seven-year intervals, and we are left to consider what might have come had he lived to fifty-six, sixty-three, or seventy years old. From that inspiration, the potential here for a memoir or a 'reminiscent' book was largely fulfilled by West's volume in the Cambridge Edition *My Lost City* (2005), after the only partially successful attempt in Edmund Wilson's 1945 miscellany *The Crack-Up*.[4]

The following chapter moves from archival discoveries to the intricacies of textual editing. 'Punctuating by Ear' is a new piece, with detailed explanations of textual variants involving punctuation and the relevant editorial decisions to be made. Matters of 'pointing'—concerning choices about the use of commas, dashes, or full points—can seem both fraught and vital: the inclusion of a dash at the end of *This Side of Paradise* is one of the most significant examples (p. 260 in West's 1996 edition). 'Editing Fitzgerald's punctuation

---

[3] F. Scott Fitzgerald, *Ledger, 1919–1938*, 2012 <https://digital.library.sc.edu/collections/f-scott-fitzgeralds-ledger-1919-1938/> [accessed 5 February 2024].

[4] F. Scott Fitzgerald, *My Lost City: Personal Essays, 1920–1940*, ed. by James L. W. West III (Cambridge: Cambridge University Press, 2005); F. Scott Fitzgerald, *The Crack-Up, with Other Uncollected Pieces, Note-Books and Unpublished Letters* [. . .], ed. by Edmund Wilson, New Directions (New York, Laughlin, 1945).

is not an easy task', West shows: 'Because he punctuated by ear, one must learn to punctuate in the same way, always keeping in mind the rules of English grammar. In preparing his texts for the Cambridge series, my assistants and I spent considerably more time on punctuation, spelling, and word division than we did on the words themselves' (p. 111). Editorial choices, then, remain provisional even as they solidify in print, for the difficulties involving variants, accidentals, and substantives are compounded by issues over how much control Fitzgerald had over his publications within the commercial marketplace. Yet with clear editorial policies and careful examination of evidence from holograph manuscripts, typescripts, proofs, first printings, marked-up copies for correction in subsequent reprintings both domestic and foreign, along with correspondence and notes, the Cambridge Edition holds an unmatched authority—even as succeeding chapters here reveal how specific textual decisions are open to reinterpretation and revision.

Textual editing gives way to textual analysis in another new essay, 'Interpreting "Jacob's Ladder"'. Fitzgerald decided to remove the story from the contents of the 1935 collection *Taps at Reveille* because of the many 'strippings' he had used in *Tender Is the Night*. A bowdlerized version was printed in the original *Saturday Evening Post* publication, so West restored both typographical features as well as expunged passages of sexual innuendo for the Cambridge Edition, incorporated as one of the additional stories in the 2007 volume *All the Sad Young Men* (pp. 333–58). The restorations to the text compel rereading involving intertextuality, connecting literary references and plot devices to sources such as Shaw's *Pygmalion*, Poe's 'The Raven', and Keats's 'Ode on a Grecian Urn'. Further analysis binds such sources to Fitzgerald's first stint in Hollywood and associates gender issues in the text with Fitzgerald's controlling treatment of his wife Zelda, his sister Annabel, and his mistress, Sheila Graham.

In perhaps the most instructive essay in this volume, 'Decisions, Decisions: Editing *The Great Gatsby*', West interweaves close attention to textual history, variants involved in different editions of the novel, the consequences of *Gatsby*'s 2021 copyright expiration, and a delineation of the prerequisites for production of a reliable edition. The archival tools available to a *Gatsby* editor are the holograph, a set of marked galley proofs, and Fitzgerald's marked first edition with thirty-seven revisions used for the second Scribner's printing. In addition, two Cambridge Edition volumes provide contrasting exemplars. The 1991 Cambridge volume, edited by Bruccoli, relied mainly on Fitzgerald's holograph text and applied 1400 changes to the Scribner's first edition. West describes the 1991 edition as having a 'rough, unfinished surface' from its holograph foundation, as opposed to the 'smooth and polished' character of West's 2019 Cambridge Variorum edition, based on the Scribner's first edition (pp. 131–32). While the validity of each approach is not at issue, the starting point of a base text and the degree of editorial intervention clearly influence the end product.[5]

Scholars will be most familiar with textual variations in editions of *The Great Gatsby* such as the spelling *Wolfsheim* or *Wolfshiem*, the final chapter's *orgiastic* or *orgastic*, the ocular debate over *retina* versus *iris*, and the mechanics of *transit* versus *compass*. But West neatly runs through many other decisions he made for the Variorum edition, so that this essay itself will be a valuable tool for the concerned editor and scrupulous reader. They will want to note all of the details, but among the cruxes to consider are the direction in which Nick Carraway walks towards Central Park (southward? eastward?), the location (and spelling) of the Queensboro Bridge (Long Island City, not nearby Astoria), the Seelbach Hotel (Louisville) or Muhlbach Hotel (Kansas City), Pammy's age (two or three?), and the mystery of the fifth guest at the Buchanans' dinner party (the topic of a *Fitzgerald Review* discussion in 2010).[6] Following evidence from the holograph manuscript, West found a logical resolution to the problem of who is being asked the question in the Metropole conversation between Gatsby and Nick: '"What place is that?" I asked Gatsby'. The Variorum editor admits to some second thoughts in a couple of other instances. At the expense of altering a single word, it would make more sense if Mendelssohn's 'Wedding March', the music playing in the Plaza Hotel scene, had 'ended' rather than 'begun' (pp. 139–40; *The Great Gatsby*, 2019, p. 153); and few would object to eliminating 'Mavromichaelis', a vestigial name for 'Michaelis' in the manuscript, from the odd interaction between the motorcycle policeman taking witnesses' names at the accident scene (pp. 140–41; *The Great Gatsby*, 2019, p. 167). Gaps between lines of text are a fraught issue in many editions, attended to with sedulous care in the Variorum. A new edition might reconsider whether to keep 'kyke' (earlier changed to 'guy' by Bantam and to 'tyke' by Penguin; pp. 144–45), or whether 'negroes', 'bucks', and 'the yolks of their eyeballs' should be amended (p. 145; *The Great Gatsby*, 2019, p. 83). What understandably seems non-negotiable to West is that the novel's epigraph and dedication should not be left out. He also rightly praises Cambridge University Press's expensive efforts to include

---

[5] Kirk Curnutt reviewed the Variorum edition with background to its publication and a thorough examination of its content, editorial principles, and the details of textual practice; see 'A Fitzgerald Potpourri', *F. Scott Fitzgerald Review*, 17 (2019), 248–71 (reviewing West's 2019 edition of *The Great Gatsby*; Zelda Fitzgerald, *Save Me the Waltz*, with an introduction by Erin E. Templeton (London: Handheld Press, 2018); Christopher A. Snyder, *Gatsby's Oxford: Scott, Zelda, and the Jazz Age Invasion of Britain, 1904–1929* (New York: Pegasus, 2019); and Jade Broughton Adams, *F. Scott Fitzgerald's Short Fiction: From Ragtime to Swing Time* (Edinburgh: Edinburgh University Press, 2019)).

[6] Robert Beuka and James L. W. West III, 'The Fifth Guest in *The Great Gatsby*: An Online Symposium', *F. Scott Fitzgerald Review*, 8 (2010), 24–32.

Francis Cugat's cover illustration as a full-colour image in the frontispiece of the 2019 edition.

In 'Le déluge: New Editions of *The Great Gatsby*', thirty-four new editions come under West's detective lens, appraised through the criteria of whether or not a base text is declared, how cruxes are handled, whether emendations are reported, whether an account of the text's history is given, whether the Cugat illustration is noted, and whether the epigraph and dedication are in-cluded. While volumes such as the Penguin Books US edition and the Norton Critical Edition pass muster, the majority fall far short of West's respectful standards for presenting this modern classic to the reading public. Profit and ineptitude mark down most of these other publications, tangled in a cycle of republication and editorial carelessness. 'I am convinced that the texts have been cross-pollinating in the night', West writes, and other righteous jabs follow. He comments on the Black Dog and Leventhal edition: 'This is a gift edition and perhaps is not meant to be read' (p. 162). On what appears to be a pilot AI-generated text, or possibly a foreign translation retranslated into a form of English, 'perhaps by an antic computer' that somehow omitted the final three pages of the 1925 original publication, he drily notes: 'One doesn't have to worry about "orgastic" or "orgiastic"' (p. 156). An inventive mind in the Mr Mintz Classics staff decided that Gatsby's meeting with the horseback-riding Tom Buchanan and the Sloans should be illustrated with a computer-generated image of a farmer and a plough-horse (p. 162). Only the most over-generous or purblind critic could see a hint of James Gatz's origins in that. Although one could easily despair at the prospect, West ends with the hope that new editions of *The Great Gatsby* will be produced with the editorial conscientiousness that the iconic novel deserves.

Described as 'some afterthoughts about the Cambridge Edition', the final essay offers fascinating insights into the editorial plans and programme for the series, and it supplements West's 2019 *Fitzgerald Review* article 'The Cam-bridge Fitzgerald Edition: Some Final Observations', that neatly summarized the history of the project, its making and make-up, as well as its distinctive character.[7] As a collected edition, the Cambridge volumes include a large number of Fitzgerald's short stories associated with the period in which his four major collections were published, and these stories are incorporated as additional texts within those collections, while other short stories earn their own separate volumes. For their perceived shortcomings, nine short stories were excluded by agreement with the Fitzgerald trustees, including the four 'Count of Darkness' stories and 'Shaggy's Morning'. Should a case have been made to add those leftovers, with suitable interpretative context, to make them

---

[7] James L. West III, 'The Cambridge Fitzgerald Edition: Some Final Observations', *F. Scott Fitzgerald Review*, 17 (2019), 18–28.

more readily available? A linguistic analysis of 'Shaggy's Morning' by Anna Ishchenko in her paper at the 2023 Fitzgerald Society conference proved that even a mongrel can be loved and appreciated.[8] About another missing piece, 'Turkey Remains and How to Inter Them', West admits both honestly and wryly, 'Why it escaped my gaze I cannot say' (p. 171). As to the rest that found a home in the Cambridge Edition, he explains that the series took longer than anticipated because of a crucial editorial policy, in collaboration with Penn State and Cambridge University Press: 'I decided to collate everything, to devote as much editorial attention to a humble story written for money as I had devoted to "The Rich Boy" and "Babylon Revisited"' (p. 172). The essential nature of that enterprise is its interpretative effort. Rather than a documentary edition, the texts reflect Fitzgerald's intentions, as determined by available evidence and the best judgement of the editor. As West explains: 'The aim is to recapture an author's active intentions—the author's desire to be read in a particular way.' That editorial method produces 'an "eclectic" text, one that has not existed before' (p. 174)—an idealized goal, but 'No intentionalist text is ever definitive' (p. 175). Therefore, the pursuit may continue in order to create something better, perhaps based on new evidence or because of publishing innovations, such as a future edition with a website for expanded annotations or interactive engagement with the text.

The Cambridge Edition of the Works of F. Scott Fitzgerald, then, stands in our historical moment. The final chapter's title, 'The Cambridge Edition and the Cambridge Plumber', rests on an anecdote about a plumber who reported, after a thorough inspection of the plumbing in the accommodation that West's family rented in Cambridge, England, that 'There is nothing to be done' (p. 176). So the occupants simply made do, just as scholarly editing ultimately works within the limitations of evidence, and sometimes time, fate, and fortune. Nevertheless, *Business Is Good* demonstrates how much needed to be done in order to produce the Cambridge Edition, and this volume will not be the last contribution to be appreciated from one of America's pre-eminent scholarly editors, whose assiduousness, open-mindedness, tact, and honesty have given us the foundational texts of the Cambridge Edition and so much more guiding scholarship to build upon.

LIVERPOOL HOPE UNIVERSITY   WILLIAM BLAŽEK

---

[8] Anna Ishchenko, '"In the front yard I howled. I don't know why": F. Scott Fitzgerald and an Experiment in Non-Human Writing', F. Scott Fitzgerald Society Conference, Linnaeus University, Växjö, Sweden, 28 June 2024; F. Scott Fitzgerald, 'Shaggy's Morning', *Esquire*, 1 May 1935, pp. 26, 160 <https://classic.esquire.com/article/1935/5/1/shaggys-morning> [accessed 5 February 2024].

ALL THE ISLANDS THE ISLAND: THE CRAFTING OF CORTÁZAR'S 'LA ISLA A MEDIODÍA'

> Delos y Mykonos, donde creo haberme acercado por un momento a una zona que rebasaba lo humano [. . .] ese pulso del mundo que siempre me pareció Delos a mediodía.
>
> (Julio Cortázar)[1]

Introduction

This is the latest in an ongoing series of essays whose principal aim is to explore in detail how and why Julio Cortázar came to write certain of his most iconic stories as and when he did by identifying previously overlooked literary sources and tracing the various ways in which he drew on and adapted them, often carefully modifying elements of the original texts in ways that reveal much about his own particular aesthetic principles and purposes.[2] From these investigations there emerges a picture of the writer very much at odds with that of the Romantic-cum-Surrealist myth of Cortázar as a wholly intuitive, spontaneous creator of or entranced conduit for *cuentos*, a myth which he himself was always keen to cultivate.[3] What we find instead is a meticulous craftsman, whose finest, most disconcertingly immersive stories are often the product of subtle and evidently quite conscious processes of selection, assimilation, and transformation of specific source material—however instinctive and unformulated his initial enthusiasm for the latter may have been.

'La isla a mediodía'

In the case of 'La isla a mediodía' (the focus of the present study) no such enquiry into the story's origins would appear to be necessary, as Cortázar provided a vivid description of its genesis in a letter to his editor, Francisco Porrúa, dated 1 November 1965, shortly after he had written it:

En el aire, entre Teherán y Viena, tuve un minuto maravilloso; a mediodía, desde un cielo límpido, vi las Cícladas o las Espóradas, el Egeo casi negro rodeando esas tortugas pedregosas. Pensé [...] Bueno, lo que pensé o viví se tradujo en un cuento breve, de unas 7 páginas.[4]

---

[1] Julio Cortázar, letter to Carlos Fuentes, 4 May 1966, in *Las cartas del Boom*, ed. by Carlos Aguirre and others (Madrid: Alfaguara, 2023), pp. 131–37 (pp. 133, 135). This letter does not appear in the five volumes of *Cartas* (see n. 4 below).

[2] Previous pieces include 'Straight from *The Horse's Mouth*? On the Origins of Cortázar's "El perseguidor"', *Bulletin of Spanish Studies*, 94 (2017), 1601–22; and 'Why Enghien? A Note on Cortázar and Proust', *Bulletin of Spanish Studies*, 97 (2020), 235–57.

[3] The *locus classicus* of Cortázar's self-portrayal as a sort of unconscious medium through which stories would emerge unheralded and seemingly fully formed remains 'Del cuento breve y sus alrededores', in *Último Round* (1969; repr. Barcelona: Destino, 2004), pp. 42–55 (esp. pp. 46–47).

[4] Julio Cortázar, *Cartas*, ed. by Aurora Bernárdez and Carles Álvarez Garriga, 5 vols (Buenos

Modern Language Review, 119 (2024), 502–24, doi:10.1353/mlr.00005

This account would make 'La isla' a classic product of that quasi-daemonic process of possession and imaginative exorcism or 'translation' that Cortázar deemed essential to the creation of 'todo cuento plenamente logrado, y en especial los cuentos fantásticos'.[5] Formally and expressively too, 'La isla' exhibits all those qualities which, according to Cortázar, raise the finest stories above the level of the merely 'literary' and imbue them with a seemingly irresistible, almost visceral force, i.e. the systematic suppression or concealment of all traces of extradiegetic narration and the radical stripping away of merely decorative description and circumstantial detail ('lo meramente accessorio') so as to create an impression of 'autarquía'; an imperceptibly quickening narrative rhythm building to an irresistible crescendo; a denouement that is at once unexpected, disconcerting, and yet seemingly inevitable. Yet for all its undeniable immediacy of impact, 'La isla' also furnishes the reader with sufficient cultural and literary co-ordinates to signal what might be at stake both existentially and ethically in the story, and thus a basic philosophical framework within which to interpret it. Perhaps most obviously, both the title and the setting point to the influence of Nietzsche. In *Thus Spoke Zarathustra* (1884–85), Nietzsche (in)famously heralded the 'great noontide' which allegedly marked the emblematic watershed at which the *Übermensch* would leave a depleted, morally rotten Western humanity definitively behind, while in the earlier *The Birth of Tragedy* (1872) he had celebrated pre-Socratic Greece as the repository of a vital, Dionysiac energy that, he claimed, had been fatally banished from modern life by an ever more stultifying and ultimately lethal rationalism.[6] These twin notions are surely (and, I would suggest, consciously) echoed in 'La isla', in which the protagonist, Marini, determines to slough his benumbed, hyper-civilized self (referred to, with obvious symbolic overtones, as '[el] hombre viejo': 'La isla', p. 131) when he encounters an Aegean island seemingly untainted by modernity whose origins, Cortázar is careful to inform the reader, lie in the remote, pre-Hellenic past.[7]

Aires: Alfaguara, 2012–13), III, 193. The story was first published in *Primera Plana*, 171 (April 1966) and subsequently included in *Todos los fuegos el fuego*, which appeared that same year. The edition to which I will be referring throughout appears in *Todos los fuegos el fuego* (Madrid: Alfaguara, 2014), pp. 123–33.

[5] 'Del cuento breve y sus alrededores', p. 46. Cortázar uses the same term ('traslado') to describe this process in the essay as he does in the letter (ibid.).

[6] Given that few times of day have been as culturally and metaphorically overdetermined as noon, I am far from suggesting that Nietzsche is the only source for Cortázar's title and subject matter, but rather simply the most immediately relevant one. It is clear from all Cortázar's writings, both fictional and other, that he was closely acquainted with Nietzsche's work. His enduring interest in an often idealized ancient Greece, meanwhile, is evident from his earliest writing, not least the posthumously published *Imagen de John Keats* (1950).

[7] When researching the island, Marini discovers that 'huellas de una colonia lidia o quizá cretomicénica' have been discovered there, indicative of a culture that pre-dates Socratic Greece by a millennium or more ('La isla', p. 126). Cortázar's fictional Xiros may well be based on the

Despite Cortázar's insistence on textual autonomy, context of different sorts also proves helpful. The story's central theme—that of the seductive but potentially fatal allure of antique forces associated with ancient Greece, too long and too forcefully repressed—is also explored in 'Las Ménades' and 'El ídolo de las Cícladas' (also from *Final del juego*), making of the three tales a loose but mutually enlightening triptych.[8] Meanwhile, its final, perplexing twist is strikingly reminiscent of the shattering conclusion to Ambrose Bierce's 'An Occurrence at Owl Creek Bridge' (1890).[9] Other possible literary antecedents include Borges's story 'El milagro secreto' and perhaps even Hans Castorp's dream in Thomas Mann's *The Magic Mountain* (1924), involving as it does an ultimately double-edged vision of what, initially at least, appears to be an age-old Mediterranean idyll. Both works play on the sometimes yawning discrepancy between clock time and, broadly speaking, psychological time, which may also figure in 'La isla'.[10] Cortázar was, of course, also familiar with the 'island' stories and novels of Verne, Stevenson, Wells, and Poe, and his personal library includes an edition of Melville's *Typee* (1846) published as recently as 1960.[11]

It is also worth recalling that as early as 1945 Cortázar had made a somewhat eccentric translation (still in print) of that paradigm of 'island literature' *Robinson Crusoe* (1719), a novel he later rehashed as bludgeoning postcolonial critique in the form of the radio play *Adiós, Robinson* (1970s), in which Crusoe

---

real Cycladic island of Syros, whose history has been traced back at least as far as the early Bronze Age, and where many of the figurines of the type which features in 'El ídolo de las Cícladas' (from *Final del juego* (1956/64)) were discovered.

[8] Also apposite here is the long trilingual poem 'Gre / cia / ce / ece 59', and especially its disillusioned final section, which features a 'vuelo de reconocimiento' over the Greek islands which reveals '*Ningún dios, todos muertos. Nada que señalar*'. See Julio Cortázar, *Salvo el crepúsculo* (1984; repr. Madrid: Alfaguara, 2009), pp. 159–69 (p. 169). Gustavo Pellón provides a superb, detailed reading of this poem, of obvious relevance to the present study, in his 'Cortázar and the Idolatry of Origins', in *Julio Cortázar: New Readings*, ed. by Carlos J. Alonso (Cambridge: Cambridge University Press, 1998), pp. 110–29. However, I find his brief comments on 'La isla' itself (pp. 125–26) and his somewhat abrupt conclusions concerning Cortázar's Hellenism in general (p. 127) more questionable.

[9] Indeed, Cortázar had already, and quite explicitly, glossed Bierce's famous tale in one of his earliest *cuentos*, 'Profunda siesta de Remi' (1939) (one of a series of 'Plagios y traducciones' from the posthumously published *La otra orilla* (1945)), somewhat contrivedly adding a further, knowing twist to that of the original.

[10] The Borges story, published in *Ficciones* (1944), is an obvious 'local' source, but Cortázar clearly knew Mann's novel well, indicating that, in part at least, he had written *Rayuela* specifically as 'una especie de anti-Thomas Mann', citing *The Magic Mountain* (which he repeatedly mischaracterizes as a 'didactic' work) as his particular target. See *Clases de literatura*, ed. by Carles Álvarez Garriga (Buenos Aires: Alfaguara, 2013), pp. 211–12, 224. For Castorp's dream, which contains various features that recur in Cortázar's story, see Thomas Mann, *The Magic Mountain*, trans. by John E. Woods (New York: Vintage, 1995), pp. 480–89.

[11] The library is held at the Fundación Juan March in Madrid and may be consulted online. For the Melville, see <www.march.es/es/coleccion/biblioteca-julio-cortazar/ficha/typee--5603> [accessed 27 March 2024].

and Friday return to a now heavily developed Juan Fernández by aeroplane—Marini's mode of transport. One or two brief references, as well as certain elements of the plot, suggest that he may knowingly have been reworking, indeed sometimes inverting, aspects of Defoe's novel in the story.[12]

Yet, whatever the pertinence of the various possible antecedents and intertexts outlined above, in what follows I shall endeavour to show that, irrespective of its anecdotal origin, 'La isla' is in fact overwhelmingly indebted to a number of English literary sources, which are themselves variously and illuminatingly interlinked: a story by D. H. Lawrence published almost forty years previously, and near contemporary works by Aldous Huxley and, above all, William Golding, whose influence I consider decisive and ubiquitous, running to the level of fine textual detail. As we shall see, these texts share, borrow, transform, and redeploy a panoply of ideas, literary precedents, narrative syntagms and scenarios, structural devices and motifs, all of which to a greater or lesser degree inform Cortázar's story.[13]

Lawrence

> We do not travel to go from one hotel to another, and perhaps see a few side-shows. We travel to get away from a world we hate, which is the world of man as we have made it. We travel, maybe, with a secret and absurd hope of setting foot on the Hesperides, if only for half an hour: of running our boat up a little creek and landing in a Garden of Eden. No good! There is no Garden of Eden on this commercial and predatory earth. The Hesperides never were. Abandon all hope of a quick trip to paradisal places. There aren't any.
>
> (D. H. LAWRENCE)[14]

The only volume by Lawrence remaining in Cortázar's personal library is a 1959 edition of *Sons and Lovers*, but it is evident from both his critical

---

[12] For example, aside from the broad similarities between the core scenarios of the two works, Crusoe reports that, shortly after being shipwrecked, 'for a while I run about like a Mad-man', while the increasingly obsessed Marini is referred to mockingly by the pilots as 'el loco de la isla' ('La isla', p. 127). Later, Crusoe discovers the sole, unidentified survivor of a shipwreck on the beach, whereas in the story Marini's seems to be the body that the locals discover. See Daniel Defoe, *Robinson Crusoe*, ed. by J. Donald Crowley (Oxford: Oxford University Press, 1997) pp. 47, 188–89.

[13] Huxley's admiration for Lawrence and his work, and the immense (though far from unquestioned) influence of the latter on his own, have been copiously documented. Huxley, in turn, was one of the young Golding's favourite writers, and his influence is detectable in many of Golding's novels, not least *Lord of the Flies*. Cortázar, as we shall see, was familiar with all three.

[14] D. H. Lawrence, review of H. M. Tomlinson's *Gifts of Fortune*, in *Introductions and Reviews*,

writings and especially his correspondence that he knew the English writer's work well.[15] In both of Cortázar's major essays on the short story Lawrence is cited as a paragon of the genre, while *The Plumed Serpent* is mentioned in *Teoría del túnel* (1947) and 'Situación de la novela' (1950) as an example of both the *poetismo* and the radical existential critique which he saw as defining features of the contemporary novel (*Teoría* also makes a passing reference, in the same vein, to *Kangaroo* (1923)). His 'Vida de Edgar Allan Poe', meanwhile (originally the prologue to an edition of Poe's complete prose works, which Cortázar translated in the early 1950s), shows that he was familiar with Lawrence's *Studies in Classic American Literature* (1923). He had also read at least some of Lawrence's poetry.[16] Perhaps even more significantly, a letter to Mercedes Arias from Mendoza (where Cortázar was teaching at the Universidad Nacional de Cuyo), dated as early as 21 August 1945, reveals that he was planning to work on a seminar series on Lawrence, Wolf, and Huxley at the end of that year.[17] As far as I have been able to ascertain, no record of that particular course remains, but the outlines of those that have survived all testify to the remarkable breadth of his reading of both primary and critical sources and the meticulousness of his preparation.[18] Cortázar also shared the English writer's fundamental conviction that Western civilization as a whole had been veering fatally off course since the rise of Socratic reason.[19] Thus, four years later, writing to his friend Fredi Guthman, he refers more exten-

---

ed. by N. H. Reeve and John Worthen (Cambridge: Cambridge University Press, 2005), pp. 291–96 (p. 288).

[15] See <www.march.es/es/coleccion/biblioteca-julio-cortazar/ficha/sons-and-lovers--3701> [accessed 27 March 2024].

[16] 'Del cuento breve y sus alrededores', p. 43; 'Algunos aspectos del cuento' (1962–63), in Julio Cortázar, *Obras completas* (henceforth *OC*), ed. by Saúl Yurkievich with Gladis Anchieri, 6 vols (Barcelona: Galaxia Gutenberg, 2003–07), VI: *Obra crítica*, pp. 370–86 (p. 381); *Teoría del túnel*, ibid., pp. 45–125 (p. 110); 'Situación de la novela', ibid., pp. 268–90 (p. 280); 'Vida de Edgar Allan Poe', ibid., pp. 304–69 (pp. 349, 355–56); 'Poesía inglesa contemporánea' (review), ibid., pp. 195–96 (p. 195).

[17] *Cartas*, I, 228–31 (p. 231). Nor is this Cortázar's first refence to Lawrence. In a much earlier letter to Luis Gagliardi, dated Chivilcoy, 9 November 1941, he speculates on 'la influencia de Sigmund Freud y D. H. Lawrence' on the work of Sartre, specifically the latter's story 'La Chambre', which he had read in translation (as 'El aposento') in *Sur* (*Cartas*, I, 135–39 (p. 137)). This suggests that he may already have been familiar with Lawrence's highly idiosyncratic works on psychoanalysis, *Psychoanalysis and the Unconscious* (1921) and *Fantasia of the Unconscious* (1922).

[18] These are listed in Jaime Correa's *Cortázar en Mendoza* (Buenos Aires: Alfaguara, 2014), pp. 235–42.

[19] Like Cortázar, Lawrence, in both life and literature, often sought refuge from what he viewed as the catastrophe of Western modernity in an idealized, 'pagan' Mediterranean, which features prominently in the travelogues *Twilight in Italy* (1916), *Sea and Sardinia* (1921), and the posthumously published *Etruscan Places* (1932), as well as poems such as 'Sicilian Cyclamens', 'The Greeks Are Coming', 'The Argonauts', 'Middle of the World', and 'For the Heroes Dipped in Scarlet'. For the latter see D. H. Lawrence, *The Complete Poems*, ed. by Vivian de Sola Pinto and Warren Roberts (London: Penguin, 1993), pp. 310, 687–89.

sively to Lawrence in a passage of obvious relevance to 'La isla a mediodía' as well as cognate stories such as 'El ídolo de las Cícladas':

Pienso que será magnifico saltar hacia atrás, desde Europa siglo XX a las mesetas originales, fuera del tiempo, a salvo de la historia. ¿Se despertarán en el occidental las resonancias de contacto, las armónicas, frente a su escenario primitivo, su punto de partida? Creo que sí; por lo menos, algunas experiencias como las de D. H. Lawrence en Taos, y las de ese americano que vivió veinte años entre los indios de Nuevo Méjico, hasta aprender no solo el idioma y las costumbres, sino llegar a pensar como ellos y sentir como ellos... El extremo desarrollo espiritual del hombre puede coincidir mejor con su extremo primitivismo, que los términos medios estilo 'misionero' o 'antropólogo'.[20]

How Cortázar came to learn of Lawrence's alleged 'experiencias en Taos' (they were, in fact, very different from what he imagined) remains unclear, but the most likely sources were the essays of *Mornings in Mexico* (1927) (especially 'Indians and Entertainment', 'The Dance of the Sprouting Corn', and 'The Hopi Snake Dance'), the novella *St Mawr* (1925), and the titular story of *'The Woman Who Rode Away' and Other Stories* (1928), itself written in Taos in 1925.[21] This latter work relates the experiences of a Californian woman in present-day New Mexico who, weary of modern life, flees her home and her failing marriage and ends up as the delirious victim of a ritual sacrifice at the hands of a an age-old, indigenous tribe.[22] The essentials of the plot are so similar to those of Cortázar's 'La noche boca arriba' (from *Final del juego*) that one suspects a direct influence. And that might be of significance to the present study, since the story on which, I shall argue, Cortázar is drawing in 'La isla a mediodía' comes from the same collection. I am referring to the redolently titled 'The Man Who Loved Islands', which also charts a man's complete and ultimately fatal withdrawal from contemporary society and its myriad perceived ills.[23] The protagonist, Cathcart, is, in certain respects, a

[20] *Cartas*, I, 296–99 (p. 297). Lawrence's possible influence on 'El ídolo de las Cícladas' will be the subject of a future study.

[21] Lawrence's other pieces relating to his time in and around Taos ('Taos' (1923), 'Pan in America' (1926), and 'New Mexico' (1928)) were initially published independently in journals and gathered and edited after Lawrence's death in 1930 by Edward D. McDonald in *Phoenix: The Posthumous Papers of D. H. Lawrence* (London: Heinemann, 1936). This collection would almost certainly have been less accessible to Cortázar but, given his insatiable reading habits, it is entirely possible that he had come across it.

[22] D. H. Lawrence, *'The Woman Who Rode Way' and Other Stories*, ed. by Dieter Mehl and Christa Jansohn (Cambridge: Cambridge University Press, 1995), pp. 39–71. The collection also includes another story, 'Sun', which involves an only partially successful and temporary flight from the horrors of industrialized modernity (in the form of New York) to an idealized Mediterranean (pp. 19–38).

[23] *'The Woman Who Rode Away'*, pp. 151–73. The story (first published independently in 1927) initially appeared only in the American edition (the one Cortázar is most likely to have encountered), since Compton Mackenzie, on whom the often ridiculed protagonist was clearly (though not straightforwardly) based, threatened to sue Lawrence were the work to be published

hyperbolized, caricatural incarnation of a type of (exclusively male) character illustrated and explored more earnestly in many of Lawrence's later novels, essays, and poems, the most developed examples of which are perhaps Birkin, from *Women in Love* (1920), Somers, from *Kangaroo*, and Mellors, from *Lady Chatterley's Lover* (1928).[24] All are intent on cultivating a deep, isolate sense of selfhood, sheltered from and untarnished by the anonymizing rituals and routines of an increasingly automated and insensate mass society but intimately attuned to the greater rhythms of the Cosmos.[25] Cathcart shares their abhorrence, but takes their quest for restorative apartness to what are ultimately self-destructive extremes, the story as a whole reading like an extended, often sardonic gloss on Donne's famous dictum. Indeed, Cathcart's debacle has been viewed by at least one critic as an example of what J. G. Ballard termed 'reverse Crusoeism', putting him in stark contrast with a character such as Birkin, who, despite envying Alexander Selkirk (the model for Defoe's character) his solitude, like Mellors craves seclusion only in order to cleanse himself before, at least in principle, reconnecting with his fellow men.[26]

The story relates Cathcart's departure from the mainland and his successive sojourns on three increasingly remote and hostile islands. The first two he abandons at least partly because they retain too many of the trappings of and ties with his former, enervatingly civilized life.[27] On the third, the text inti-

in book form in England. The threat was later dropped, and it was published posthumously in *The Lovely Lady* (1933), being repeatedly anthologized thereafter. For details of the spat see '*The Woman Who Rode Away*', 'Introduction', pp. xxi–lxv (pp. xxxv–xxxix).

[24] There is a substantial critical bibliography on the story, and many other interpretations of Cathcart's character and fate have been offered. For example, a number of commentators have viewed it as an exercise in self-critique and its protagonist as a damning self-portrait of his creator and the latter's own, repeatedly adumbrated but ultimately abortive, attempt to found a Utopian community, which he initially named Rananim but later referred to simply as 'the Island'. See e.g. Stefania Michelucci, 'A Man Who Loved Islands: D. H. Lawrence and the Paradox of Rananim', in *Vite di Utopia*, ed. by Vita Fortunati and Paola Spinozzi (Ravenna: Longo, 2000), pp. 27–38; Jill Franks, '"The Man Who Loved Islands": D. H. Lawrence and his Island Scheme', in her *Islands and the Modernists: The Allure of Isolation in Art, Literature and Science* (Jefferson, NC: McFarland, 2006), pp. 105–38 (esp. pp. 107–21). For a clear and detailed summary of Lawrence's uniformly disastrous attempts at establishing Rananim see George J. Zytaruk, 'Rananim: Lawrence's Failed Utopia', in *The Spirit of D. H. Lawrence*, ed. by Gamini Salgado and G. K. Das (London: Macmillan, 1988), pp. 266–94.

[25] I have written extensively on this aspect of Lawrence's work in relation to Pablo Neruda's poetry, and to avoid excessive recapitulation I would refer the reader to my '"Caballero solo": Eliot, Lawrence . . . Porter?', *MLR*, 113 (2018), 117–29 (esp. pp. 119–22).

[26] See Frederick R. Karl, 'Lawrence's "The Man Who Loved Islands": The Crusoe Who Failed', in *A D. H. Lawrence Miscellany*, ed. by Simonetta de Filippis and Nick Ceramella (Naples: Loffredo, 2004), pp. 265–79; D. H. Lawrence, *Women in Love*, ed. by David Farmer and others (London: Penguin, 1995), p. 108. Tellingly, Birkin first tells Ursula Brangwen of his loathing of the 'huge aggregate lie' of a contemporary humanity that obliterates all individuality, in Chapter 11, entitled 'An Island' (*Women in Love*, pp. 123–33 (p. 126)).

[27] On the first island, in marked distinction to Marini, he sets himself up as a sort of benign patriarch of an autonomous, quasi-feudal community that he is singularly ill-equipped to govern, and it is here that he is most obviously the butt of the narrator's irony. Subsequently, however, and

mates, after becoming too weak and disoriented to flee, he dies in a snowstorm in what, finally, is absolute, inhuman isolation.[28] There are obvious parallels here with Marini's quixotic trajectory in 'La isla'. Like Cathcart, Marini craves a total break, both physical and spiritual, with the dehumanizing protocols of twentieth-century life (symbolized, as all the story's commentators note, by the aeroplane and its programmed, endlessly repeated flight paths), even if the latter is drawn towards what he imagines as a sun-drenched, pre-Hellenic idyll rather than a barely habitable lump of rock in the freezing waters off Britain.[29] Both characters, in sum (albeit in quite different ways), embody that categorical rejection of Western modernity and yearning for some imagined sense of primal, spontaneous 'being-in-the world' shared by their creators, and both seem to end up dead as a consequence. These broad overlaps in theme and plot alone are worthy of note, but more striking still are what appear to be the specific, conscious echoes of Lawrence's story in Cortázar's, several of which I shall now examine.

Both stories refer explicitly to the rise of mass tourism and its pernicious effects on unspoilt wildernesses and/or changeless, ancestral ways of life. The hapless Cathcart, increasingly beset by financial worries (throughout the first two sections of the story, money acts as a sort of synecdoche for all of contemporary society's malaises), is forced to sell his first island to 'an hotel company who were willing to speculate in it' by turning it into a 'handy honeymoon-and-golf island' ('The Man', 160).[30] The phrase, twice repeated (p. 161), drips with irony, and Cortázar is equally scathing. The island on which Marini becomes fixated is said to remain unsullied, 'al margen del circuito turístico', but a stewardess warns him 'No durará ni cinco años [. . .] Apúrate si piensas ir, las hordas estarán allí en cualquier momento, Genghis Cook vela' ('La isla', p. 151).[31] Even more suggestive are the similarities

particularly on the third island, the caustic humour recedes and a more (bleakly) philosophical tone emerges.

[28] As Karl points out, the increasingly misanthropic and solipsistic Cathcart is in fact much closer in character to Birkin's friend, the egotistical industrialist Gerald Critch, whose icy fate Lawrence perhaps deliberately has him share ('The Crusoe Who Failed', p. 269).

[29] There are, initially at least, classical Utopian echoes in Lawrence's story too, though they are treated with sometimes blunt irony. Once settled on the first island, for example, Cathcart sets about compiling a 'book of reference to all the flowers mentioned in the Greek and Latin authors', absorbed in the process of 'tracing flower after flower as it blossomed in the ancient world' as an antidote to ugly, capitalist modernity. And he wonders, rather deludedly in the context, 'why it should not be the happy Isle at last [. . .] the last small isle of the Hesperides, the perfect place' ('The Man', pp. 153, 156).

[30] Money plays a comparable though less prominent role in 'La isla', where Marini's fetishization of the island as a pre-capitalist Arcadia causes him to downplay the fact that the subsistence of its inhabitants depends on trade with the mainland, in which he plans to participate ('La isla', pp. 126, 131). Similarly, paying for his lodging is his primary concern upon arrival (p. 131).

[31] Thomas Cook is similarly maligned in 'Gre / cia / ce / ece 59' (p. 164). Lawrence himself refers to Thomas Cook with equal contempt ('the great adventure of death, where Thomas Cook

between the respective protagonists' relationships with women. On the second island, Cathcart begins an affair with a girl called Flora, his widowed housekeeper's daughter, but does so out of a 'kind of pity' (p. 164) so that the union is a disaster, 'mechanical, automatic', governed by the 'automatism of sex' rather than the 'fresh new delicacy of desire' that he hoped might arise from the 'new stillness of desirelessness' which he had been nurturing within himself (p. 164).[32] Consequently, 'the island was besmirched and spoiled' (p. 165). Flora duly becomes pregnant and Cathcart feels obliged to marry her, even though throughout the pregnancy he is 'meditating escape' (p. 166). When their daughter is born, he settles his remaining property on Flora and pays her to leave (which, he tartly notes, 'did arouse her interest' (p. 166)) before fleeing unannounced and unaccompanied to the final island. We find an analogous, though far more tersely articulated, narrative embedded in 'La isla'. Marini has a fiancée, Carla (even the bisyllabic, Italian(ate) names are similar), whom he increasingly neglects as a consequence of his obsession. When, having moved back in with her family, she writes to tell him that she has decided to abort their child, like Cathcart he gives her two months' wages before she pointedly has a friend inform him that she is considering marrying a presumably wealthy dentist ('La isla', pp. 126–27). Unmoved, he initially replaces her with a series of empty and repetitive sexual encounters, mostly with seemingly indistinguishable stewardesses and determined solely by the flight schedules, and this soulless carnal merry-go-round only heightens his desire to visit the island. Both characters, then, attempt to leave behind capitalist modernity by spurning one of its cornerstones—the bourgeois family and its exigencies.

There are further, less developed but still significant, links between the stories. Just as Cortázar provides us with certain markers to indicate the pre-Hellenic antiquity of Xiros, so Lawrence deliberately locates his islands in 'the celtic sea' in order to lend them an air of untrammelled, 'primitive' vitality, and makes reference to ancient, Druidic religious rites, including ritual sacrifice ('priests, with golden knives and mistletoe [. . .] old men of an invisible race, around the altar stone') ('The Man', pp. 153, 161). Now,

---

cannot guide us') in the poem 'Glad Death' (*The Complete Poems*, pp. 676–77 (p. 677)). The description of Xiros cited above also recalls Lawrence's evocation of an unblemished, archaic Sardinia, on the cusp of being swallowed up by the 'railroads' and 'omnibuses', which, he says, 'has no history, no date, no race, no offering [. . .] It lies outside; outside the circuit of civilization' (*Sea and Sardinia*, ed. by Mara Kalninis (Cambridge: Cambridge University Press, 1997), p. 9).

[32] Here Cathcart momentarily sounds much more like Birkin or Mellors, or indeed the speaker of a poem such as 'Manifesto', perhaps providing evidence of Lawrence's claim, made in a letter to his publisher in response to Mackenzie's threat, that the story is not merely an extended piece of mockery but that 'the Man who Loved Islands has a philosophy behind him, and a real significance' (quoted in *'The Woman Who Rode Away'*, 'Introduction', p. xxxvii). Something similar might be said of Marini, who himself initially cuts a somewhat ridiculous figure—at least in the eyes of those around him. For 'Manifesto' see *The Complete Poems*, pp. 262–68 (esp. pp. 266–68).

whereas Marini is drawn towards this sense of the primordial, Cathcart is initially repelled by these remote historical ghosts, though for a reason which again connects the two characters—his fear of and subsequent attempt to elude 'the terrors of infinite time' (p. 152). Both protagonists share a revulsion at the chronometric hell of contemporary Western life and of the tyranny of time more generally, but whereas Cathcart's progressive and ultimately vertiginous loss of temporal co-ordinates contributes to his eventual demise, Marini seems unable completely to overcome his ingrained reliance on strict routine, symbolized by the automatic checking of his watch when he hears the aeroplane, an episode carefully foreshadowed at the start of the story ('La isla', pp. 124, 125, 131).[33] This repudiation of measured, clock time gives way, in both works, to a celebration of what is imagined as pure space. Lawrence is characteristically expansive:

Only he still derived his single satisfaction from being alone, absolutely alone, with the space soaking into him [. . .] No other contact [. . .] Only space, damp, twilit, sea-washed space! This was the bread of his soul! ('The Man', p. 170)

Cortázar, once again, is far more economical. Immediately after Marini has torn off his watch, in frustration at his continued dependency on it (though, tellingly, he does not discard it, merely putting it in his pocket), he muses 'No sería fácil matar al hombre viejo, pero allí en lo alto, *tenso de sol y espacio*, sintió que la empresa era posible' ('La isla', p. 131, emphasis added).[34]

Both writers also progressively blur the boundary between subjective and objective experience. Cortázar does this in especially dramatic fashion, and the ambiguity he generates is central to the overall effect of the story and our capacity to make sense of it (I shall say much more about this in the following sections), whereas Lawrence's treatment of and references to this perceptual confusion are more sporadic and less pivotal. Nevertheless, his influence may still be detectable. On the first island Cathcart is increasingly prone to 'Uncanny dreams, half-dreams, half-evoked yearnings', while on the second 'his spirit was like a dim-lit cave under water' and he begins to feel that 'I am turned into a dream'. On the third, 'he felt as if he were dissolving' and, 'barely conscious [. . .] no longer realized what he was doing', mistaking the heads of

[33] In Cathcart's case, having fled the 'otherworld of undying time' on the first island, on the second 'the years [blend] into a soft mist' and, prior to his entanglement with Flora, he felt that he had reached 'the rare, desireless levels of Time'. On the third, now utterly alone, 'he kept no track of time', and we are told that, just before he dies, 'Time had ceased to pass' ('The Man', pp. 152, 163, 165, 170). The phrase 'No llevaba demasiado la cuenta de los días' also appears in Cortázar, but to describe the hazy limbo between Marini's sightings of the island rather than his experience on/of the island itself ('La isla', p. 128).

[34] The increasingly nightmarish ticking of a watch also features at a critical moment in 'An Occurrence at Owl Creek Bridge', just before the noose is released. See *The Collected Writings of Ambrose Bierce*, with an introduction by Clifton Fadiman (London: Picador, 1988), pp. 9–18 (p. 11). We also find a comparable reference in Huxley (see below).

seals for 'the black heads of men swimming in his bay'. At the close, now a
sort of sickening 'wraith', he can no longer even distinguish the seasons ('The
Man', pp. 159, 163, 169, 173). Cortázar, meanwhile, prefigures the manifold,
tantalizing uncertainties which permeate the concluding section of his story
with Marini's rather less subtle thought that 'volar tres veces por semana a
mediodía sobre Xiros era tan irreal como soñar tres veces por semana que
volaba sobre Xiros' ('La isla', p. 125). There are also correspondences, though
they may be fortuitous, between the episodes in which the respective protagonists react to the unwelcome return of civilization towards the close of the
stories. When a boat unexpectedly arrives on the third island (interestingly,
it is said to arrive 'suddenly, swooping down', rather like the aeroplane in
'La isla'), Cathcart experiences the intrusion as 'repulsive', a 'violation', 'an
uncleanness on the fresh earth' ('The Man', p. 169). Marini, meanwhile, on
hearing the whirring of the aeroplane's engines, 'se dijo que no miraría el
avión, que no se dejaría *contaminar* por lo peor de sí mismo' ('La isla', p. 160,
emphasis added).

Huxley

> 'Where are you now?', Susila asked.
> Without turning his head in her direc-
> tion, Will answered, 'In heaven, I suppose,'
> and pointed at the landscape.
> 'In heaven—*still*? When are you going to
> make a landing down here?'
> (ALDOUS HUXLEY)[35]

Huxley was, from early on, an important writer for Cortázar.[36] As indicated
above, Cortázar was already planning to lecture on Huxley's work in 1945.
In 1947, meanwhile, he wrote an enthusiastic review of *The Perennial Philo-*
sophy (1945) for the magazine *Cabalgata*, in which he also singled out *Point,*
Counterpoint (1928), *Brave New World* (1932), and *Eyeless in Gaza* (1939)
as 'ápices intelectuales de nuestras cuatro primeras décadas' (*OC*, VI, 166).
Huxley is also mentioned twice in *Teoría del túnel* (*OC*, VI, 73, 116), while in
his review of *Adán Buenosayres*, published two years later in *Realidad* (*OC*,
VI, 253–60), he compares Huxley favourably to Marechal as a philosophical
novelist (pp. 257–58). In 'Situación de la novela' he describes Huxley as a
'magnífico novelista', albeit one of the 'continuadores de la línea tradicio-
nal' rather than a pathbreaker (p. 280). *Los premios* (1960) was likened by

---

[35] Aldous Huxley, *Island* (1962; repr. London: Vintage, 2005), p. 271.
[36] In 'Los pescadores de esponjas' (*OC*, VI, 540–45), an essay dedicated to Ramón Gómez
de la Serna published in *Clarín* in 1978, he looks back and recalls 'los primeros panatallazos
sobrecogedores' he experienced on reading Huxley 'a los veinte años' (pp. 541–42).

one early critic to *Point, Counterpoint*, while Huxley is alluded to directly in *Rayuela* (1963) in his capacity as a creator of dystopias. A number of critics have also remarked on his deeper, compositional influence on that novel, especially its metafictional dimension.[37] The possible influence of the same novel on *Rayuela* is examined by Elizabeth Escalante Herrera.[38] The key parallel is that of the embedded novelist figures, Edouard, Quarles (also co-opted by Borges in 'Examen de la obra de Hebert Quain'), and Morelli, who offer a sort of running commentary on the text as it unfolds. *Point, Counterpoint* also features memorably in one of Cortázar's final stories, 'Diario para un cuento', where the narrator recalls the scene in which Spandrell awaits his killers while listening to his favourite Beethoven quartet.[39] His library includes a 1959 edition of the essays *The Doors of Perception* (1954) and *Heaven and Hell* (1956), written in the wake of Huxley's experiments with mescalin.[40] In the former, Huxley details the radically liberating effects of the drug on the subjective experience of time, which seemed to lose all rational measure, so that minutes and centuries became indistinguishable. He remarks at one point, 'I could, of course, have looked at my watch; but my watch, I knew, was in another universe.'[41] This particular reflection surely brings Marini's dilemma to mind. In the latter, he compares the visionary experiences induced by mescalin to the 'Other Worlds' of the 'heavens and fairylands of folklore and religion', the 'lovely islands' where man might allegedly exist in 'his primal state of innocence', citing, among many others, the Garden of the Hesperides and the Islands of the Blest as examples (*The Doors of Perception*, pp. 72–74). These observations, of obvious relevance to 'La isla a mediodía', were subsequently revisited and amplified in Huxley's final novel, *Island* (yet another!), whose plot is triggered when Will Farnaby, an initially cynical journalist in the pay of a rapacious oil baron, runs his boat aground in a squall on the shore of Pala (yet another variation on the Crusoe narrative), an island whose inhabitants have formed a purportedly Utopian community grounded philosophically in precepts culled from various Eastern religions (principally Buddhism) and related meditation techniques, but also in the controlled use of a hallucinogen named moksha (after the Buddhist/Hinduist notion of liberation from the

[37] On the inside cover of the first French edition of the novel, *Les Gagnants* (Paris: Fayard, 1961), Henri Hell claims that 'ce roman remarquable évoque le meilleur Aldous Huxley, celui de *Contrepoint*'.
[38] Elizabeth Escalante Herrera, 'The Novel within a Novel: Gide, Huxley, Cortázar' (unpublished Ph.D. thesis, University of South Carolina, 1977).
[39] 'Diario para un cuento', in *Deshoras* (1983; repr. Buenos Aires: Alfaguara, 2017), pp. 111–42 (pp. 137–38).
[40] See <www.march.es/es/coleccion/biblioteca-julio-cortazar/ficha/doors-perception-and-heaven-and-hell--3673> [accessed 27 March 2024] The hard copy is heavily marked and annotated.
[41] Aldous Huxley, *The Doors of Perception; Heaven and Hell* (London: Flamingo, 1994), p. 10.

cycle of birth and death).[42] Schoolchildren learn, via induced trances, how to distort or telescope time, so that minutes of clock time can be experienced as hours. When Farnaby, increasingly sympathetic to the islanders, asks a teacher how this is achieved, the latter replies:

Nobody knows how [. . .] but all those anecdotes about drowning men seeing the whole of their life unfolding in a few seconds are substantially true. (*Island*, p. 205)[43]

Later, Farnaby himself is suddenly engulfed by 'a vision as brief and comprehensive and intensely circumstantial as a drowning man's' in which many of the horrors he has witnessed on his extensive travels as a journalist seem simultaneously to return (*Island*, p. 232). In the final chapter, he takes moksha and has an ecstatic trip very similar to the one recorded by his creator in *The Doors of Perception*, before returning abruptly to reality to find the island in the grip of a violent, foreign-backed military coup which, the reader suspects, heralds his own imminent demise.

There are obvious parallels with 'La isla'—some broadly thematic or structural, others more concrete—in all of the above, but it is the idea of the unaccountably expanded consciousness of the drowning man that is perhaps most relevant and leads us directly to the last and, I would argue, principal source of the story.

Golding

> This is an island. At least I think it's an island.
>
> (William Golding)[44]

The most memorable feature of 'La isla a mediodía' is surely the sudden, disorienting shift in focalization which occurs in the final sentences and forces the reader to re-evaluate the nature of Marini's experiences on the island and indeed question whether and in what manner he visited it at all. For almost the entire narrative we have remained very close to Marini's perspective on

[42] The novel opens with him 'lying [. . .] like a corpse', caught between fitful wakefulness and prolonged, delirious dreams, which replay painful episodes from his past. Initially the reader, like the character, cannot easily distinguish the two (*Island*, pp. 7–12). It will end in comparable fashion.

[43] In fact, Huxley had already experimented with such ideas in the earlier novel *Time Must Have a Stop* (1944), in which the consciousness of a character, Eustace Barnack, who apparently dies of a heart attack in Chapter 12 (of thirty) lingers in a sort of timeless limbo until Chapter 28, inexplicably (and often comically) aware of relatives trying to contact him via a series of seances. He had also treated the 'drowning man' scenario in largely comic mode in *Those Barren Leaves* (1925), where one of the central characters, Chelifer, is knocked unconscious in a boating accident in Italy and eventually washed up on a beach to find 'sympathetic spectators surrounding my corpse' (*Those Barren Leaves* (London: Vintage, 2005), pp. 133–40 (p. 135)).

[44] William Golding, *Lord of the Flies* (1954; repr. London: Faber and Faber, 1997), p. 2.

events, but now fleetingly view the scene from that of the islanders who surround an unidentified corpse on the beach and who, disconcertingly, are said to be 'como siempre [...] solos en la isla' ('La isla', p. 133), before the story concludes abruptly in a classic instance of *saber callar a tiempo*.[45] Now, Cortázar had frequently employed this type of stratagem in earlier stories in order to deliver that 'knockout blow' which he identified as one of the indispensable features of the genre, but the precise form it takes here suggests the direct and, it turns out, pervasive influence of a specific literary precedent.[46] I am referring to William Golding's novel *Pincher Martin* (1956), which follows in minute, harrowing detail (Golding also uses an intensely concentrated form of free indirect discourse to keep the reader in claustrophobic, often repellent proximity to his protagonist's agonized consciousness) the tribulations of the titular character, who, thrown overboard somewhere in the North Atlantic when his destroyer is torpedoed by a German U-boat, struggles to a remote, rocky outcrop where he spends six days clinging to life before finally succumbing.[47] Or so the reader initially supposes. Then, however, in the final chapter, the focus changes dramatically, just as it does in Cortázar's story. The scene now shifts to an unnamed island, where a naval officer, Davidson, has come to recover a body that has washed ashore. It is revealed on the final page that the body is Martin's, but an even greater surprise awaits the reader. When the islander who discovered the corpse tentatively asks whether Martin would have suffered, Davidson reassures him, in what are the novel's final words, 'Don't worry about him. You saw the body. He didn't even have time to kick off his seaboots.'[48] Just as in 'La isla', this closing revelation obliges

[45] Unsurprisingly, almost all the story's commentators dwell on this climactic sequence, with several pointing out that the ambiguity here results from a much earlier transitional passage, which begins with Marini's face pressed almost erotically against the inside of the aeroplane window ('Con los labios pegados al vidrio'). Here a series of conditionals (supposedly detailing what Marini *would* do in order to reach to the island) are suddenly interrupted by a preterite ('Desembarcó'), which seems to indicate that he has actually arrived ('La isla', p. 129). What none mentions, however, is that any sense of the 'fantastic' that arises here is wholly the product of Cortázar's subtle manipulation of that staple mode of *realist* prose narrative, *style indirect libre*, which blurs first- and third-person viewpoints (Cortázar himself referred to it as a 'primera persona disfrazada': 'Del cuento breve', p. 44) and prevents the reader from acquiring any reliable external viewpoint on the action. It is a further irony, also passed over by critics, that a story which places so much emphasis on the visual depends entirely for its final effect on the reader's complete *inability* to see what is going on 'behind' the printed text. For a lucid summary of Cortázar's narrative strategy here, see Peter Standish, *Understanding Julio Cortázar* (Columbia: University of South Carolina Press, 2001), pp. 63–64.

[46] Aside from 'Profundo sistema de Remi' (cited above), these include 'Carta a una señorita en París', 'Lejana' (from *Bestiario* (1951)), 'Continuidad de los parques', 'El río', and 'La noche boca arriba' (from *Final del juego*). Cortázar uses the boxing analogy in 'Algunos aspectos del cuento', p. 375.

[47] Like Lawrence's story, Golding's novel is, inter alia, a sort of hellish anti-Robinsonade, and indeed includes multiple, sometimes blackly comic references to Defoe's original.

[48] William Golding, *Pincher Martin* (London: Faber, 1984), p. 208. Martin had apparently freed himself of his boots three pages into the novel (p. 10), and they feature as a motif throughout.

the reader to reassess the nature and significance of everything that has come before. If Martin died right at the start of the novel, what are we to make of the experiences related over the subsequent two hundred pages? Were they, as in Bierce's story (a common literary precursor, which is unequivocal in this respect), the horrendously protracted and increasingly incoherent meander-ings and hallucinations of his fading consciousness in the moments preceding death?[49] Or do they rather invite a supernatural, metaphysical, or other type of allegorical reading? I shall return to these crucial interpretative questions presently. For the moment, I wish merely to underline the remarkable simi-larity in both the central narrative premise and its structural manipulation in the two works—a similarity which even extends to the characters' names, with Cortázar's reading like a minimally Italianized anagram of Golding's. All this, I would argue, is anything but coincidental, since it turns out that Cortázar had almost certainly read *Pincher Martin* shortly before he wrote 'La isla'. Originally published by Faber in 1956, it appeared in two Penguin editions in 1962 and 1964, and Cortázar owned a copy of the latter.[50] Furthermore, he also possessed a 1960 edition of *Lord of the Flies*, another island novel which features an aeroplane crash (though in this case one that occurs prior to the commencement of the narrative proper and is referred to only in flashback) and culminates with a scene on a beach involving another abrupt alteration of narrative viewpoint.[51]

And the resonances of Golding's novel in Cortázar's story do not end with the basic narrative set-up and dizzying final twist. They range from specific plot details to a series of shared motifs and even particular turns of phrase, and I shall address the most important of these in turn. Regarding plot, Cortázar prepares the ground for the unsettling denouement via a seemingly innocuous but, in retrospect, vital piece of foreshadowing, when Marini, peering down on the island from the aeroplane, imagines its inhabitants looking up with equal fascination at the alien reality on high ('los pescadores alzarían apenas los ojos para seguir el paso de esa otra irrealidad': 'La isla, p. 125).[52] Shortly

---

[49] A number of early reviewers identified Bierce's story as a specific source for the novel. For a summary, see Arnold Johnston, 'The Miscasting of Pincher Martin', in *Critical Essays on William Golding*, ed. by James R. Baker (Boston: Hall, 1988), pp. 103–16 (p. 104).

[50] See <www.march.es/es/coleccion/biblioteca-julio-cortazar/ficha/pincher-martin--5876> [ac-cessed 27 March 2024].

[51] See <www.march.es/es/coleccion/biblioteca-julio-cortazar/ficha/lord-flies--3838> [accessed 27 March 2024]. Golding was, of course, consciously rewriting, in darkling mode, what he viewed as ludicrously romanticized island novels such as R. M. Ballantyne's *The Coral Island* (1857), to which he has the mysterious captain somewhat improbably allude on the final page. Golding's second novel, *The Inheritors* (1955), concludes with an even more remarkable switch of narrative perspective, though I have no evidence that Cortázar had read it.

[52] This is one of several instances in the story of that surreptitious, cumulative 'softening up' of the reader which paves the way for the killer punch to which Cortázar, extending the boxing metaphor, alludes in 'Algunos aspectos' (p. 375).

afterwards, immediately before he decides to visit the island, he again picks out 'un pescador que debía estar mirando el avión' (p. 128), but at the close *he* will apparently be the one looking up at the aeroplane as it crashes. In the novel, on the other hand, the shipwrecked Martin imagines how his island might look from an aeroplane and consequently makes a pattern with stones to attract attention (*Pincher Martin*, pp. 107–08, 126). Cortázar has effectively inverted that scenario for his own purposes. Certain key sentences further link the two texts. So, as soon as Martin conceives of the possibility of being rescued by air:

His *ears began to fill* with the *phantom buzzing of planes*. He kept *looking up* and *fell at once*, cutting himself. (*Pincher Martin*, p. 110, emphasis added)

In 'La isla', meanwhile, we read:

Se dejó caer de espaldas, entre las piedras calientes, resistió sus aristas y sus lomos encendidos, y *miró verticalmente el cielo*; lejanamente, le llegó el *zumbido de un motor*.
    Cerrando los ojos, se dijo que no miraría el avión. ('La isla', p. 131, emphasis added)

Much of the wording is so close here that it is difficult to believe that this is not a direct borrowing, though again there is a significant transposition: Martin is so desperate to get away from his island that he thinks he hears an aeroplane; Marini, equally anxious to remain on his, struggles to suppress every trace of his former existence.

    When it comes to motifs, we are told repeatedly that the ailing Martin appears to perceive everything on the island distortedly, as if through an increasingly blurred window. So, for example:

Sometimes a pebble would be occupied entirely by a picture as though it were a window, a spy-hole into a different world or other dimension. (*Pincher Martin*, p. 26)

He looked at the sea. All at once he found that he was seeing through a window again [. . .] He *leaned to peer round the window frame* but it went with him. (*Pincher Martin*, p. 82, emphasis added).

The hallucination sat on the rock and at last he faced it through his *blurred window* [. . .] He bent forward until his *bleared window* was just above his right instep. (*Pincher Martin*, pp. 194–95, emphasis added)[53]

Marini, of course, initially glimpses the island through the aeroplane window, which simultaneously enables and restricts his vision:

Al enderezarse la isla *se borró* de la ventanilla. ('La isla', p. 124, emphasis added)

Se inclinó sobre una ventilla de la cola. ('La isla', p. 124, emphasis added)

[53] For further references to this increasingly skewed perceptual window see *Pincher Martin*, pp. 45, 67, 97, 102, 130, 138–39, 182.

Pero Marini siguió pensando en la isla, mirándola cuando se acordaba o cuando había una ventanilla [. . .] Todo estaba falseado en la visión inútil y recurrente. ('La isla', p. 125)

Todo era también *borroso* y fácil y estúpido hasta la hora de *inclinarse* sobre *la ventanilla* de la cola, sentir el frío cristal como un límite del acuario, donde lentamente se movía la tortuga dorada en el espeso azul. ('La isla', p. 128, emphasis added)

Again, the precise phrasing, especially the detail of the respective protagonists leaning over in order to pursue a moving image beyond an obstructive limit, looks too close to be fortuitous, and although Martin's window is primarily metaphorical and Marini's physical, the latter is clearly freighted with symbolic significance, functioning as one of those many thresholds or interfaces in Cortázar's work which connect different planes or facets of reality, offering, to borrow Golding's own phrase, 'spyhole[s] into a different world or other dimension'.[54]

These observations concerning the inherent inadequacies and frustrations of particular modes of perception are further extended in both works via a series of allusions to pictures, photography, and film. When Martin appears to be regaining his bearings, initially he is only able to perceive in the form of isolated, seemingly arbitrary 'pictures that came and went inside his head [. . .] small and remote' (*Pincher Martin*, p. 25).[55] Later, now actively endeavouring to piece together the elusive shards of his past which sporadically flash through his lurching, splintered consciousness, Martin laments that 'I am an album of snapshots, random, a whole show of trailers of old films' (pp. 132–33)—static, disconnected snippets or truncated excerpts rather than a coherent, continuous self.[56] In Cortázar's story, the same media constrain or cloud Marini's view, whether figuratively or materially. On his second sighting of the island, he makes out what is described as 'el *dibujo* de unos pocos campos cultivados' ('La isla', p. 124, emphasis added). Subsequently he 'sacó una foto de Xiros pero le salió borrosa' (p. 127) and later considers filming 'el paso de la isla' so as to be able to 'repetir la imagen en el hotel' (p. 128), but ultimately deems these partial, ersatz views to be no substitute for first-hand experience of the island.[57]

[54] To take just one, parallel example, the comparison of the aeroplane window to the glass of a fish tank cited above clearly and perhaps consciously recalls the *mise en scène* of 'Áxolotl' (from *Final del juego*), where the aquarium wall that separates man and axolotl is as symbolic as it is concrete. Interestingly, Golding makes use of the aquarium in a very similar way in *Pincher Martin*, when Martin, staring at fish in a rockpool on the island, suddenly and seamlessly finds himself transported to a scene from his past, looking at 'bottles at the back of the bar [. . .] through the aquarium' (p. 134).

[55] For further, related references see *Pincher Martin*, pp. 50, 93. After this, analogies involving photography and film take over.

[56] For further, related references see *Pincher Martin*, pp. 159, 162, 173, 190.

[57] Here Cortázar is surely referring back to the interplay between photography and film which

Golding's text is replete with often—and increasingly—grotesque references to Martin's eyes and especially his mouth, which are also replicated in 'La isla'. As he is cast against what turns out to be the rock, his eyes are said to be 'needlessly open' (*Pincher Martin*, p. 22), and there are several further allusions to their either being wide open or opening, especially in the early part of the text when he is struggling to orient himself (pp. 43, 46, 58, 91–92, 124).[58] Cortázar makes subtle and sparing use of the same motif. When Marini appears to reach the island he is greeted by Klaios, whom he takes to be 'el patriarca', and who 'le habló lentamente, mirándole en los ojos' ('La isla', p. 129). This seemingly trivial detail proves to be of paramount importance since, shortly afterwards, Marini, after hearing the aeroplane approaching and initially trying to ignore it by 'cerrando los ojos', suddenly opens them at the precise moment at which it plunges into the sea. Then, at the close, when the islanders surround the body, a woman implores 'Ciérrale los ojos', though they remain hauntingly open (p. 133).[59] The intimations remain inconclusive, but they all point to the possibility that, if Marini reaches the island at all, it is only as he somehow drags himself, dying, out of the wreckage and onto the beach.[60] The rest of the story, from just after the point at which we see him with his lips

formed the basis of 'Las babas del diablo', from *Las armas secretas* (1959). For a detailed analysis of the limitations of and sometimes paradoxical relationship between the two media in that earlier story, see my *Questions of the Liminal in the Fiction of Julio Cortázar* (Oxford: Legenda, 2000), Chapter 2 (especially pp. 85–106). Interestingly, Lawrence makes a very similar observation in *Etruscan Places*, when he refers to the need to see 'not as a camera does when it takes a snapshot, not even as a cinema camera, taking a succession of instantaneous snaps; but in a curious rolling flood of vision, in which the image itself seethes and rolls; and only the mind picks out certain factors which *shall* represent the image seen' ('*Sketches of Etruscan Places' and Other Essays*, ed. by Simonetta de Filippis (Cambridge: Cambridge University Press, 1992), p. 127).

[58] In Bierce's story the protagonist also closes his eyes (to picture his family) and then opens them immediately prior to what the reader assumes will be his execution; then, just before the close, we are told that his eyes 'felt congested; he could no longer close them' ('An Occurrence', pp. 11, 17). The repeated opening and closing of the eyes, blurring the frontier between inner and outer experience, imagination and concrete perception, is also a pivotal feature of both Farnaby's initial return to consciousness and his concluding trip in *Island* (pp. 9–10, 263–65, 269–70, 274, 276, 278–79) and, though used more sparingly, of Chelifer's near-death experience in *Those Barren Leaves* (pp. 136–38).

[59] The women in the story may provide yet another link with Golding, though in the context they also have a more diffuse, faintly atavistic air about them. As Martin descends into delirium, he repeatedly thinks he sees a ghostly old woman whom he associates with a terrifying cellar from his childhood (*Pincher Martin*, pp. 175, 192–93). On the island, Marini encounters two women who, disconcertingly, 'lo miraron asombradas antes de correr a encerrarse' ('La isla', p. 130). They later fleetingly reappear speaking 'animadamente' to Klaios and his son while 'lo miraban de reojo' (p. 131). It is one of these women who asks for his eyes to be closed, suggesting that the two scenes might in fact be almost simultaneous. For the origins of the motif in Golding, see John Carey, *William Golding: The Man Who Wrote 'Lord of the Flies'* (London: Faber, 2009), pp. 15–17, 193.

[60] This is further suggested (but, again, never confirmed) by the fact that the islanders cannot comprehend 'cómo había tenido fuerzas para nadar a la orilla y arrastrarse desangrándose hasta ahí' ('La isla', p. 133). The reader, witness throughout to Marini's obsession, can.

pressed against the window, would occur in his distended, 'drowning man's' consciousness after the crash, which he himself had precipitated.[61]

When it comes to the motif of the mouth, Golding's text is deliberately, distressingly relentless, whereas Cortázar is at his most compellingly succinct. Its treatment and implications, however, are remarkably similar in both works. From the outset and throughout, Martin's mouth is described, via a series of increasingly grotesque, defamiliarizing periphrases, as a sort of autonomous, alien appendage operating independently of its owner, uncontrollably pouring out an often incomprehensible stream of bubblings, gurglings, quackings, spluttering and snoring noises rather than articulate speech.[62] The sole reference to the mouth in 'La isla' is figurative, but it is equally graphic and perturbing and also implies an uncanny *dédoublement*. When Marini appears to drag the dying man from the water he sees that he is 'sangrando por una enorme herida en la garganta', which is likened to a '*boca repugnante que llamaba a Marini* [. . .] *le gritaba entre borbotones algo que él ya no era capaz de oír*' ('La isla', p. 133, emphasis added). This is the last we see of Marini in the story, which further implies that the body he seemingly recovered was in fact his, the choked cries his own death throes.[63] The specific terms employed in this passage are almost identical to some of Golding's. Early in the novel, for instance, we are told that 'The sound began in the *throat*, *bubbled* and stayed there. The *mouth* took no part but lay open' (*Pincher Martin*, p. 34, emphasis added), while towards the close 'His *mouth said things but he could not hear them* so did not know what they were' (p. 171, emphasis added).

In addition to all of the above, there are also various isolated phrases and descriptive passages common to both texts. Particularly noteworthy are the deliberately mystifying depictions of the sinking of Martin's ship and the aeroplane crash, which include a number of common elements, albeit differently configured:

---

[61] This was certainly one of the ways in which Cortázar initially conceived of the ending. While correcting the proofs he informed Francisco Porrúa, in a letter dated 6 December 1965, that he had intended to imply that 'Marini vivió sus horas de dicha en un plano que ya no es el de la realidad cotidiana, o también que le fue dada la recompensa de vivir esas horas mientras su cuerpo terrestre caía al mar junto con el avión y moría en la playa' (*Cartas*, II, 206–10 (p. 208)).

[62] See e.g. *Pincher Martin*, pp. 7–8, 13, 17–19, 22, 25, 28–30, 34–37, 46, 67, 78, 80, 90, 93, 102, 129, 138–40, 144, 145–46, 167, 171–73, 178, 180, 186, 188–94, 197–98. Martin's mouth is referred to variously as a 'gate in the lower part of the globe', 'the hole under his window', 'the opening under his bristles' etc. (pp. 93, 138, 140).

[63] There is also an interesting resemblance here with a line from Lawrence's long poem 'New Heaven and Earth', in which the world-weary speaker, looking on at the ravages of the First World War, laments 'When I saw the torn dead, I knew it was my own torn dead body'. The entire poem explores the possibility of completely abandoning the 'old world' and 'the old life' so as to become a reinvigorated 'madman in rapture' who, 'my hand flung like a drowned man's hand on a rock', is 'thrown upon the shore' of 'a new world of time' (*The Complete Poems*, pp. 256–61 (pp. 257, 259–60)). The parallels with the story are patent and multiple, though they may be entirely casual.

He searched the circle for wreckage or a head, but *there was nothing*. She had gone *as if a hand had reached up* that *vertical* mile and *snatched her down in one motion*. (*Pincher Martin*, p. 18, emphasis added)

Vio [. . .] *la caída vertical* sobre el mar [. . .] *no se veía más que la blanda línea de las olas*, una caja de cartón oscilando absurdamente cerca del lugar de la caída, y casi al final [. . .] *una mano fuera del agua*. ('La isla', p. 132, emphasis added)

In both cases the unaccountable absence of debris suggests that all may not be as it seems. We also find in Golding a comparably pointed reference to the confusion of dream and wakefulness experienced by Marini (see above):

How difficult it was to distinguish between sleeping and waking when all one experienced was a series of trailers. (*Pincher Martin*, p. 173)

And finally, both texts feature a moment when it dawns on the protagonist that, for reasons he is unable fully to comprehend (and which prove especially ironic in Marini's case), he will never leave the island:

The thought became words that tumbled out of his mouth: 'I shall never get away from this rock!' (*Pincher Martin*, p. 162)[64]

Supo sin la menor duda que no se iría de la isla, que de alguna manera iba a quedarse para siempre en la isla. ('La isla', p. 130)

There are, of course—besides the fundamental one of genre—many differences between the two works, only the most obvious being that whereas Martin (closer to their common ancestor, Crusoe, in this respect) yearns to escape from an island he views as a sort of hell, Marini longs to visit one that he imagines as a prelapsarian paradise. Perhaps the most intriguing of these relates to the degree of ambiguity operative in the texts. In particular, the novel ultimately makes it clear that Martin has died and that his is the body recovered by Davidson, whereas Cortázar only ever hints that the corpse is Marini's. So, in the story we are left with unresolved possibilities which no rereading can entirely reconcile, whereas in the novel the reader is seemingly compelled to try to make at least some sense of the text, given that we *know* that Martin died within minutes of his being thrown overboard. Or at least so its author thought. Indeed, Golding, rebutting all discrepant readings, was adamant that almost the entire novel is a *post mortem* narrative that unfolds in a sort of personal purgatory, making it essentially a fable or, to use his own preferred term, myth.[65] Many early reviewers and critics balked at this 'supernatural' dimension to the narrative and its 'trick' ending, but in fact,

---

[64] On just one occasion Marini refers to his island as 'un peñón solitario' (p. 158), echoing Golding's description of Martin's rock, which in turn seems knowingly to hark back to the 'Piece of a Rock' to which Crusoe clings when his ship is wrecked (*Robinson Crusoe*, p. 45).

[65] See e.g. his letter to the *Radio Times* of 21 March 1958, quoted in Carey, *William Golding*, pp. 195–96. John Peter identified Golding as essentially a fabulist in 'The Fables of William

as Carey and others before him have pointed out, Golding does not hold a hermeneutic monopoly on his novel, and the text itself is considerably less clear-cut than his interpretation suggests.[66] Not only does the sheer, suffocating profusion of often gruesome sensory and psychological detail militate against narrowly allegorical readings, the text also provides at least one major clue that all Martin's experiences on the rock may be hallucinated *in extremis* rather than literally purgatorial, in the form of a decaying tooth whose contours correspond closely to those of the rocky outcrop (*Pincher Martin*, p. 174).[67] Indeed, bizarre though it may seem, I would not be surprised if Cortázar, who had a predilection for inserting the most extravagantly recondite of literary jokes or acknowledgements in his stories, were paying tacit homage to Golding's technical virtuosity here in his seemingly throwaway reference to the 'dentista de Treviso'.[68] Conversely, if what Golding conceived of as a theological allegory is enriched by the injection of radical ambiguity, Cortázar's ostensibly more worldly narrative is perhaps intermittently compromised by the inclusion of glaringly symbolic elements, though perhaps in the context of his work as a whole a quest such as Marini's could hardly remain entirely free of more generic resonances. So, while the name Marini may be an oblique nod to Golding's character, it also points directly to the sea, which plays so prominent a role in the story.[69] Similarly, Marini initially

Golding', *Kenyon Review*, 19 (1957), 577–92. Golding welcomed the designation in principle but preferred the term 'myth', as 'I think a myth is a much profounder and more significant thing than fable', which he saw as 'an invented thing on the surface' (quoted in Arnold Johnston, 'The Miscasting of Pincher Martin', p. 9).

[66] For a useful summary of the early, predominantly negative, critical responses see *William Golding: Novels 1954–67*, ed. by Norman Page (London: Macmillan, 1985), pp. 24–26. Interestingly, Angus Wilson commented that Golding's concluding coup was more appropriate for a short story than a novel, and Cortázar evidently agreed. See Jack I. Biles, *Talk: Conversations with William Golding* (New York: Harcourt, 1970), p. 69. Coincidentally, Golding, who later became much more open to alternative interpretations of his work, initially insisted on the primacy of authorial intention in trenchant opposition to Lawrence's recommendation to trust the tale, not the teller, which he dismissed as 'absolute nonsense' when the notion was put to him by Frank Kermode in a BBC interview (Biles, *Conversations*, p. 54).

[67] This is by far the most extended and explicit passage, but Golding, very like Cortázar in this respect, has in fact subtly prepared the reader for this apparent revelation via a series of earlier references to teeth and the toothlike shape of the rock (*Pincher Martin*, pp. 16, 30, 77–8, 90–1, 139, 154). Cortázar provides what retrospectively become identifiable as multiple hints (Marini's oddly instantaneous friendship with 'los jóvenes', his inability to 'pensar o elegir', his jumping into the sea from a rock, his being borne by 'corrientes insidiosas', his swimming to the shore, his 'golpeándose en las rocas y desgarrándose un brazo'—there are many more) which suggest that, when he appeared to be settling into life on the island, he may in fact have been dying amongst the wreckage ('La isla', p. 129–30, 132).

[68] See e.g. my comments on his use of the 'bola de cristal' as a deceptively Proustian leitmotif in 'Las armas secretas' ('Why Enghien?', pp. 249–50). In fact, Golding also makes just a single reference to 'the dentist's chair' in *Pincher Martin* (p. 139).

[69] As Golding indicated to Kermode, his character's full name, Christopher Hadley Martin, was chosen deliberately for its (ironic) echo of Saint Christopher, the Christ-bearer. See Frank

thinks that the island is called Horos, which is rather crudely suggestive of time, escaping whose stranglehold is his principal motivation.[70] The cases of Lawrence and Huxley are pertinent here too. Despite the former's professed loathing of allegory, 'The Man Who Loved Islands' clearly draws on elements of fairy tale or fable, both structural and stylistic, though here it is perhaps the form itself that is treated ironically, at least at the outset.[71] Huxley, meanwhile, freely conceded that the narrative action of *Island* was crushed under the weight of its relentless expositional philosophizing.[72] Perhaps, given its intrinsic peculiarities and history, the island genre necessarily entails at least a suggestion of allegory, more or less (de-)emphasized by its practitioners. If so, Cortázar's tale, despite its occasional missteps, is unusually successful in eschewing the types of excess and/or limitation associated with the more conventional or, to use Northrop Frye's term, naive manifestations of the form so roundly condemned by Lawrence (*Apocalypse*, 61).[73]

Conclusion—No Island is an Island

> That's the kingdom one would like to live in—the kingdom of Ancient Greece, purged of every historical Greek that ever existed, and colonized out of the imaginations of modern artists, scholars and philosophers.
>
> (ALDOUS HUXLEY)[74]

None of the above is intended to give the impression that Cortázar wrote 'La isla a medodía' by sitting at his desk with copies of Lawrence, Huxley, and

Kermode, *Puzzles and Epiphanies: Essays and Reviews, 1958–1961* (London: Routledge and Kegan Paul, 1962), p. 208. Martin was also formerly a professional actor, a fact which Golding manifestly uses to create a sense of his being an Everyman in the *Theatrum Mundi*, and furthermore likens himself to Atlas and Prometheus, thereby explicitly endowing his predicament with a mythical dimension (*Pincher Martin*, p. 164). Additionally, his six days and nights on the rock clearly (and ironically) mirror those of the Creation in Genesis. Excepting Marini's name, Cortázar avoids all such emblematizing.

[70] Peter Beardsell has suggested that the name Xiros is itself symbolic, echoing the Spanish verb *girar* and thereby suggesting a critical turning point. Conversely, Alberto Manguel and Gianni Guadalupe indicate that the name Xiros has acquired symbolic status as a consequence of its role in the story, of which they provide an oddly inaccurate summary. See *Siete cuentos*, ed. by Peter Beardsell (Manchester: Manchester University Press, 1994), p. 84; Alberto Manguel and Gianni Guadalupi, *The Dictionary of Imaginary Places*, rev. edn (London: Bloomsbury, 1999), pp. 718–19.

[71] For Lawrence's wholesale dismissal of allegory see *Apocalypse* (1931), ed. by Maria Kalnins (London: Penguin, 1995), p. 61. His critical champion, F. R. Leavis, reads the story as a *Märchen* in his *D. H. Lawrence, Novelist* (1955; repr. Harmondsworth: Penguin, 1978), pp. 324 ff.

[72] See his letter to Myrick Land in *Letters of Aldous Huxley*, ed. by Grover Smith (London: Chatto and Windus, 1969), pp. 929–30 (p. 930). Interestingly, given his considerable indebtedness to Huxley and his own acknowledged penchant for the fabular, Golding also considered the former's chief w eakness (one, he felt, that he shared, though perhaps to a lesser degree) to be his privileging of ideas over character, i.e. his tendency to allegorize, even in novels such as *Point, Counterpoint* (Biles, *Conversations*, pp. 5–8).

[73] Northrop Frye, *Anatomy of Criticism* (1957; repr. Princeton: Princeton University Press, 2020), pp. 90 ff.   [74] *Those Barren Leaves*, pp. 177–78.

Golding and assembling a montage of strategically tweaked borrowings and allusions, or indeed that he always drew on those sources consciously. What I would argue, rather, is that if the chance sighting of one of the Cyclades provided the germ of the story, it fell on particularly rich and abundant literary ground, and what ended up as a single, supposedly pristine island has in fact been fashioned out of an entire archipelago. A work of thoroughgoing assimilation and reinvention, it offers a prime illustration of Eliot's maxim that it is better to steal than to imitate, or of that combative cannibalization of one's forebears which, for Harold Bloom, offered a potential release from the 'anxiety of influence'.[75] Indeed, it is worth comparing 'La isla' in this respect to two other stories in the same collection, 'Reunión' and 'El otro cielo', which draw explicitly and at times reverentially on specific literary works and can seem contrived and stilted as a consequence, curbed by their overt indebtedness. Here, by contrast, Cortázar's range of reference is both broader and more artfully synthesized and camouflaged. And that receptivity and eclecticism is revealingly at odds with the tunnel vision and monomania of his protagonist. Marini, in his way, is as much a Puritan as his predecessor Crusoe, but, in terms of its compositional principles, the text in which he features is considerably more Catholic. Neither, needless to say, is or ever could have been remotely pre-Hellenic, but that, intentionally or otherwise, may ultimately be at least part of the story's point.[76]

CHRIST CHURCH, OXFORD   DOMINIC MORAN

[75] See Harold Bloom, *The Anxiety of Influence* (New York: Oxford University Press, 1973). As it happens, Cortázar's creative larceny is as nothing compared to Golding's, whose primary source was a novel with almost the same title and an identical narrative premiss—Henry Taprell Dorling's *Pincher Martin O.D.* (1916), published under the pseudonym 'Taffrail'! Crucially, In Dorling's novel Martin is saved, but otherwise Golding plunders it for material.

[76] But not, perhaps the whole point, as Pellón assumes when he describes Marini's apparent death as a 'mercy killing' perpetrated by his creator to put his delusional character out of his misery ('The Idolatry of Origins', p. 126). That Marini's attempt to 'return to the source' may founder does not render the story's critique of the world which he flees any less potent. And even Lawrence, in a coda to the seemingly desolate passage used as an epigraph above, notes that 'Yet, *in our very search* for [the Hesperides], we touch the coasts of illusion and come into contact with other worlds' (*'Gifts of Fortune'*, p. 288, emphasis added). Which, as Derrida might have said, is not nothing.

BETWEEN WASTE STUDIES AND POSTCOLONIAL THEORY: WASTED LIVES, NECROPOLITICS, AND ENVIRONMENTAL (IN)JUSTICE IN MARCOS HERRERA'S *LA MITAD MEJOR*

[E]l basural está en su casa.
(MARCOS HERRERA)[1]

According to the Polish-born sociologist Zygmunt Bauman, modern capitalism and economic 'progress' have generated as a side effect an ontological category of humans categorized as waste: useless, devoid of value, surplus to requirement.[2] Drawing on Bauman alongside Frantz Fanon, Giorgio Agamben, Hannah Arendt, and Georges Bataille and building on Michel Foucault's notion of biopower, Cameroon-born philosopher Achille Mbembe makes a case for 'necropolitics'. This death-driven system of domination, he argues, characterizes the modern state, which imposes its sovereignty by dictating who has the right to live. The corollary—the sovereign right to kill—for Mbembe, stems from enduring structures of coloniality and constructions of racialized Others that endure and prevail in the twentieth and twenty-first centuries. As he argues in relation to the ultimate example of necropolitics, the Holocaust, the roots of Nazi terror lay in 'a class-based racism that, in translating the social conflicts of the industrial world in racial terms, ended up comparing the working classes and "stateless people" of the industrial world to the "savages" of the colonial world'.[3]

The present essay offers an insight into the contribution that Mbembe and other postcolonial theorists such as Rob Nixon make to the ever-growing field of Waste Studies in the Age of the Anthropocene—a contribution that, as Martín Fernández Fernández argues, has been largely neglected.[4] Examining this link is urgent for two main reasons. First, in order to understand the roots and the impacts of the current waste crisis, we need to understand its relation to environmental (in)justice by delving into the intersections of race, class, and gender that play into our everyday relationships with waste. Secondly, working at the crossroads between waste theory and postcolonial studies reveals that the contemporary conflation of power, politics and war (against the racialized Other) denounced by Mbembe results not only from historical

---

[1] Marcos Herrera, *La mitad mejor* (Madrid: 451 Editores, 2009), p. 49. Throughout, page numbers referring to this edition are given parenthetically in the body of the text.

[2] Zygmunt Bauman, *Wasted Lives: Modernity and its Outcasts* (Oxford and Malden, MA: Polity, 2004).

[3] Achille Mbembe, 'Necropolitics', *Public Culture*, 15 (1 January 2003), 11–40 (p. 19) <https://doi.org/10.1215/08992363-15-1-11>.

[4] Martín Fernández Fernández, 'A Necropolitical Approach to Waste Theory', *Revista Canaria de Estudios Ingleses*, 86 (2023), 147–56 <https://doi.org/10.25145/j.recaesin.2023.86.09>.

Modern Language Review, 119 (2024), 525–45, doi:10.1353/mlr.00006

events, human actors, and social factors, but also from other-than-human beings, processes, and environments.

In what follows, I explore the links between wasted lives, violence, and 'death-worlds' (Mbembe) through *La mitad mejor* (2009), a novel by the Argentine writer Marcos Herrera. In this metafictional text, set in Buenos Aires' slums and suburbs, the protagonist Mulno is a journalist and investigator. The plot revolves around the three stories he is investigating: the mysterious self-immolation of a young boy in a train shed; the hallucinogenic drugs manufactured from worms collected from a waste dump; and an illegal boxing business featuring doped fighters. Within these interconnected strands of the narrative, the figure of the waste-picker remains, as in Aira's 2004 novel *La villa*, a ghostly absent–present figure, who (dis)appears in the novel because of his entanglement in plots involving clandestine work, informal informants, criminal networks, drug trafficking, and contract killing. As I argue, Herrera builds his novel not only on plots and characters, but also on more obscure 'unplots' and racialized 'uncharacters'—the tramp Eusebio, the scrapyard worker Celofán, the pimp Leira's Indigenous sex workers—who are exposed to heightened levels of stigma and violence. At the same time, some of the urban spaces themselves, whether the peripheries or slums of Buenos Aires, the city's polluted rivers, or waste dumps, take on new forms of agency that locate the other-than-human at the centre of such Mbembian 'death-worlds'. An allegory of the consequences of Western modernity and its structural war against its colonial Others, *La mitad mejor* is read in what follows as a powerful dramatization of the production of 'wasted lives' that has roots in hierarchies as racist, classist, and sexist as they are intertwined with multiple environmental injustices. Before delving into *La mitad mejor*, I begin with a brief theoretical introduction to present the points of connection (and disconnection) between the three principal theorists with whom Herrera's novel will be brought into dialogue: Bauman, Mbembe, and Nixon.

Theoretical Strands

Introducing his notion of 'wasted lives', Bauman draws on Agamben's characterization of the *homo sacer*, who in Roman religion was the cursed human, set apart from society, located outside the rule of law, and stripped of any rights or protection. Killing a *homo sacer* was not a punishable crime in Roman law nor could it constitute a sacrifice to the gods, because the life in question was considered devoid of value. Bauman translates this idea into the modern context: 'wasted lives' are the modern-day *homo sacer*, neither protected by human rights nor actually supported by any affirmative legislation.[5] In Bau-

---

[5] Bauman, *Wasted Lives*, p. 32.

man's work, the disposable, dispensable, surplus life of modernity's outcasts takes on sociological reality for different contemporary subjectivities: the un-employed; the urban poor; the migrant; the refugee; the prisoner; and so on. Through the effects of political order, legal structures, military interven-tions, imprisonment, ghettoization, and other strategies, these subjects are transformed into the Other upon which the modern state or other sovereign forms rely to construct themselves as ordering, hegemonic entities. Useful though Bauman's work is for our present purposes, it does have a number of lacunae which will be filled by bringing postcolonial theory into dialogue with Herrera's novel.

With a line of argument inspired almost exclusively by European figures—Sigmund Freud, Italo Calvino, Mary Douglas, and Tim Jordan—Bauman largely neglects the historical roots of the modern construction of 'outcast' in the European process of colonization and its enduring legacy of coloniality. Furthermore, the question of violence—and especially the fact that the 'wasted lives' of modern capitalism are disproportionately vulnerable to a range of dif-ferent forms of violence—is largely left untouched by Bauman. These blind spots are amply explored by Achille Mbembe, whose postcolonial perspec-tive allows him to explore the historical causes and effects of modernity's 'death-worlds'. Through his notion of 'necropolitics', Mbembe explores why and how society's constructed surplus is treated with violence and cruelty that go unpunished. As he puts it, 'contemporary forms of subjugation of life to the power of death' lead to the production of a category of human forced to remain in ontological states located between life and death.[6] Like Bauman, Mbembe builds on Agamben's insights to argue that the form of the camp—whether the facility for refugees, the prison, the suburb, or the slum—has become a pervasive way of organizing and controlling unwanted human lives. He takes a significant step beyond Bauman, however, in situating this construction of 'camps' explicitly in colonial and postcolonial contexts, from plantation slavery in Latin America to the Gaza Strip in Israel/Palestine. Race, in this context, is crucial: since the first days of European coloni-alism, the Western invention of race has led to a relation of superiority/subservience between White colonizer and Brown/Black colonized which has shaped power relations until the present. For Mbembe, plantation slavery epitomizes a foundation of present-day necropolitics: colonialism, he argues, 'thrived by excreting those who were, in several regards, deemed superfluous, a surfeit within the colonizing nations'.[7] 'In the context of the plantation', Mbembe argues, 'the humanity of the slave appears as the perfect figure of a shadow. Indeed, the slave condition results from a triple loss: loss of a "home,"

[6] Mbembe, 'Necropolitics', p. 39.
[7] Achille Mbembe, *Necropolitics* (Durham, NC, and London: Duke University Press, 2019), p. 10.

loss of rights over his or her body, and loss of political status.'[8] In many ways, then, the plantation slave is a precursor to the contemporary 'living dead',[9] stripped of humanity through a process that Fernández Fernández—bringing together Bauman's and Mbembe's theories—terms *'racist wastification'*.[10]

In Latin America, theorists and activists have sought to make sense of diverse manifestations of necropolitics in relation to different manifestations of unchecked violence. María José Rodríguez Rejas, from a Mexican perspective, characterizes post-2009 neoliberalism as a continuous 'war against the poor':

Se teme al 'otro' porque es pobre y a eso se van sumando los demás componentes del estereotipo (color de piel, migrante, gitano, 'es barrio'). Si además se es joven la percepción de amenaza aumenta. Los medios de comunicación conservadores alimentarán los fantasmas al igual que las empresas de seguridad, encantadas de vender alarmas y rejas. Una parte de la población demandará mayor presencia de los cuerpos de seguridad del Estado y estará más dispuesta a ceder su autonomía a cambio de sentirse seguros. Como resultado, la criminalización de la pobreza y la criminalización de la protesta crecen.[11]

With reference to Mexico's violence-based neoliberal economy, drug war, and hyper-consumerism, the Tijuana transfeminist activist and intellectual Sayak Valencia develops a complementary concept—'gore capitalism'—to theorize the link between the exercise of neoliberal economic power and the cinematic genre of 'gore' through the over-representation and banalization of 'exceedingly brutal and horrifying forms of cruelty'.[12] On the other side of the continent, the Argentine lawyer, activist, and prison educator Alberto Sarlo— writing about a Buenos Aires prison that houses some of the city's most marginalized inhabitants—denounces 'este pacto silencioso con la muerte de los "nadies"':

El hecho de que los tres muertos semanales en centros de tortura estatales sean marginales, sean negros, sean chorros, explica el porqué de que el periodismo —institución reaccionaria y conservadora como pocas—, y la sociedad toda, acepte este genocidio por goteo. Somos racistas, pero no nos gusta que nos reprochen nuestro racismo. Somos cómplices por omisión y muchas veces por acción.[13]

Reading between the lines of *La mitad mejor*, I address the following questions: What are the different forms of violence narrated in this novel? How does Herrera use plot, character, and setting to expose these acts, experiences,

---

[8] Mbembe, 'Necropolitics', p. 21.

[9] Ibid., p. 40.

[10] Fernández Fernández, 'A Necropolitical Approach', p. 151.

[11] María José Rodríguez Rejas, 'Neoliberalismo y guerra contra los pobres: la construcción social del doblegamiento y la derrota', *Viento Sur* (2019) <https://vientosur.info/neoliberalismo-y-guerra-contra-los-pobres-la-construccion-social-del/> [accessed 1 April 2024].

[12] Sayak Valencia, *Gore Capitalism* (South Pasadena, CA: Semiotext(e), 2018), p. 137.

[13] Alberto Sarlo, *Espectros del pabellón: el hedor de la tortura* (Guadalajara: Editoriales Cartoneras, 2021), pp. 17–18.

or modes of violence? To what extent does Herrera's use of layered narratives allow him to avoid entering into what Sarlo terms a 'silent pact with the death of the *nobodies*' and to denounce—rather than being complicit in—different forms of systemic racism and classism?[14] Finally, how are these 'nobodies' connected to their deteriorated, polluted, and wasted environments?

To address these questions, I bring Herrera's narrative into dialogue with three interrelated bodies of theoretical work—Waste Studies, Postcolonial and Decolonial Studies, and Environmental Justice—in order to trace the multiple interconnections between plots, characters, and settings, and to interpret those entanglements both against the historical backdrop of modernity/coloniality and in the contemporary context of the climate emergency. Through the course of my critical analysis, I bring to the fore Rob Nixon's concept of 'slow violence', a form of violence that contrasts with the dominant form of violence that characterizes late capitalism, the spectacular, short-lived event that can be captured in a shocking news flash.[15] Against this excessive focus on the visible, momentary act or event, Nixon calls for greater attention to be paid to a slower, less spectacular form of violence: the violence of environmental injustice which 'occurs gradually and out of sight, a violence of delayed destruction that is dispersed across time and space, an attritional violence that is typically not viewed as violence at all'.[16] As he suggests, the relative invisibility of slow violence forces us to engage with representational and narrative challenges: 'how to devise arresting stories, images, and symbols adequate to the pervasive but elusive violence of delayed effects'.[17] My hypothesis is that this is precisely what Herrera's novel achieves.

Below, I offer a response to Nixon's call to attend to that which 'occurs gradually and out of sight', arguing that Herrera's novel 'plots and gives figurative shape to formless threats whose fatal repercussions are dispersed across space and time'.[18] Herrera does so, I argue, through interwoven plotlines built on entangled forms of violence; through literary techniques ranging from narrative ellipsis ('unplots') to highly sensorial description; and through a novel that constantly spills out from its fictional camps to gesture towards multiple connected realities. Engaging with each of these elements helps us to offer an answer, through Herrera's narrative, to Nixon's question: 'How do we bring home—and bring emotionally to life—threats that take time to wreak their havoc, threats that never materialize in one spectacular, explosive, cinematic scene?'[19] The essay finishes with a response to some of the pressing

[14] Ibid., p. 18.
[15] Rob Nixon, *Slow Violence and the Environmentalism of the Poor* (Cambridge, MA: Harvard University Press, 2011).
[16] Ibid., p. 2.
[17] Ibid., p. 3.
[18] Ibid., p. 10.
[19] Ibid., p. 14.

questions posed by Nixon as well as to my earlier suggestion that alternative 'waste theories' might be found in creative forms in Latin American cultural production.[20]

Plotting the Violence of 'Wasted Lives'

Let us begin by examining the interconnecting plotlines around which the narrative of *La mitad mejor* revolves. The internal narrator–investigator Mulno, described by the external narrator as 'una mezcla de periodista, investigador privado y alcahuete *freelance*', is the point of connection between three stories: 'Estaba metido en tres asuntos: 1) la historia del pibe que se prendió fuego, 2) las consecuencias del basural norte, 3) boxeo clandestino con púgiles dopados' (p. 44). Mulno's belief that the three stories he is investigating can be separated into three distinct subject matters, in different folders with separate labels, is dismantled only at the very end of the novel, when he suddenly realizes that his three folders are one and the same thing: 'el caos de un loco que se divierte conmigo. Soy el peón en un tablero de ajedrez curvo, trucado, malparido. El jefe debe ser el tipo que me contrató sin mostrar la cara' (p. 155). The boss he refers to is La Foca, the mafioso mastermind who pulls the strings of all his subordinates; his 'gran máquina [. . .] gobernaba prostíbulos, contrabando, robos y, por supuesto, políticos y policías' (p. 35). As well as being connected through certain key characters such as the big boss and the journalist–intermediary, the plotlines are also brought together through the common themes of poverty, marginality, and violence. The violent plots in which Herrera's characters are involved on one level produce the sensationalistic scenes of instant mediatic gratification against which Nixon presents his notion of 'slow violence': violence as it is represented and reproduced by corporate media. These plots are fast-paced, sensational, and gruesome; they 'have a visceral, eye-catching and page-turning power'.[21] Yet they are also underpinned by the same structures—modern capitalism, coloniality, and structural racism—that fuel another, much less visible kind of violence: the apparently 'slow' violence of environmental injustice.

The novel's first strand deals with the self-immolation of the nineteen-year-old gang member Jeremías (Jere). We are taken straight into the heart of the action told from the perspective of another street kid, his friend Jinete:

Jere era un muchacho de diecinueve años. La voz de la experiencia para Jinete. Compartían el hambre y aventuras furtivas por las que hubieran podido terminar encerrados por un juez adúltero, alcohólico y agorafóbico al que habían tenido el gusto de cono-

---

[20] Lucy Bell, 'Place, People and Processes in Waste Theory: A Global South Critique', *Cultural Studies*, 33 (2019), 98–121 (p. 118).
[21] Nixon, *Slow Violence*, p. 3.

cer. En esa oportunidad, solo les propinó una encendida filípica inconexa que ellos entendieron como una amenaza. (p. 16)

Already the theme of violence, (in)justice, and corruption is brought to the fore, and Herrera's syntax explicitly links the hunger of the boys with their involvement in La Foca's criminal network. Violence and abuse of power are implied in the judge's 'encendida filípica' ('impassioned harangue'): the adjective 'encendida' connects this menacing figure of authority and Jere's death through self-immolation, and thus creates a link between the so-called justice system and the violent death of the young man. Jinete tries to rescue Jere, throwing himself into the flames, but he is unable to move his friend's burning body or find anything with which to extinguish the fire. Jere's story, therefore, comes full circle: his physical and economic precariousness (his hunger and poverty) lead him to become involved in a series of adventures that spiral out of his control and cause him to commit suicide. As is revealed later, he had little choice: since his two escape attempts had failed (p. 18), his only other option was to be killed by La Foca's assassins El Perro and Pico. Like the plantation slave, one of the blueprints for contemporary necropolitics in Mbembe's theory, Jere's agency is reduced to 'rebellion and suicide, flight and silent mourning'.[22]

The significance of Jere's self-immolation lies in the knock-on effects it has on the spiralling participation of multiple characters in La Foca's clandestine networks (p. 17). La Foca's regime is a necropolitical system of terror and death, based on authoritarian and hierarchical structures that rely on henchmen and *sicarios* to maintain control. In Chapter 5, the *sicarios* Pico and El Perro—whose names, like many of Herrera's characters, associate them with the bodily and the animalistic—come after Jinete and torture his 'brother' Herminio (one of the street kids taken in by the Christian 'benefactor' Juan) in the hope of receiving information about Jinete's whereabouts, whom they have presumably been charged to kill to avoid further repercussions deriving from Jere's death. In a graphic scene of violence, they throttle Juan, terrorize all his 'children', and cut off Herminio's ears (p. 59). Later on, Juan's foundlings take revenge by torturing and killing the *sicarios*. El Perro's torture is particularly gruesome: they tie him to a tree 'como un matambre', before Herminio cuts off his ears and indiscriminately plunges his knife into different parts of his body. This ruthlessness is underlined by the way he carries out his vengeful act 'ignorando los gritos atenuados por el trapo, ignorando los forcejeos inútiles' (p. 124). Everyday life, for these characters, is characterized by ritualistic and cyclical forms of violence that are underpinned by the 'wastification' of human life: what Bauman terms 'human waste' or what Mbembe, in relation

---

[22] Mbembe, 'Necropolitics', p. 21.

to the colonial myth of the 'savage', refers to as 'animal life'—in both cases, a life that is subhuman.[23]

The spiralling of violence takes its most extreme turn in the third plotline investigated by Mulno, revolving around La Foca's clandestine boxing operation. Jinete's plan to take revenge on La Foca for the killing of his friend Jere assumes much larger proportions once he gets involved with Ho Chi Minh, a rival gang leader named after the Vietnamese revolutionary communist leader who, according to the Marxist student–tramp Pitufo, 'fue capaz de conducir a todo un pueblo sometido por el imperialismo' (p. 64). This struggle points to the coloniality of power that underlies the violent lives of Herrera's characters: a coloniality of power that negates them as subjects, on the one hand, and against which they resist, on the other. Furthermore, it places in political context—global colonial capitalism—the gang's constant flirtation with death: 'había muchas posibilidades de que algunos quedaran tiesos en esa arena' (p. 95). As Mbembe suggests, the predominant means by which Marxism has manifested itself throughout history is via

[l]abor militarization, the collapse of the distinction between state and society, and revolutionary terror [. . .] In other words, the subject of Marxian modernity is, fundamentally, a subject who is intent on proving his or her sovereignty through the staging of a fight to the death.[24]

This fight to the death is dramatized by Herrera through Ho Chi Minh and his 'soldiers' alongside their operation to steal cashboxes from La Foca's clandestine boxing ring. Having sourced four Uzis from ex-policeman Petete, Jinete and Corona storm into the illegal boxing match, sowing terror by shooting indiscriminately, injuring and killing several people. Under the cover of this distraction, Ho Chi Minh and his 'soldier' Ficha Martínez go in to steal the cashboxes, killing the four guards and three cashiers they find in their way, and leaving behind a veritable blood bath. The gang escapes by car, accelerating away, after just a few blocks, from the (corrupt and complicit) policemen who intercept them. They continue to evade the police and drive on, planning to escape from La Foca's reach by crossing the Argentina-Paraguay border (p. 152). The plotline is left hanging with Ho Chi Minh's wishful assertion: 'es cuestión de sobornar a un par de gendarmes borrachos, y chau' (p. 152). The reader is left with the intuition that the only possible denouement involves corruption and lawlessness, and that the cyclical violence of the narrative will continue.

Perhaps, however, the key narrative strand for understanding the deeper structures underlying Herrera's narratives of violence is the second on Mulno's list: that of the valuable hallucinogenic drug distilled from worms

[23] Ibid., p. 24.
[24] Ibid., p. 20.

harvested from the waste heap. This is the plotline about which the reader is given the least information, though it has various links with the other plots: the manufacture and trafficking of the drug is masterminded by La Foca and the substance ends up in his basement; like the drugs used to dope the boxers in the underground ring, the hallucinogens are produced by the crazed Professor Griley; and of course, like the other stories, it is being investigated by Mulno. But it is only in two fairly short fragments that we are presented with the story, the two points at which Mulno manages to extract information from a 'linyera' (tramp)—Eusebio, who lives on and off the dump—in exchange for a few glasses of wine and a plate of food (p. 47). Eusebio knows about the expensive worm-based drugs because his brother is a municipal waste worker, but refuses to tell Mulno who his brother is. He asks Mulno not to tell anyone that he had told him the story because 'lo pone en peligro' (p. 48). A vicious cycle of poverty, precariousness, and violence emerges here: he reveals the secret only because of his desperate poverty, illustrated by the way in which 'se zambulle en el el plato de lentejas' (p. 48); yet his poverty leads him to act in ways that endanger him, that make his physical existence even more precarious and render him vulnerable to organized crime. Mulno's assumption that he is a 'paranoid tramp' is contrasted with the tramp's very real feeling of vulnerability: 'Mi hermano me mata si se entera que yo conté' (p. 48). After dismissing the tramp as paranoid, Mulno simply leaves without considering the possible impact of his meddlings on his interlocutor: the vulnerable Other.

Herrera's narrative, through its ellipses, contributes to this effect of othering, as the reader never discovers the fate of this minor character. The only time he reappears is when Mulno returns to seek further information. Under Mulno's violent threats—'si no me contás algo interesante, te fajo' (p. 75)—Eusebio tells him about Cilirius, who later turns out to be another of La Foca's men: a racialized character, 'ese negro, colorado y gigante', a devil ('mandinga') who turns up at the waste heap one night, commanding the lorries to transport the worms to La Foca's underground base (p. 75). That is the last time Eusebio appears in the plot. He is too minor, too surplus to matter: he is reduced to a 'shadow' (Mbembe) in the narrative and within the corresponding underground economy—the 'reino de la Foca', the sovereign power that possesses the right to kill, which is in turn served by the corrupt journalist Mulno, who has the power to render invisible and silence the Other. The suggestion, then, is that even within the category that Bauman terms 'wasted lives', there is a pecking order, with some subcategories of 'wasted lives' not even deemed worthy of a narrative ending.

'Unplots' and Racialized 'Uncharacters'

What is left out is often as important as what makes the cut for Mulno's metaplots. Why is it that Mulno does not pursue Eusebio's story? Because he cannot? Or because he simply can't be bothered? Given Mulno's dismissive view of the only two characters associated with the waste dump he bothers to meet, Eusebio and Leira, one might assume the latter. As mentioned above, he uses the pejorative term 'linyera' in reference to Eusebio and refers to Leira as 'el salvaje del basural', using a word that links Leira with the hares that Juan's 'children' hunt and kill for food: 'Mucho tiempo de hervor para los animales. Era carne dura, salvaje' (p. 12). This term also connects the 'uncharacter' of Leira to his sex workers: the 'indias' (p. 23) whom Leira has 'tamed' for his economic gain (p. 27), and whom he had obtained on one of the hunts ('cacerías') organized by 'gangsters de cuarta categoría' that worked for La Foca (p. 23). A relation is therefore forged by the narrator's discourse between the human characters and the other-than-human animals on which they feed.

The term 'salvaje' recalls the racist discourses and imagery of savagery and barbarism used by Domingo Faustino Sarmiento in his 1845 nation-building narrative *Facundo, o Civilización y barbarie*,[25] suggesting a link between contemporary 'wasted lives' and historical, colonial structures of classism and racism in Argentina and across the world's colonies. As Mbembe puts it:

> That colonies might be ruled over in absolute lawlessness stems from the racial denial of any common bond between the conqueror and the native. In the eyes of the conqueror, savage life is just another form of animal life, a horrifying experience, something alien beyond imagination or comprehension.[26]

Racial inequalities and the spectres of coloniality recur across Herrera's narrative through 'uncharacters' who barely feature or fade into the background. The character Celofán, for example, is thus named because he is 'colorido pero transparente' (p. 66). The effacement of this racialized 'uncharacter' links him to the Indigenous prostitutes in La Foca's brothel, the 'indias' who 'habían perdido su nombre', have been 'baptized' as Lorena and Araceli, and who 'belong' to Leira (pp. 23–24). These women are the epitome of María Lugones's 'menos que seres humanos'.[27] They are chased away from their Indigenous community (the unnamed 'isla', presumably in the Paraná Delta) and caged like animals (pp. 23–24). They are treated as meat rather than humans: 'la carne se iba organizando según su calidad, su baqueta y su edad' (p. 23).

---

[25] Domingo Faustino Sarmiento, *Facundo, o Civilización y Barbarie* (Buenos Aires: Biblioteca del Congreso de la Nación, 2018).

[26] Mbembe, 'Necropolitics', p. 24.

[27] María Lugones, 'Hacia un feminismo descolonial'. *Revista La Manzana de la Discordia*, 6.2 (2011), 105–19 (p. 108).

And the ones left over—once they were no longer attractive to clients—are used to star in 'films pornográficos con ejecuciones. Sin trucos: películas con sacrificios humanos que se comercializaban en el norte de Europa' (p. 23). Aside from these gruesome details, we never gain access to their perspective: they are denied dialogue, voice, or subjectivity. This 'unplot', with its plural 'uncharacters', gestures out towards the ever-expanding networks of human trafficking in Argentina and beyond. Around the time this novel was published, twenty Indigenous women were freed by the police from captivity in Chaco, Córdoba, Buenos Aires, and Santa Cruz. As described in a newspaper article in *Página 12* published the same year as the novel:

Las indígenas eran colonizadas para que sean miradas de otra manera. Estaban el captador, el transportador y el que producía a las mujeres en un salón de belleza, que las vestía y las peinaba para cambiar su aspecto de mujeres indígenas. Después, estaba el colocador que las encerraba en bares, whiskerías, pooles y locales privados. Las enrejaban como bestias y debían dormir, comer, hacer pis y caca en un solo box. Sólo podían salir para ejercer la prostitución y, si se negaban, eran golpeadas, quemadas con cigarrillo en la espalda y privadas de alimentación. No tenían posibilidad de salir de su cautiverio y eran sistemáticamente violadas por sus explotadores.[28]

In Mulno's 'journalism', in contrast to the real trafficking story above, this ring of trafficked sex workers do not merit their own plotline. As expendable characters forced to enact literal sacrifices in pornographic films marketed for European audiences, they are dehumanized through the colonial filters of sexism, classism, and racism.[29]

This narrative erasure is reflected in the geographical marginality of the waste dump. Whereas the two plots to which Mulno devotes most attention occur at the heart of Buenos Aires, the location of the second plot, the Basural Norte, is 'abandonado y horrible' (p. 74). This fictional waste dump appears to be a reference to the real-life, CEAMSE-run complejo ambiental Norte III, which lies in the José León Suárez province of Greater Buenos Aires, on the land of three different municipalities—Tigre, San Martín, and San Miguel— flanked by a river (Río de la Reconquista), a motorway (Camino del Buen Ayre), and two main *villas* (informal settlements), Villa Adelina and Villa Ballester.

The environmental aspects and impacts of this location loom over the entirety of the novel. As we shall see, the waste dump is not a mere setting or background image, but instead functions as an ever-present, threatening Latourian other-than-human agent in the novel, which impacts on the lives of the characters and on the development of the plot. In the following section,

[28] Anon., 'Piden que la lucha contra la trata se reglamente y cuente con más fondos', *Página 12*, 9 Oct. 2009 <https://www.pagina12.com.ar/diario/suplementos/las12/13-5234-2009-10-09.html> [accessed 1 April 2024].

[29] Lugones, 'Hacia un feminismo descolonial', p. 108.

I contend that another kind of violence—what Nixon terms 'slow violence'—underlies every aspect of the narrative: its plots, settings, characters, imagery, and language. Herrera's street kids, *villeros*, and waste workers not only seek to survive and make money in the city through clandestine and violent employment, such as drug and human trafficking, pimping, robbing, and even contract killing, activities that lead many of them to become victims of violence. They are also exposed to 'slow violence' in the form of harmful or even fatal living and working conditions.

Environmental Injustice and Unplotted Violence

Violence is the fuel that drives the plot and La Foca's powerful clandestine machine, ignited by the spark of the less visible but nonetheless powerful effects of poverty and inequalities linked to race, class, and gender. Living in the vicinity of the Basural Norte, the protagonists of this drama—many of whom are 'perpetrators' or 'criminals' in the eyes of the (corrupt) justice system represented in the novel—are themselves victims of dangerously unsanitary living conditions and aggressive pollutants in the air that they breathe, the rivers from which they fish, and, consequently, the food that they eat.

As in Andrés Neuman's *Bariloche*, whose narrative, discursive, social, and material networks of waste I have analysed in a previous article,[30] Herrera reveals from the very start of the novel the material connections between his characters, their bodies, and their surroundings. The novel opens thus:

Leira supo por la temperatura que era mediodía. Tres rayas furiosas pasaban por la persiana rota y ablandaban la oscuridad. Evitó a la familia que se arremolinaba semidesnuda: los niños, su mujer, la madre de su mujer iban y venían correteando, llorando, peleando, cambiando de forma y cambiando a su vez las formas monótonas del verano. En el rancho, en los alrededores del río, en el enorme basural permanentemente alimentado por los camiones que llegaban de la ciudad, la familia de Leira buscaba ocupaciones para matar el tiempo. (p. 9)

On implicit and explicit levels, this passage foregrounds the relationship between the 'wasted lives' of Leira and his family and their degraded living conditions—the makeshift house which is flanked by the waste heap. Rising at midday every day (because of his nocturnal work as a pimp), Leira is woken up by the heat and the light, which is described here not as life-giving or comforting, but rather as a violent illumination, a set of 'rayas furiosas' that pierce through the broken blind—a metonym for the ramshackle conditions in which the family lives. His family, presented as a set of entities constantly changing form, are introduced to the narrative as energetic and material entities rather

---

[30] Andrés Neuman, *Bariloche* (2008; repr. Barcelona: Anagrama, 2024); see Lucy Bell, 'Narrative, Nature, Society: The Network of Waste in Andrés Neuman's *Bariloche*', *MLR*, 110 (2015), 1045–66.

than human beings. As well as pointing towards Leira's indifference toward his children, this description is suggestive of the deep connection between human bodies and more-than-human environments that propels the plot: the notion of transcorporeality put forward by Stacy Alaimo, 'where human corporeality [. . .] is inseparable from "nature" or "environment"'.[31] It is no co-incidence that, while the sunrays and the waste dump are anthropomorphized through human emotions and states such as fury and hunger, the children are metamorphosed—or even meteomorphosed, to use a term coined by Italian artist and academic Paolo Scoppola for his 2015 art installation[32]—through the attribution of whirlwind-like characteristics to their movements.

The interconnections between bodies and their surroundings are further emphasized in Herrera's vivid description of Leira's morning rituals, the regularity of which is underlined by the use of the imperfect tense:

Después de calentar agua, se iba con el mate y el termo a revisar las líneas.
   Le gustaba quedarse un rato mirando el agua. Sobre todo si había sol y los reflejos bailaban haciendo que la turbidez marrón pareciera cargada de pedacitos de enorme espejo roto que hubiera caído del cielo [. . .] En general había algo. Un surubí, una boga, algún amarillo. Leira orinaba largamente, ponía carnada nueva, tiraba otra vez las líneas y, después de tomarse unos mates, limpiaba los pescados. Luego volvía al rancho y prendía el fuego. Salaba el pescado y lo ponía en la parrilla. (p. 10)

These routine actions illustrate on a micro-scale the transcorporeal connections between the human body and more-than-human environment, between waste and consumption: Leira fishes and eats from the same river into which he excretes his bodily fluids. The poetic image of the river's reflections as the shards of a huge broken mirror is an ominous one, pointing to its dangerous, harmful qualities and foreshadowing the later revelation that Juan's wife drowned in this very river—another 'unplot' to which the reader never gains access. These in turn suggest different plots, the kind of unplotted plots that Nixon terms 'slow violence'. By slowing down the pace of the narrative as the character stops for a while to look at the water, Herrera draws attention to important details—the muddy brown colour of the water, for example—that remind the reader that this ever-moving, life-giving body of water becomes a 'death-world' (Mbembe) as its course passes through the Basural Norte.

The connections between waste and consumption become yet more explicit in the following paragraph, which shows Leira defecating in his makeshift toilet, a hole in the ground surrounded by wooden planks:

Las letrinas de los corazones humanos tenían su representación en esa realidad llena de moscas. Asoció: cagar=comer=coger. Cuando salió, caminó. Los mosquitos habían empezado a volar, invisibles, zumbando en el aire pesado y húmedo. (p. 10)

[31] Stacy Alaimo, *Bodily Natures* (Bloomington: Indiana University Press, 2010), p. 238.
[32] <https://www.paoloscoppola.com/en/works/meteomorphosis/> [accessed 6 April 2024].

In one sense, the equivalence he draws between shitting, eating, and screwing is an existential reflection of his indifference towards life and, perhaps, his struggle for survival, whereby his life is reduced to a set of base functions. In another sense, the association between excreting and ingesting is quite literal. On a material level, Leira's latrine, full of flies, is so close to where he cooks and eats that he is inevitably feeding himself and his family with their own waste: through Leira's crude terms, Herrera synthesizes Alaimo's notion of transcorporeality. Within a narrative that, as we have seen, is replete with references to racialization and coloniality, this transcorporeal connection between humans and their excrement is inevitably political. As Arjan Appadurai puts it:

The 'politics of shit'—as Gandhi showed in his own efforts to liberate the lowest castes, whom he called *Harijans*, from the task of hauling upper-caste ordure—presents a node at which concerns of the human body, dignity and technology meet.[33]

Beyond the Indian context to which Appadurai is referring here, Mike Davis in *Planet of Slums* insists on this politics of shit: 'shit still sickeningly mantles the lives of the urban poor'; in poor mega-cities from Nairobi to Mumbai, 'constant intimacy with other people's waste [...] is one of the most profound of social divides'.[34] Against this background, Leira's 'wasted life' points to a much more literal aspect of the notion of 'waste lives' than that which was perhaps intended by Bauman: it gestures towards forms of living *off* waste, of which the most extreme example in Herrera's novel is the tramp Eusebio, who lives on the dump.

Waste Dumps and Water Pollution: Beyond Slow Violence

In *La mitad mejor*, the connections between river, excrement, and consumption are not mere metaphors, images of moral degradation or judgements about Leira's 'dirty work', his occupation as a pimp.[35] There is no omniscient narrator here to make any such judgement, and the meta-author Mulno is as morally questionable as the characters on whom he is reporting. Instead, the wider implication is that the river is quite literally filled with waste from the dump and sewage from the surrounding *villas*, and polluted further by the fumes from the heavy traffic on the ironically named Buen Ayre motorway that runs alongside it. In turn, these biological and chemical pollutants are ingested by the fish, which are then eaten by the *villeros* who fish in the

---

[33] Arjan Appadurai, 'Deep Democracy: Urban Governmentality and the Horizon of Politics', *Public Culture*, 14.3 (2002), 21–27.

[34] Mike Davis, *Planet of Slums* (London and New York: Verso, 2007), p. 138.

[35] Blake Ashforth and Glen Kreiner, '"How Can You Do It?": Dirty Work and the Challenge of Constructing a Positive Identity', *Academy of Management Review*, 24 (1999), 413–34.

river. Later on, Juan draws attention to this fact, telling Leira that his fish 'no van a tardar en estar intoxicados por las porquerías del basural' (p. 113). In addition, pests such as 'los mosquitos invisibles' (p. 10) for which the rubbish dump and polluted river constitute the perfect breeding ground, are able to carry these diseases far beyond the direct areas of contamination.

This fictional scenario echoes some alarming realities, of which Herrera was doubtless aware. A 294-page report published two years prior to the publication of *La mitad mejor* contains a damning indictment on the state of Río de la Reconquista in the province of Buenos Aires, on which the fictional river is based. In the report, which demonstrates that the Reconquista is one of the most polluted watercourses in Argentina, there are multiple references to contamination caused by sewage and rubbish dumps, both municipal and clandestine:

La baja cobertura de los servicios sanitarios y la presencia de basurales no controlados condiciona un alto riesgo de contaminación bacteriana y las consiguientes enfermedades de transmisión hídrica (diarreas, hepatitis, parasitosis, etc).[36]

Because of the migratory character of waste—its ability to be carried and transported by water, air, soil, but also pests (rodents and insects)—bacteria spread with ease and, consequently, the surrounding populations suffer from a high incidence of ailments including but not limited to diarrhoea, eye and skin conditions, neurological disorders, and chronic diseases.[37] According to the report, these represent 'una dramática realidad en los hospitales y centros de salud de los barrios más humildes de [la] ciudad [de Buenos Aires], que encuentran su origen en el contacto o cercanía con basurales'.[38]

These hybrid human and other-than-human processes play out as largely invisible dramas, occurring within the digestive tracts of tiny, sometimes invisible insects, the cytoplasm or intracellular compartments of particular host cells, and the thin protective layers that separate human and animal bodies from what is supposedly 'outside'.[39] Like the forms of chemical and radiological 'violence' explored by Nixon, these biological phenomena, from a narrative perspective, are 'open ended, eluding the tidy closure, the containment, imposed by the visual orthodoxies of victory and defeat' that govern 'spectacle-driven corporate media'.[40] The power of Herrera's fictional narrative, then, is that it shows us different forms of visible, gruesome violence

---

[36] *Informe Especial Cuenca del Río Reconquista* (Buenos Aires: Defensor del Pueblo de la Nación, Fundación Ambiente y Recursos Naturales, 2007), p. 107.

[37] Ibid., p. 167.

[38] Ibid.

[39] Bruce Alberts and others *Molecular Biology of the Cell* (New York: Garland Science, 2002), available (for searching only) at <https://www.ncbi.nlm.nih.gov/books/NBK21054/> [accessed 1 April 2024].

[40] Nixon, *Slow Violence*, p. 6.

while hinting at other modes of violence. He does so through a narrative device that echoes a long line of Argentine short-story writers, from Esteban Echevarría through Horacio Quiroga and Jorges Luis Borges to Julio Cortázar: suggestion, or what Hemingway referred to as the 'tip of the iceberg' technique. What the environmental report says and condemns, Herrera's novel *suggests*, refraining from any moralistic discourse and leaving readers to reach their own conclusions.

Nixon's concept of 'slow violence', though, is somewhat misleading in this context. The waste dump by which the *villa* is flanked grows at an alarming rate. Leira has to ask his neighbour Juan for his shovel on a weekly basis to bury the waste that threatens to engulf his precarious home, 'porque una de las paredes de su rancho daba contra el basural, que crecía demasiado rápido' (p. 11). The idea that the rubbish dump is growing too quickly reflects not only Leira's struggle for survival, but also the urgency of the global waste crisis: in Argentina alone, one tonne of waste is generated every two seconds, and 16.5 billion tonnes of rubbish is produced every year.[41] The sheer speed of the global waste crisis is crystallized in the narrative pace, which seems to accelerate as Leira drunkenly shovels eleven wheelbarrow-loads of rubbish forty metres away from his precarious house:

La basura se acumulaba avanzando como una ola lenta y sólida. Rascó el sudor que bajaba por su cara, por su pecho y empezó a palear. [. . .] Primera carretilla: nada. La gran marea de colores sin lógica y olores muertos. Podredumbre, mugre, amasijo, latas. Toda esa masa ni se enteraba del trabajo de Leira. [. . .] Segunda carretilla [. . .] (pp. 90–91)

The not-so-slow violence of the waste dump is depicted through a range of natural and supernatural images—a wave, a tide, a 'cadáver congelado', and a monster 'que amenazaba tragarse todo' (p. 91)—that evoke different senses: the sound of a giant wave; the smell of a frozen corpse in a morgue; the image of a giant monster indifferently gobbling away the trash. Herrera thus resists privileging visibility over the invisible, and thus violence above what Nixon alternately calls slow violence, environmental violence (p. 7), and 'uneventful' violence (p. 8). Instead, Herrera foregrounds what might be termed 'out-of-sight violence', forcing the reader to *live waste*, to experience it in all its ugliness through different senses.

This passage constitutes a potentially brilliant answer to Nixon's question: 'How do we bring home—and bring emotionally to life—threats that take time to wreak their havoc, threats that never materialize in one spectacular, explosive, cinematic scene?'[42] By suggesting in multiple ways that the reader is

---

[41] Ignacio Sala, 'Un Aconcagua de basura', *Anccom*, 9 October 2020) <http://anccom.sociales. uba.ar/2020/10/09/un-aconcagua-de-basura/> [accessed 1 April 2024].
[42] Nixon, *Slow Violence*, p. 14.

encouraged to experience the rubbish dump *with* and *in relation to* the character Leira and the internal narrator Mulno, Herrera's prose evokes a mix of emotions which are dependent on the reader's subjective reaction to the waste, and wasted lives, depicted. As Gay Hawkins argues in *The Ethics of Waste*, acknowledging our 'different relations with [waste]' enables us to escape from the human/non-human duality that has long characterized modern Western society's relationships to waste.[43] Understanding our complex and subjective relations to our discards, in Hawkins's view, also enables us to break down the paralysing, moralizing oppositions that impede our productive engagement with the waste crisis, a series of oppositions that she encapsulates thus: 'the capacity of humans to destroy nature with their waste renders them morally bankrupt, and the capacity of nature to function as a dumping ground renders it passive and denatured'.[44] Herrera engages sensorial, relational, and affective modes of *reading waste* that are open to different and divergent feelings: disgust, of course, but also perhaps horror (of the grotesque waste-monster and its powerful jaws), sympathy (for an otherwise unsympathetic, misogynistic character), or guilt (for being complicit in the global waste crisis).

Between Life-Worlds and Death-Worlds

By 'living waste', I refer to the narrative techniques employed by Herrera to bring the waste dump closer to the reader through a combination of sensory perception and vivid emotion. Like the dump in Neuman's *Bariloche*, Herrera's depiction of the *basural* as a moving, semi-solid mass, an anthropomorphic form with huge jaws, points to the threat that it poses to the characters due to its living quality, as an agent capable of producing powerful effects on other living things. By juxtaposing descriptions of the 'cuerpo podrido' (p. 92) of the waste heap and Leira's own body, the narrator suggests the transcorporeal connections between the two entities, but also lends another—more environmental—dimension to Mbembe's necropolitics.

As suggested throughout the narrative by the encroachment of the toxic waste dump on Leira's home, identity, and existence, living in and with waste can easily tip over into *living as waste*. This character, in many ways, is the ultimate 'living dead', his body in the balance between different forms of death: cancer or cirrhosis, bullet or stabbing (p. 91); slow violence or human-on-human violence. Environmental politics, Herrera's novel suggests, is an ever-more important aspect of necropolitics in the age of the Anthropocene.

This not-so-slow violence, unsurprisingly, is not experienced equally by all characters. As is becoming abundantly clear in a growing body of scholarship

[43] Gay Hawkins, *The Ethics of Waste: How We Relate to Rubbish* (Lanham, MD: Rowman & Littlefield, 2006), p. 22.
[44] Ibid., p. 15.

on environmental injustice and decolonial ecology, the effects of 'slow violence' in postcolonial capitalism are disproportionately felt by poor, racialized communities. As Nixon insists, 'casualties of slow violence—human
and environmental—are the casualties most likely not to be seen, not to
be counted'; they are 'disposable casualties' or what Bauman in relation to
modern capitalism refers to as 'wasted lives'.[45] As Herrera's narrative makes
clear, while the privileged classes live in clean, sanitary, healthy conditions, it
is the poor who have to—literally—live in/with/on/off other people's waste.
When Mulno claims that he is an anthropology student investigating the
waste dump, Pico tries to dissuade him from his choice of subject by pointing
out that 'va a ser mejor que hagas un trabajo sobre otra cosa. Ahí te podés
arruinar la salud' (p. 49). Pico's comment suggests the socially accepted idea
that higher levels of economic, educational, and cultural capital—those, in
this case, of a university student in Buenos Aires—should preclude one from
exposure to hazardous working conditions, from environmental violence.[46]
Dirty work and dirty living, then, are the domains of the underclasses.[47]
Thought of by Juan as 'una basura humana, mierda con patas' (p. 85) and
told by Perla that he was always 'bastante basura' (p. 119), Leira is the prime
example of this: living in waste, he *becomes* waste in the eyes of society and,
as such, becomes a disposable casualty of not-so-slow violence.

In the journalist Faldetti's spruce, state-of-the-art office, viewed through
Mulno's eyes, 'cualquiera [. . .] sentía la obligación de estar limpio y bien
vestido' (p. 10). By contrast, getting or staying clean in the slum or by/on the
rubbish dump is a constant struggle. Juan tries to educate his foundlings to
value hygiene, insisting that they wash their hands with soap before dinner
and smelling their hands to check on them (p. 13), but this process is shown
to be largely futile as the children play around in the dirt (p. 19). To add insult
to injury, the street kids Juan has taken into his makeshift home are selected
precisely because of their ill health: 'elegía a los que estaban en malas condi-
ciones: descalzos, lastimados, enfermos, perdidos en Poxi Ran' (p. 13).[48] Later,
when they help the injured Juan into the car, their bodies are seen in close-up:
'fue empujado por un montón de manos flacas. Antebrazos quemados por

[45] Nixon, *Slow Violence*, p. 13.

[46] See *Just Sustainabilities: Development in an Unequal World*, ed. by Julian Agyeman and others
(Cambridge, MA: MIT Press, 2003).

[47] There is a comprehensive body of work, principally in sociology and anthropology, on
so-called 'dirty work', including Shirley K. Drew and others, *Dirty Work: The Social Construction
of Taint* (Waco, TX: Baylor University Press, 2007); and Blake E. Ashforth and Glen E. Kreiner,
'Dirty Work and Dirtier Work: Differences in Countering Physical, Social, and Moral Stigma',
Management and Organization Review, 10 (2014), 81–108. For a powerful set of counter-narratives
and an examination of the different 'forms of living' represented by waste work, see Kathleen
M. Millar, *Reclaiming the Discarded: Life and Labor on Rio's Garbage Dump* (Durham, NC: Duke
University Press, 2018).

[48] Poxi Ran is an adhesive commonly used as a cheap drug.

el sol, tiras de músculos flacos' (p. 88). Suffering from a range of conditions linked to homelessness, poverty, malnutrition, violence, and drugs, their only chance of shelter is perversely located in an area that, as Juan himself is well aware, is toxic and harmful.

Herrera's characters are not unaware of the injustice of their living conditions. In the novel, Juan unsuccessfully attempts to ignite a protest among the *villeros* against the growing landfill site, telling them that the dump would carry disease and that the toxic chemicals would contaminate the river and kill the fish (p. 51). Yet the unanimous response of his neighbours is dismissive of any action: 'Vivimos de la basura, le dijeron. Sacamos botellas, cartón y fierro' (p. 51). This view points to the complex 'forms of living' that Kathleen Millar studies in depth in the context of the Rio Gramacho waste dump in Rio de Janeiro:[49] living from, returning to, and being dependent on the waste dump are the different 'forms of living' that feature in Herrera's novel and prevent any omniscient narrator—or the character Juan—from making a blanket moral condemnation of this life-world, even if it is, for many of the characters, what Mbembe would term a 'death-world'.[50] A complex set of circumstances links the *villeros* to the waste dump: they are in that environmentally damaged and damaging location because of their poverty, a poverty that also makes the waste dump perversely important to, and valued for, their immediate economic survival. As *villeros*, they simultaneously live off the rubbish dump and suffer from its effects; and as readers, we are left to decide whether the *basurero*-flanked slum gives rise to 'forms of living' (Millar) or 'forms of dying' (Mbembe): life-worlds or death-worlds.

Just as the more sensational forms of violence outlined in the first section above are underpinned by colonial hierarchies of class, race, and gender, so are these forms of not-so-slow violence, pointing to the realities of environmental racism in the Americas.[51] Deeply embedded withing their settings—the *villa*, the waste dump, the scrap yard—Herrera's characters are embodiments of the environmental racism that structures the underside of the so-called Paris of

---

[49] Millar, *Reclaiming the Discarded*, p. 9.

[50] Mbembe, 'Necropolitics', p. 40.

[51] As an example of environmental racism in the USA, Daniel Faber and Deborah McCarthy show that it is principally low-income workers and communities of colour that face the greatest exposure to harmful waste because their less privileged neighbourhoods are characterized by a greater concentration of polluting industrial facilities, power plants, hazardous waste sites, and disposal facilities, and by a lack of environmental enforcement and clean-up facilities. In Latin America, most academic work has been—rightly—centred on acts of violence committed against rural Indigenous communities, as in the *chaqueños* in Argentina, with less attention paid to urban environmental racism. See Daniel R. Faber and Deborah McCarthy, 'Neo-Liberalism, Globalization and the Struggle for Ecological Democracy: Linking Sustainability and Environmental Justice', in *Just Sustainabilities*, ed. by Agyeman and others, pp. 38–63; and Javier Rodríguez Mir, *Violencia y racismo ambiental en Argentina: resistencia y movilización de los pueblos indígenas en el Chaco. Etnografía wichí del conflicto* ([n.p.]: Académica Española, 2011).

the South. Celofán, for example, works at a scrapyard located 'en un terreno hundido [. . .] que alojaba (además de a otros perros menos afortunados que Güisqui [his dog]) montones y montones de piezas de automóviles' (p. 66). The sunken physical environment, occupied by stray dogs and piles of scrap, reflects his low social status. The only time he is given agency in the narrative is in an act of self-effacement: as mentioned above, he tells El Perro and Pico that he is called Celofán because he is 'colorido pero transparente' (p. 66). His dark skin, it seems, leads to a paradoxical social invisibility, connecting him to the 'terreno hundido' in which he works and the dogs with which he shares the scrapyard. In turn, it connects him to Leira's 'indias', the trafficked women treated like caged animals; and to Leira himself, 'el salvaje del basural'.

Bauman's category of 'wasted lives', then, takes on a distinctly racialized character in Herrera's novel. The author invites us to *feel* the very heavy, very literal weight of the waste on the lives of the characters; a weight that, as he takes pains to underline through his narrative, is (unequally) determined by intersecting categories of race, class, and gender. At the same time, he discourages the reader from becoming complicit with the necropolitical state, and from entering a 'silent pact with the death of the *nobodies*' (Sarlo), by placing within his metanarrative a highly unreliable, corrupt, and morally questionable narrator–journalist whose focus on spectacular plots leads him to neglect some of the most glaring violence committed in the novel.

Conclusion

With *La mitad mejor* as a prime example of decolonial eco-fiction, Marcos Herrera could usefully be added to Nixon's list of predominantly English-language authors, which includes writers from India (Arundhati Roy and Indra Sinha), Nigeria (Ken Saro-Wiwa), South Africa (Njabulo Ndebele and Nadine Gordimer), the US (Rachel Carson, June Jordan, and Stephanie Black), and the Caribbean (Jamaica Kincaid from Antigua) but excludes writers from Latin America: a list of 'combative writers who have deployed their imaginative agility and worldly ardor to help amplify the media-marginalized causes of the environmentally dispossessed'.[52] Herrera's violent plots and environmentally violent 'unplots' reveal how, 'in a world permeated by insidious, yet unseen or imperceptible violence, imaginative writing can help make the un-apparent appear, making it accessible and tangible by humanizing drawn-out threats inaccessible to the immediate senses'.[53] As I have demonstrated above, one of Herrera's achievements is that he manages to point towards the causes and effects of slow or not-so-slow violence, often without having to name them, and without adopting a moralizing, didactic tone.

[52] Nixon, *Slow Violence*, p. 5.
[53] Ibid., p. 15.

The deeply ingrained connections between power, violence, death, and dis-possession in the fictionalized Buenos Aires of Herrera's narrative are such that Mbembe's essay could at times be taken for a reading of Herrera's novel:

As a political category, populations are then disaggregated into rebels, child soldiers, victims or refugees, or civilians incapacitated by mutilation or simply massacred on the model of ancient sacrifices, while the 'survivors,' after a horrific exodus, are confined in camps and zones of exception.[54]

Mbembe's 'zones of exception', and the 'living dead' that inhabit them, pave the way for an interpretation of Herrera's title—*La mitad mejor*—as an ironic reference to the neat lines constantly being drawn between those whose (better) lives matter and those whose lives can or should be discarded with violence that is never held to account. The idea of a 'better half' resonates with increasingly frequent headlines stating that, for example, 'The richest 1% own almost half of the world's wealth, while the poorest half of the world own just 0.75%', or that '81 billionaires have more wealth than 50% of the world combined'.[55] Society's least valued, most degraded, most violated re-jects take human form in racialized 'uncharacters' such as Celofán, Leira, and the Indigenous sex workers, who become akin to the territory of the *villa* itself, an 'enorme descampado que, a orillas del río, recibía los desperdicios que la ciudad enviaba en camiones, monótonos, continuos' (p. 46). The pre-carious lives of Herrera's characters, living on, off, or *as* waste, are invariably shortened by plural, intersecting forms of violence. Herrera's fiction calls for a widened conception of necropolitics and its corresponding 'death-worlds', which as well as the physical, racial, and social forms foregrounded by Mbe-mbe includes and reveals the sometimes invisible forms of environmental violence.[56]

SAPIENZA UNIVERSITÀ DI ROMA   LUCY BELL

---

[54] Mbembe, 'Necropolitics', p. 34.
[55] Khanyi Mlaba, 'The Richest 1% Own Almost Half the World's Wealth and 9 Other Mind-Blowing Facts on Wealth Inequality', *Global Citizen*, 19 January 2023 <https://www.globalcitizen.org/en/content/wealth-inequality-oxfam-billionaires-elon-musk/> [accessed 1 April 2024].
[56] Mbembe, 'Necropolitics', p. 40.

REVIEWS

Pregnancy in the Victorian Novel. By LIVIA ARNDAL WOODS. Columbus: Ohio
State University Press. 2023. 194 pp. $69.95. ISBN 978–0–8142–1553–1.

The obscuring of pregnancy and the pregnant body in the Victorian novel may
explain its notable absence (at least until recently) in critical discussions of the
genre—this in spite of the fact that in multiple, perhaps even most, nineteenth-
century novels the birth of a child (or children) is central to the narrative. It is
in part for this reason that Livia Arndal Woods feels the topic is important and
necessary: the lack of attention to pregnancy thus far seems indicative of a wider
lack of interest in the maternal experience as fertile ground for critical exploration.

As Woods notes in her Introduction, the Victorian novel typically treats pregnancy with 'modesty', rarely depicting it as an embodied experience. Woods's
challenge, then, is not so much to read what is there, visible, centred, in the Victorian novel, but to explore that which is largely absent, hinted at through veiled
language and often confirmed only by the subsequent birth of a child (or rather,
appearance, as births too are typically elided from nineteenth-century fiction).
Woods rises to the challenge, and offers engaging and convincing readings of
pregnancy in a range of canonical and non-canonical Victorian novels, including
Wuthering Heights, *Ruth*, *Adam Bede*, *East Lynne*, *The Clever Woman of the Family*,
Jude the Obscure, and *The Heavenly Twins*. In a sweeping study which captures
the Victorian literary landscape from the 1840s to the 1900s, Woods explores
these texts' representations of pregnancy in relation to a range of topics, including
(im)modesty, transgression, judgement, sympathy, sensation, and diagnosis. Her
'somatic readings' of these works are astute and convincing, providing valuable
insights into the treatment of pregnancy by Victorian writers.

If this were the pinnacle of Woods's achievement in this book, it would nonetheless be a worthy and applaudable endeavour. However, as important as the
new critical explorations of these works are, the strength of the book lies also in
its wider contribution to the fields of Victorian Studies and literary criticism. In
examining the Victorian novel, Woods also looks beyond its covers to a cultural
and critical landscape which spans some two hundred years, encompassing 'the
long and wide historical arc of Anglo-American modernity and its aftershocks'
(p. 1) from the early modern witch trials to twenty-first-century restrictions on
women's reproductive rights in America and elsewhere. These connections may not
seem immediately apparent, but Woods succeeds in drawing attention to the wider
cultural and historical landscape which impacts not only depictions of pregnancy
in the Victorian novel, but our own understandings and experiences of pregnancy
in the modern world. In the Interlude which marks the centre of Woods's study,
the lived experiences of women in twenty-first-century America are placed in
direct correspondence with Mrs Henry Wood's Lady Isabel Vane. Through this,
Woods argues for the importance of presentism—long resisted and baulked at by
scholars—in the field of Victorian Studies. In closing her final chapter, Woods

highlights the consequences of recent retrograde moves in America as regards women's reproductive rights, noting that the somatic readers of the future may find themselves 'much more attuned to the pain of bearing unwanted pregnancies' (p. 155): this common plotline from the Victorian novel thus takes on new resonance in today's world.

While Woods's study thus forms part of a wide temporal and geographical canvas, she also brings the personal to bear on her critical interpretations of the novels she scrutinizes, reflecting a broader trend in critical writing of recent times. Pregnancy is a personal, embodied experience, and, as Woods eloquently argues, 'The significance of the texts we read inheres partly in the responses of our bodies to those texts' (p. 75). Twenty-first-century bodies thus become central to interpretations of the pregnant body in nineteenth-century texts. Woods is candid about the influence of her own maternal (embodied) experiences on her research, emphasizing the connections between maternal bodies and understandings of those bodies across time, space, and different cultures. There has long been resistance to bringing the personal to bear in academic writing, but Woods's study highlights the importance—indeed the necessity—of such an approach. In excavating not only Victorian novelistic depictions of pregnancy, but also the influence of embodied experiences on the researcher, Woods's work makes a convincing case for a radical revisioning of traditional critical approaches to the past and its literature.

BRUNEL UNIVERSITY LONDON JESSICA COX
doi:10.1353/mlr.00007

Literary Multilingualism in the Borderlands: The Challenge of Trieste. By MARIANNA DEGANUTTI. New York: Routledge. 2024. viii+205 pp. $170. ISBN 978–1–032–21325–5.

Marianna Deganutti's monograph is a striking study of literary multilingualism in the intricate case study of the city of Trieste, a challenging meeting point of Romance, Germanic, and Slav cultures, that was in the past a highly contentious area experiencing frequent and dramatic changes of territorial control. It is today a very good example of a borderland city with a thriving literary tradition. It is precisely the study of border literature that is the focus of the researcher's attention: 'This geographical location had an impact not only on the political and sociological dynamics dominating the area but also on its literary outputs, which will be the main focus of this analysis' (p. 2).

Deganutti takes into account some of the most representative authors working in the twentieth century in different languages and from different cultural backgrounds, but all sharing the experience of living in Trieste: Italo Svevo, Boris Pahor, Fulvio Tomizza, Claudio Magris, Virgilio Giotti, and Carolus Cergoly. Deganutti is one of the first researchers to have taken these authors into account in a unitary analysis because until recent years each one was discussed within his own national literary system. But as she points out, 'writers from Trieste may have more in common among themselves than with their country fellows' (p. 14). First of all, in

Chapter 1, she identifies a specific theoretical framework, called 'language choice', that can also be used to analyse and understand other literary phenomena in similar borderland contexts. Deganutti argues that borderland authors have at their disposal a variety of languages, one of which they decide to use. But this choice is not stable and can evolve or change over the course of a literary career. Continuing on this wave of reflection in Chapter 2, she analyses Triestine writers who decided to privilege their first language. She explicitly emphasizes that by 'first language' she does not necessarily mean either the first language acquired chronologically, or the one in which the writer's performances and skills are higher: 'There is usually one main or a restricted number of tongues used by borderland writers in their works, I name this selected language, which may be chosen according to a variety of subjective factors, the first language among the ones available in the writer's repertoire' (p. 71). In analysing the variety of languages in Trieste, it is necessary to take into account the vernacular Triestino, which is used also in literary contexts: the third chapter considers this dialect in the works of Giotti and Cergoly. The 'borderlanguaging' condition in Joyce's highly experimental work *Finnegans Wake* is the focus of attention in Chapter 4, where Deganutti defines what an 'extensive multilingual repertoire' is. She argues that

what Joyce has done differently from the other writers operating in Trieste is that he has fully exploited the dynamics of multilingualism—at the price of being less immediately understandable. Not only has he broken codes and switched to countless other tongues, but he has also cross-fertilized codes and translanguaging, destabilizing the boundaries between different tongues, both latently and manifestly. (p. 157)

Deganutti presents in the next chapter an example of a writer who has chosen neither his native nor his dominant language, but rather the dominating tongue, which had first to be learnt. This is the case of Italo Svevo: considering his way of writing, the researcher states that he 'offers more original solutions and a new way of conveying multilingualism, perhaps favoring a vertical reading, which allows the reader to penetrate the surface of the narrative and reach its multilingual core' (p. 189). Deganutti demonstrates that many Triestine writers, despite living in the same borderland conditions, have reacted differently to the multilinguistic condition of the city of Trieste. That is why, in her analysis of boundary literary systems, she proposes to speak of 'languaging instead of language' (p. 197) and consequently of 'borderlanguaging'. Having available the ability to use different languages, these authors are operating at the borders between different tongues.

One of the strengths of Deganutti's work is certainly the theorization of the term 'borderlanguaging', first used only in recent years and still in need of further study and elaboration. The other great strength is the case study of the city of Trieste: Deganutti has analysed its literary system not from the point of view of a national literary system, but from the spatial point of view of a border, which is certainly a new approach and therefore all the more worthy of attention.

University of Primorska   Jadranka Cergol
doi:10.1353/mlr.00008

Poesis in Extremis: Literature Witnessing the Holocaust. By DANIEL FELDMAN
and EFRAIM SICHER. (Comparative Jewish Literatures) London: Bloomsbury.
2024. xi+258 pp. £81. ISBN 979-8-765100-20-2.

The title of Daniel Feldman and Efraim Sicher's book suggests that this is a study
of Holocaust verse, since 'poesis', from the ancient Greek *poiēsis*, signifies, among
other meanings, 'composition (of poetry)' and shares its root with 'poem'. The
bulk of the book is indeed dedicated to verse. Part II addresses the work of
Paul Celan (Chapters 2 and 3), Czesław Miłosz (Chapter 2), Abraham Sutzkever
(Chapter 2), Dan Pagis (Chapter 3), Miklós Radnóti (Chapter 4), Władysław Szlen-
gel (Chapter 5), and Itzhak Katzenelson (Chapter 6). These poets, as well as Elie
Wiesel and Ida Fink, whose prose is analysed in Parts I and II, are united by their
experience of living under the Holocaust; apart from Miłosz, who was a righteous bystander lamenting the indifference of many of non-Jewish Poles to Jewish
suffering, all the writers were targeted by Nazi antisemitism. These poets and novelists include both survivors and those who perished; those who wrote during the
war and those who recorded their experience later; those who identified as Jewish
and those who did not. Radnóti, for example, saw himself primarily as Hungarian
and in 1943 converted to Christianity. Finally, the corpus includes works both
canonical and less familiar to anglophone readers. The focus on verse reflects the
monograph's ambition to counter the 'paucity of critical attention to Holocaust
poetry' (p. 12), which Feldman and Sicher ascribe mainly to Adorno's injunction
(often misunderstood and quoted out of context) against poetry in the aftermath
of Auschwitz. Besides being outnumbered by critical works on Holocaust prose,
studies of Holocaust verse tend to be undertaken in a single linguistic context
(e.g. Antony Rowland's presentation of English-language poets, *Holocaust Poetry*
(Edinburgh: Edinburgh University Press, 2005); Gary D. Mole's survey of French
Holocaust poetry, *Voices of Pain, Cries of Silence* (New York: Peter Lang, 2024)). In
contrast, undaunted by the linguistic diversity of their corpus, Feldman and Sicher
conduct a comparative examination of texts written in French, German, Polish,
Hebrew, Hungarian, and Yiddish. The book's attention to verse notwithstanding,
it also addresses prose. Together with the volume's subtitle—*Literature Witnessing
the Holocaust*—Sicher's essay on Wiesel's *Night* and Feldman's reading of Fink's
short stories, which bookend Part II, gesture towards the authors' understanding
of poesis as synonymous with imaginative writing. What therefore interests Feldman and Sicher is the poetics and testimonial role of verse *and* prose created by
those who lived *during* the Holocaust. Before investigating the generic categories
and discursive practices adopted by these writers, the book tests the concept of
'Holocaust poetics', which indicates a generic shift provoked by 'the constraints
that the everyday experience of Nazi genocide [. . .] imposed on romantic and
modernist [literary] conventions' (p. 2). It asks whether writers sought new idioms
or, conversely, inscribed the existing poetics only to subvert it and expose its failure
to express the inexpressible. The varied writing strategies are exemplified by Radnóti's successful 'synchroniz[ation of] versification and lyrical form with the reality

which denies the poet's existence' and Celan's 'poetics of negativity', which means his engagement with poetic traditions in order to give 'new, often ironic meaning to their use in a horrific reality' (p. 129). Whether the examined works embrace, reject, or parody established literary practices, they invariably bear witness to the unfolding calamity which was the context of their creation. For, even though, under normal circumstances, poetry's aesthetic quality outweighs its communicative purpose, in the case of the Holocaust its programmatic literariness 'enhances [. . .] testimony' (p. 16). It is not only by focusing on poetry, but also by insisting on its evidentiary value, that Feldman and Sicher's volume becomes a timely and original contribution to a relatively neglected area of Holocaust research, the study of verse. *Poesis in Extremis* is thoroughly researched, erudite, and engaging, with each chapter providing helpful historical and biographical contextualization, and deftly interweaving these paratextual details with close literary analysis. The work could have been more cohesive had it included only poetry written during the Holocaust (to reflect the title), for, however illuminating, readings of Wiesel's and Fink's prose provide incongruous bookends for the central poetry chapters. Another slight weakness is the authors' choice to frame their critique with well-worn truths about Holocaust representation, such as the aporia, where memorial obligation to Jewish victims is up against ethical and epistemological concerns proceeding from, among other sources, Adorno's judgement of post-Shoah poetry as 'barbaric'. Another such commonplace is the ambiguity of culture, which, although meant to safeguard humanity against 'bestiality', was cherished and keenly practised by many of those who masterminded and executed the worst genocide in history. Should these questions be revisited, terms such as 'barbarism', 'bestiality', and even 'humanity' ought to be approached more carefully. Scrutinizing these terms from a posthumanist perspective, which in Holocaust Studies locates the ontological origins of the Nazi genocide in the demarcation of humanity from the non-human, we can see that they can enable exclusion and hierarchization, which also happened to be the driving processes behind the Holocaust.

University of Wrocław   Helena Duffy
doi:10.1353/mlr.00009

Contested Communities: Small, Minority and Minor Literatures in Europe. Ed. by Kate Averis, Margaret Littler, and Godela Weiss-Sussex. Cambridge: Legenda. 2023. xiii+248 pp. £85. ISBN 978–1–839542–23–7.

Guided by the 'Deleuzo-Guattarian concept of minor literature as linguistic disruption, political immediacy and anticipation of an as yet absent collective' (p. 8), *Contested Communities* is an ambitious study that uncovers a complex net of relationalities, within Europe and beyond, starting from the language question within the literary domain.

Chapters by Kate Averis, Margarida Rendeiro, and Christinna Hazzard remind us of the colonial legacies of France, Portugal, and Denmark respectively: Averis focuses on Latin American expat writers writing in French, thereby detaching themselves from the tradition of Spanish; Rendeiro exposes Portugal's ongoing 'denial' (p. 54) of its colonial past by examining Afro-Portuguese literature that challenges the 'Eurocentric memory projects' (p. 55); Hazzard compares Danish representations and self-representations of the Greenlandic minority, pointing at the 'ongoing imperialism in the Arctic region' (p. 65).

The debate on cultural and linguistic hegemony within the continent drives the chapters by Catherine Barbour, Mari Jose Olaziregi, and Stefan Willer, which question the politics of (self-)translation of minor languages—Galician, Basque, and Low German respectively—into hegemonic languages such as Castilian and German, calling for 'foreignizing translation strategies that can work to counteract the invisibility' (p. 105) of '"peripheral" literatures' (p. 97), and for the establishment of strong relationships among minority languages in Europe.

The politics of marginality are nonetheless complex and intersectional, as Godela Weiss-Sussex, Pamela McCallum, and Teresa Ludden show: from Jewish women writers in early twentieth-century Germany, and narratives of the new migrant communities emerging in a hostile Britain, to reflections on translation, absence, and non-identity in Terézia Mora's Hungaro-German *Das Ungeheuer*, Europe appears still to be strictly reliant on its nation states and thus establishes, socially and privately, hierarchical relationalities on the basis of otherness.

Otherness, nonetheless, also becomes a way to 'overcome exclusionary discursive tendencies and move beyond the nation where subjectivity is coded male and the migrantized woman remains an "unsubject"' (p. 213), as Áine McMurtry demonstrates in her posthuman reading of German Afrofuturism. Similarly, it is an integral part of the creative process in Madalena Gonzalez's chapter on multilingual minority theatre, which exposes the linguistic and cultural affinities of the Breton, Cornish, and Welsh European peripheries, and in Margaret Littler's exploration of Berkan Karpat's and Zafer Şenocak's poetic production, where medieval Sufi poetry meets modern science and technology to create a '"new man"' evoking Gilles Deleuze's '"dissolved self"' (p. 167).

These chapters exemplify how 'literature [. . .] actively participates in social processes and changes' (p. 134), but crafting a new, multilingual, and diverse Europe also depends on the participation of publishing houses and public reading spaces: on this note, Simone Brioni and Shirin Ramzanali Fazel dialogically expose the difficulties of publishing faced by migrant authors. Briony Birdi's sociological study of minority Black British and Asian British fiction shows how libraries play a crucial role in diversifying the taste of the British readership and in broadening our 'interpretation of terms such as "fiction" and "literature"' (p. 94).

Transnational projects easily lend themselves to the thorough scrutiny of the absences they allow. There is in fact a gap in literature from the Scandinavian peninsula and the Baltic countries, which speaks for academic collaborations yet to be established and geographies yet to be fully embraced by the European literary landscape. The case of Eastern Europe is more complex. In fact, McCallum and Ludden move the volume's axis eastwards by analysing narratives of Eastern European migrants in the UK and Germany respectively. Yet within the novels they explore, the Eastern European characters remain an otherness, a reflective surface held in the face of Britain and Germany and their representative characters, who are thereby prompted to think about themselves in relation to these stranger others. The volume nonetheless succeeds in minoritizing Europe, highlighting its rich and complex inner and outer relations, and opening a space for further explorations.

It is undeniable that Averis, Littler, and Weiss-Sussex have crafted a masterful piece of edited work that is coherent in its theoretical positioning and diverse in its methodology. It would be a mistake not to recognize how the careful editorial work does not just bring together some penetrating essays that would be of interest to the specialized reader, but also makes of *Contested Communities* the material representation of the Deleuzo-Guattarian rhizome that constitutes the theoretical cornerstone of the volume. This is a valuable text for researchers in the fields of European transnational literature and multilingualism.

UNIVERSITY OF YORK   ALICE FLINTA
doi:10.1353/mlr.00010

City Scripts: Narratives of Postindustrial Urban Futures. Ed. by BARBARA BUCHENAU, JENS MARTIN GURR, and MARIA SULIMMA. Columbus: Ohio State University Press. 2023. xii+240 pp. $59.95. ISBN 978-0-8142-1552-4.

City Scripts offers a new way to think about the relationship between cities on the page and the cities in which we live, between representations of urban life and the lived experiences of urbanites. The editors of and contributors to this collection turn to and theorize the concept of the *script* as a particularly useful way to make sense of how the stories we tell about cities shape the way we design, construct, and inhabit them. In this volume's Introduction, Barbara Buchenau, Jens Martin Gurr, and Maria Sulimma thoroughly examine and explicate the analytical possibilities of 'city scripts' by drawing upon the various ways in which the term 'script' is deployed: theatrical scripts, social scripts, religious scripture, and other types of script. City scripts, the editors suggest, 'communicate and negotiate various understandings of the city' by combining 'figural expressions', 'narrative expositions', and 'media affordances' (p. 11), packaging these combinations in 'stark condensations and abbreviations' that are readily available to social actors to deploy and act upon in a wide range of contexts (p. 9). In addition to theorizing the essay collection's organizing concept, the Introduction provides a very useful entrée to the emerging field of Literary and Cultural Urban Studies, noting the field's shift away from literary texts written primarily by white male authors and its more recent 'broadening of the corpus to include nonliterary *pragmatic* texts' (p. 7).

To highlight what the editors refer to as 'postclassical literary urban studies', the volume's first group of essays focuses on the ways in which city scripts are embedded in non-fictional, pragmatic texts such as graffiti, architecture, street design, planning documents, and city monuments and sculptures—texts that have traditionally been the subject matter of a social-science brand of urban studies (p. 6). While the type of urban texts to which authors in the first section apply the concept of city scripts may depart from classical literary urban studies, their essays simultaneously suggest a continuity within the field by pointing to the value of urban theorists such as Michel de Certeau in thinking through the analytical possibilities of city scripts. Florian M. Deckers and Renee M. Moreno, for instance, turn to de Certeau's concept of the 'tactic' to ground their analysis of Black Lives Matter graffiti in Denver as expressions of 'counterscripting' that 'inscribe themselves into urban space in order to rescribe local and translocal urban tales of belonging, social cohesion, and political action' (p. 28).

The second group of essays returns to the more traditional purview of literary urban studies (i.e. urban poetry and prose) but does so with the intention of seeing what new modes of interpretation the concept of city scripts makes possible. At times, the notion of script feels like a stand-in for more familiar categories such as narrative patterns, literary conventions, and genres. At others, as in Sulimma's smart essay about the appearance of bodegas and cafés in contemporary gentrification fiction, the notion of the script serves as a source of theoretical inspiration and creativity. Sulimma proposes the concept of 'microscripts' as a useful variation on the volume's organizing concept of city scripts: while city scripts 'seek to inspire grand visions of/for a city's past, present, or future', Sulimma suggests that 'microscripts are short and condensed moments in a larger story that in an off-hand and incidental manner transport an observation or insight about life in a city' (p. 140). When read through the lens of microscripts, passages about acts as mundane or 'subnarratable' as buying and drinking coffee can, in Tommy Orange's *There There* (2018) and Ottessa Moshfegh's *My Year of Rest and Relaxation* (2018), signify much larger 'discourses surrounding gentrification, individual responsibility, and structural change' (pp. 140, 141).

The final group of essays examines the relationship between the city scripts and some of the big ideas that have shaped our understanding of cities for some time— ideas such as decline, creativity, and futurity. The contributors to this section are particularly interested in the ways in which these city scripts animate broader public discourses about urban life and thus inform urban policies, planning decisions, and personal experiences. It is fitting that Barbara Eckstein and James A. Throgmorton's essay concludes the section and volume; their *Story and Sustainability: Planning, Practice and Possibility for American Cities* (Cambridge, MA: MIT Press, 2003), which brought together the fields of literary studies and urban planning, is an important part of the intellectual tradition that *City Scripts* seeks to extend. Speaking from his perspective as a former mayor and member of his city's city council, Throgmorton makes a compelling case for the value of this volume's contribution to literary and cultural urban studies—one that resonates with my own experience as a member of my city's planning commission: 'My experience revealed a great deal about how, specifically, stories (and scripts more broadly) influenced what people advocated, what city councils do, and what external constraints and incentives affected a city's actions' (p. 218).

BRIGHAM YOUNG UNIVERSITY   JAMIN CREED ROWAN
doi:10.1353/mlr.00011

A New Anatomy of Storyworlds: What Is, What If, As If. By MARIE-LAURE RYAN.
   Columbus: Ohio State University Press. 2022. x+226 pp. $89.95 (ebk $49.95).
   ISBN 978-0-8142-1508-1 (ebk 978-0-8142-8226-7).

While the concept of 'storyworlds', or world-building, precedes the advent of cognitive narratology, it rose quickly to prominence with the pioneering work of
David Herman and has long been central to Marie-Laure Ryan's work. In her
latest monograph Ryan defends the utility of the concept against competing models
and develops a new approach to the study of world-building in narrative which
is distinct from four dominant schools of narratology: the rhetorical approach;
the feminist approach; the cognitive approach; and the unnatural approach (p. 9).
Ryan's 'What Is, What If, As If' approach is an alternative allowing for a necessary
ontological distinction to be made between factual representations of the real world
('what is'), fictional representations of imaginary worlds ('what if'), and the game
of pretence that apprehends what-if worlds *as* what-is worlds ('as if') (pp. 8–9). This
'as-if effect' might seem to evoke what Coleridge famously described in *Biographia
Literaria* as 'that willing suspension of disbelief', but Ryan is precise about what she
means: it is, at the very least, an 'acceptance of the narrative as true of its reference
world' and, at best, 'an immersive sense of presence in the storyworld' (p. 9). Inspired by the possible worlds theory of the philosopher David Lewis and by Kendall
Walton's 'make-believe' conception of 'fiction as a game with its own rules' (p. 37;
in *Mimesis as Make-Believe* (Cambridge, MA: Harvard University Press, 1990)),
Ryan returns to the significance of this 'as-if' effect in a discussion of fictional truth
in Chapter 1 and elaborates further as she compares and contrasts her preferred
theory of fiction with four rivals in Chapter 2. While Ryan's theory may initially
sound more like a pithy formulation summarizing existing conceptualizations of
storyworlds than an innovative 'new anatomy', its theoretical specificity and origins
will become increasingly clear as the reader moves through the volume.

   Drawing on her encyclopaedic knowledge of narratology and its adjacent dis-
ciplines from decades of research, Ryan deftly navigates controversial debates in
narratology (from the classification of autofiction to the revival of Ann Banfield's
and S.-Y. Kuroda's non-narrator theory from the 1980s in Sylvie Patron's optional-
narrator theory in *Le Narrateur* (Paris: Lambert-Lucas, 2016) and *Optional Narrator Theory* (Lincoln: University of Nebraska Press, 2020)). She is unflinching in
her claims throughout, declaring, for instance, that 'there is no such thing as a
feminist narratology' and rejecting two foundational contributions from rhetorical
narratology: the definition of narrative as communication and its notion of the
implied author (p. 12).

   A New Anatomy of Storyworlds necessarily begins by grounding narratology in the
concept of world. Each of its subsequent chapters re-examines a different core narratological concept that either strengthens or troubles the centrality of the notion of
storyworld. These are: truth (Chapter 1), fiction (Chapter 2), narrator (Chapter 3),
character (Chapter 4), plot (Chapter 5), mimesis and diegesis (Chapter 6), parallel
worlds (Chapter 7), impossible worlds (Chapter 8), virtual worlds (Chapter 9), and

transmedia worlds (Chapter 10). Ryan's ambitious first chapter tackles the pertinence of truth in the contemporary moment and for the discipline, arguing that discourse types should be distinguished according to the conception of truth and validity we are using (p. 21). Chapter 2 usefully organizes four theories of fictionality around their answers to crucial questions such as whether counterfactuals and thought experiments constitute fiction according to each of the theories, and it gives the reader a glimpse of how Ryan might teach the subject in a classroom. Although Ryan's explanation of 'counterfactuals' in this sort of review necessarily lacks the theoretical specificity that would be found in works by Hilary P. Dannenberg (now 'Duffield'), it is nevertheless a useful overview of the topic. Ryan's last two chapters will be of particular interest to scholars working on virtual reality (VR) technology and digital fiction, where she traces the historical development of both (pp. 162–67) and distinguishes interactivity from immersion (pp. 167–70) with extraordinary precision.

The chapters are of a digestible length and the writing is engaging and lucid with much to offer both well-versed narratologists and students new to narrative theory alike. Characteristic of this volume are formulations such as the following, where Ryan achieves that rare balance between provocation and insight: 'Nineteenth-century positivism called myth a superstition. Fiction never suffered the insult. In the language game of fiction, the false is regarded as true, but the player knows that it is only a game' (p. 31). Ryan does not forget to contextualize and state the origins of key concepts and movements as she problematizes core tenets of narrative theory. Whatever school of narratology readers associate themselves with, Ryan's numerous provocations will no doubt illuminate, inspire, and excite.

JUSTUS LIEBIG UNIVERSITY GIESSEN   DENISE WONG
doi:10.1353/mlr.00012

Subsurface. By KAREN PINKUS. (posthumanities, 67) Minneapolis and London: University of Minnesota Press. 2023. 219 pp. £93.30 (pbk £21.99). ISBN 978–1–5179–1478–3 (pbk 978–1–5179–1479–0).

This is a rather experimental book located at the intersection of the natural sciences and the humanities. Karen Pinkus sets up an exercise in which the history of geology and past fantasy texts about the subsurface of the Earth are juxtaposed with contemporary anxieties in which the subterranean is understood very differently. What once seemed a space of mystery, possibility, and adventure now seems a forbidding antagonist to human hubris, an object of often destructive extractivism, source of fossil fuels but also the possible burial site of emissions. Pinkus mostly eschews the term 'Anthropocene', but, humans being essentially creatures of the surface, she stresses in images of the subsurface a pervasive 'rupture' or 'crack' or 'crevasse' between the past and the present in general human and social self-understanding, dated, pragmatically, from around the turn of the twenty-first century.

The exercise of stark juxtaposition is aware of its own lack of traditional scholarly foundations. Nevertheless, the central claim of a vast gap between past and present understandings can seem overdone. Compare how Christophe Bonneuil and Jean-Baptiste Fressoz, in *The Shock of the Anthropocene* (2015; translated by David Fernbacher (London: Verso, 2016)), read the so-called Anthropocene through several centuries of controversy about the destructive effects of capitalist exploitation, leading them to attack 'the media cliché of an inadvertent environmental destruction and a quite recent awakening' (p. 73).

In each chapter well-referenced accounts of contemporary debates—about climate change, geo-engineering, carbon sequestration, and so on—are juxtaposed with readings of historical texts, including Jules Verne, *Journey to the Centre of the Earth* (*Voyage au centre de la Terre*), *The Black Indies* (*Les Indes noires*); George Sand, *Laura*; Arthur Conan Doyle, *The Lost World*; E. T. A. Hoffmann, *The Mines of Fallun* (*Die Bergwerke zu Falun*). There is also consideration of some premodern geological texts (e.g. Georgius Agricola; Loius Figuier, *The World before the Flood*; Athanasius Kircher, *Mundus Subterraneus*). The subsurface conceived as a space of rich capitalist possibility finds some precedent in these versions of the ancient theme of descent to the underworld, but some are frankly escapist fantasies. Might they demand more wariness about making big claims for their importance when reading the present? The question of the status of Verne, Conan Doyle, et al. as 'literature', 'serious' or otherwise, is raised rather casually. Agamben's theory of literature as a reliquary of the mythic (pp. 78–79) is drawn in, but phrases such as 'from a literary point of view' (p. 60) or 'reading as literature' (p. 78) remain rather question-begging, raising issues of the very varied and contrasting cultures of readership for all the texts taken up, historical and contemporary; consider, for example, that Verne was writing with adolescent male readers in mind. Might something have been made of other arguments about nineteenth-century geology, for instance that the influential gradualism postulated for processes of change by Charles Lyell (and Charles Darwin on evolutionary change) was a factor in the development of literary realism?

Chapter 1, on 'cracks', stands out, studying various modes of representing or mapping geological entities, such as the familiar image of a vertical column in which past epochs are represented as a series of marked layers. Pinkus traces both the fragility and the cultural power of various understandings of the geological, how they construct themselves spatially and temporally through such concepts as 'strata' or 'epochs', and such overarching questions as how the subsurface can be assumed to mirror the surface. Chapter 2, with the theme or keyword of 'extraction', offers readings of the subsurface understood as a space of resources for capitalism or for utopian fables that evade the realities of exploitation, such as Verne's *The Black Indies*. Chapter 3, on burial, concerns the theme of disposal underground, carbon sequestration, and repression, while Chapter 4 turns to the shallow space between subsurface and surface, the soil (with material on carbon sinks and carbon accounting). Chapter 5 speculates on possible futures for the subsurface.

Throughout the book there is a sustained self-conscious staging of how figures of depth and surface, above and below, the apparent and profound, etc., inhabit and often structure critical and ordinary discourse about knowledge and ignorance.

Such staging, however, also becomes a mannerism and the conflation of literal and figurative terms for mining, exploration, seeing/reading beneath the surface, and so on can even make crucial passages exasperatingly opaque. The book is written in an allusive coterie mode that projects its readers as intellectual insiders au fait with ongoing work in the environmental humanities. If one of the strategic goals of ecocriticism remains to influence the more general culture and public thinking in which environmental issues are conceived, it is of dubious help to introduce a summary argument from Deleuze and Guattari with '*As readers will know*, the two French thinkers focus' (p. 39, emphasis added).

In sum, *Subsurface* offers a moderately rich source of reference on modern debates on the subsurface that could be stimulating to other thinkers in the environmental humanities, but seems at times weak and even impressionistic in overall or strategic argument.

University of Durham   Timothy Clark
doi:10.1353/mlr.00013

Localizing Christopher Marlowe: His Life, Plays and Mythology, 1575–1593. By Arata Ide. Martlesham: Brewer. 2023. xxi+422 pp. £85 (ebk £24.99). ISBN 978–1–84384–693–2 (ebk 978–1–80543–142–8).

Arata Ide's provocative book aims to 'challenge the established narrative of Marlowe studies' (p. 1) and to 'offer new readings about these fragmentary documents' (p. 2) with the aim of elucidating Marlowe's social experience rather than the man himself. He is in fact quite dismissive of 'the current thriving business of biography' (p. 3), his main beef being that biographers of Marlowe guess things, but he is not above a bit of speculation himself: he suggests, for instance, that Greene's hostility to Marlowe (which he sees as the main and wholly unreliable source for the idea that Marlowe was an atheist) might be traceable to Greene's putative connections with the Norwich faction at Corpus (p. 57), and he starkly and startlingly declares that *Tamburlaine* was 'written to comply with the urgent request of the Privy Council' (p. 22), a statement for which I would very much like to see some evidence.

Ide also promises to draw attention to 'hitherto overlooked sources' (p. 2), and in this respect the book is more satisfying. Chapter 2, 'Marlowe in the Community of Canterbury Scholars', does indeed yield a possible new sighting of Marlowe in April 1587 accompanying a fellow student on a trip to pawn a borrowed cloak, though I think it is pushing it a bit to describe this as firm evidence of 'Marlowe's faithful dealing with his friend' (p. 73). Ide is interesting too on the italic hand of Marlowe's supplicat (different from the secretary hand found on the Benchkin will), but we are in the realm of speculation again when he suggests that the use of italic may be in imitation of Abraham Tilman, also a scholar from the King's School, Canterbury, whom he thinks Marlowe admired. Chapter 3, 'The Origin of the Rumour against Marlowe', makes the intriguing suggestion that going to Rheims could be about making money rather than religion (p. 92), and Ide again finds a possible sighting of Marlowe in the form of a payment being made in the presence of 'marlin' (p. 111).

Most eye-catchingly of all, the final chapter in this section, 'Marlowe and the Privy Council', introduces a document which, if it really does say Marlin rather than Martin, might suggest that Marlowe went to Padua.

The book opens with a timeline which includes the date of Greene's christening but omits Shakespeare's, and this sets the tone for Ide's project of situating Marlowe primarily within the world of Cambridge university politics. The several illustrations include a plan of the room allocations for Parker scholars which Ide uses to suggest that Marlowe shared a chamber with Samuel Beadle rather than, as previously supposed, Robert Thexton and Thomas Lewgar; again Ide takes this as signalling Marlowe's 'comradeship' with Beadle (p. 74), though any boarding school survivor knows that proximity may not breed affection. I was more convinced by the suggestion that another Corpus Christi scholar and playwright, Nathaniel Woodes, can be traced through these documents in ways which, Ide suggests, allow us to 'localiz[e]' his play *The Conflict of Conscience* 'in the context of Norwich in the 1570s' (p. 50).

Most surprisingly, Ide declares that 'the methodology I apply in *Localizing Christopher Marlowe* prevents us from examining all his work' (p. 21), as a result of which there is literally not one word about *Edward II* and surprisingly little about *Doctor Faustus* (with what there is focusing more on stories and theories about early performances rather than the play itself). Even the chapter on 'Dido, Elizabeth I, and the University Playwrights' is not so much about the play as about the two distinct versions of Dido, the chaste and the amorous (a subject on which Ide is very good); he also suggests that Dido's mention of Meleager's son (p. 165), which is apparently Marlowe's invention, might allude to William Gager's *Meleager* (1582) and hence implicitly to Philip Sidney, who is considered too in the chapter on 'Tamburlaine's Prophetic Oratory and the English Holy War', which connects the play to Sidney's funeral and the myth of Arthur, and is interesting on the importance of prophecy to Tamburlaine himself (though some of the discussion of Israel and genocide makes disturbing reading in ways the author could not have predicted). This is followed by '*The Jew of Malta* and the Diabolic Power of Theatrics', which rather surprisingly connects the play to contemporary work on Dover harbour and speculates that Marlowe might have known Reginald Scot. Finally, in 'Plays' comes 'Ramism, Thomas Nashe, and the "new sects of secularitie"'. There are very brief glances at *Doctor Faustus*, *The Massacre at Paris*, and *Tamburlaine* again, but the bulk of the discussion takes us back to religious tensions at Cambridge, confirming that it is Cambridge politics and contemporary documents rather than Marlowe the dramatist that energize the book and invite the attention of readers.

SHEFFIELD HALLAM UNIVERSITY   LISA HOPKINS
doi:10.1353/mlr.00014

The Activist Humanist: Form and Method in the Climate Crisis. By CAROLINE
LEVINE. Princeton and Oxford: Princeton University Press. 2023. xv+202 pp.
£20. ISBN 978-0-691-25058-8.

Caroline Levine's monograph develops positions articulated in her justly celebrated
and influential 2015 book, also published by Princeton, *Forms: Whole, Rhythm,
Hierarchy, Network*. There, Levine purposed to turn 'literary criticism [. . .] upside-
down' (p. 122) by questioning discriminations 'between the *formal* and the *social*'
(p. 1), by 'reading aesthetic forms as responses to given social realities' (p. xi), and
by querying whether 'smashing or evading' said forms would really 'advance social
justice' (p. xii). Instead, she argued, 'formless or antiformal experiences have [. . .]
drawn *too much* attention' (p. 9), and that 'All politics, including revolutionary
political action, will succeed only if it is canny about deploying multiple forms'
(p. 18). The social, political, and environmental crises informing Levine's readings
almost ten years ago have only intensified, as has the need for some kind of radical
if not revolutionary response to what she now deems our 'acute precarity' (p. xiii).

Like *Forms*, Levine's latest book seeks to 'make sense of all formed things in the
world' (p. xii)—that is, any 'arrangement of elements, any ordering or patterning'
(p. 23) in any aesthetic or social context—but also tries to provide just such a response: 'a justification for practical political action as an integral part' of 'aesthetic
study', and a way to 'use formalist strategies drawn from the arts to redescribe
political power' (p. xii). While Levine accepts that 'one of the core assumptions of
humanistic pedagogy' is that 'reading a passage or an image in the classroom' facilitates 'an informed and responsible citizenry' (p. 139), she also asserts that though
'the humanities tend to valorize the works of art that revolutionize consciousness',
they rarely offer 'any specific course of action to redress [. . .] wrongs' (p. xii). Yet,
if, like Levine, we conceive of an 'unfamiliar canon' (p. 84) and draw on a 'motley
assortment of narratives' (p. 21), we see that 'we need many forms to know the
world' (p. 33) and that 'blueprints for social life are everywhere: in the middle of
a Rossetti poem, [in a mural] on the wall of the post office, in Austen fanfiction'
(p. 121). Historicizing and close textual analyses—'reading for fine distinctions' and
revealing 'the contingency of practices' (pp. 22–23)—therefore remain central to
Levine's inclusive and resistant methods.

The big difference between the two books, as Levine remarks with reflexive self-
criticism, is the way her new work tries to offer what the older one did not: a
'sketching out' of 'shapes and arrangements' that might come *after* we have ap-
prehended 'instability, complexity, and open-endedness' in our cultural analyses
(pp. xii–xiii). This leads into Levine's critique of anti-instrumentalism, viz. readings and positions 'set [. . .] against all constraints, all rules, all plans' (p. 6).
Anti-instrumentalism might seem like a liberatory response to 'neo-liberal precarity' (p. 8), but it is a dangerous, disaggregating, disempowering dead end. It sustains
'a libertarian logic' (p. 53), and has been all too easily co-opted in the past (by
the CIA, notes Levine) and the present: 'Climate denial is itself oddly consonant
with the humanistic values of opacity and open-endedness' (p. 7). To imagine only

'hopes—but not plans' (p. 9), to remain 'in the pause before action' in the 'daily work of teaching and writing in the aesthetic humanities' (p. 10), and to shy away from prescribing or 'crafting new rules' (p. 53), means that ground is ceded to those who have no problem imposing their authority.

As she is clear about the progenitors of this anti-instrumentalism and its 'disturbance of means–end thinking' (p. 3), from Kant to Adorno, Levine is explicit about the influences that have led her to this point: feminism, 'the Birmingham school of cultural studies' (p. 20), with its analyses of popular cultures, and Raymond Williams's Cultural Materialism, through affirming '*Form is a materialist concern*' (p. 27). Marx barely merits a mention, which is curious since Levine is informed by the perspective that 'beliefs and values grow out of material [. . .] arrangements' and those arrangements 'produce us as much as we produce them' (p. 28). Indeed, a good subtitle for this book might well have been 'the point is to change it', echoing Marx on philosophers who have only 'interpreted the world', in his *Theses on Feuerbach* (1888).

Countering anti-instrumentalism licenses Levine to offer compelling close readings of diverse cultural texts which affirm that not all forms and structures are bad: 'the forty-hour work week' might appear 'a rigid institutional form' but has value for precarious workers in a gig economy (p. 44). Borders and roads might coerce and exploit, but 'routines, pathways, and enclosures' can keep 'life going', enabling what Levine says the Potawatomi philosopher Kyle Powys Whyte terms '*collective continuance*' (p. xiv).

While Levine's argument perhaps overlooks the commitments of Critical Race Theorists, who deconstruct discourses *and* advocate for change, in the best possible way this is a kind of politicized Structuralism: 'a formalist scholar can analyze the shapes and patterns of a *Bildungsroman* or a school system' (p. 24). Arguably, too, this approach threatens to homogenize diverse experiences and representations, but Levine recognizes that 'Pop songs and prison labor are not, in fact, the same at all' (p. 92).

The final section of the book is perhaps the most intriguing and idiosyncratic. Levine offers a 'Workbook', setting out daily activities and tasks a humanist activist might undertake from a standing start to effect political action in a few weeks (pp. 150–57). The potential of this section is significant: one could imagine it being incorporated into a course on the humanities and social justice, for example. But it might have been augmented by engaging with the work of someone like Jane McAlevey, especially her necessarily exacting and, yes, prescriptive guide to building democracy within and beyond the workplace, *No Short Cuts: Organizing for Power in the New Gilded Age* (Oxford: Oxford University Press, 2016). Indeed, a key 'form' in society—trade unions—barely gets a mention here; odd, since the final word is, as it should be, 'Solidarity!' (p. 159).

NORTHUMBRIA UNIVERSITY ADAM HANSEN
doi:10.1353/mlr.00015

Marcel Proust. By MICHAEL WOOD. (My Reading) Oxford and New York: Oxford
   University Press. 2023. xiii+130 pp. £18.99. ISBN 978-0-19-284582-5.

This short book appears within Oxford University Press's 'My Reading' series, one
purpose of which is to provide a forum for unconventional forms of critical writing
on major authors (p. v). Michael Wood's contribution on Marcel Proust offers a
suitably singular approach. While it revisits well-known scenes and themes from
A la recherche du temps perdu and its precursors—examples include the goodnight
kiss, the Dreyfus Affair, jealousy, knowledge and memory—the study does not read
like an introductory guide. Instead, it favours a suggestive style one senses is aimed
primarily at reframing the perspectives of seasoned readers returning to the work.
In the Preface, for example, Wood announces, rather elusively, that his areas of
focus will be 'a change of track, a distant cause, a national crisis, an incomplete
occurrence, a suspension of life, a displacement of justice, a parade of appearances'
(p. viii). The chapters 'move broadly between different worlds'—neurosis, politics,
law, and romance are cited as examples. These worlds 'meet up quite often', but the
implications of Wood's critical juxtapositions will be largely left to the reader to feel
out (p. viii). There are frequent epigrammatic formulations: 'We are to be haunted
by truths we have never known, and we are to make these truths available to others
in writing' (p. 8). Or 'The interesting question is why a story that can't be true is
so important for its teller' (p. 33). Wood's keyword is 'event', which is interpreted
and explored in various ways: both 'Proust's work as an event and [. . .] events
in relation to that work itself' (p. vii). For Wood, Proust's own use of the word
testifies to his love of its 'mixed implications of certainty and slippage', the French
author deploying it as 'a sort of interpretative magic wand' (p. xi). Interwoven with
the idea of the Proustian event is a consideration of 'rhetorical extravagance' as a
'major element in Proust's modernism' (p. 4). Later on, Wood identifies a habitual
Proustian trait as 'exaggerating wildly and also implying that *only* an exaggeration
will get us anywhere near the truth of the matter' (p. 58). This claim offers one way
to think about a recurrent emphasis in Proustian criticism: that the narrator of *A
la recherche du temps perdu* is most compelling in those moments when the reader
has cause to question his reliability, coherence, or even his basic sanity. Wood
also returns frequently to failure and 'a sense of significant impossibility' (p. 2) as
privileged Proustian concerns, with the novel dramatizing 'an exploration of time
that was always also a dream of its defeat' (p. 117). Wood's discussion of canonical
Proustian passages is elevated by his engagement with recently published materials
from the archive of Bernard de Fallois—for example, an earlier version of the goodnight kiss episode that is now available to readers via *Les Soixante-quinze feuillets
et autres manuscrits inédits* (Paris: Gallimard 2021)—as well as with frequent and
insightful reflections on translation from French into English. A discussion of the
grammatical strangeness, in French, of the famous Proustian incipit announces an
analysis of Proust's 'many discreet subversions of language' (pp. 20–21). Wood's
easy movements across the expanses of Proustian writing are thus grounded by his

attentiveness to linguistic detail, and readers willing to embrace his suggestive style will find much to stimulate reflection in this brief yet far-reaching study.

UNIVERSITY OF BATH

RICHARD MASON
doi:10.1353/mlr.00016

The Zombie in Contemporary French Caribbean Fiction. By LUCY SWANSON. (Contemporary French and Francophone Cultures) Liverpool: Liverpool University Press. 2023. x+208 pp. £110. ISBN 978-1-80207-799-5.

The figure of the zombie has long been misunderstood and misrepresented in academic and mainstream Western discourse. Widely thought to have originated in the French Caribbean, the Caribbean zombie, rooted as it is in 'the context of chattel slavery' (p. 2), has often been mobilized as a 'sensational symbol of Haitian and Caribbean culture in media particularly of the Global North' (p. 171), functioning to reinforce a Western vision of the region as 'a land of death and political dysfunction' (p. 3). It is such reductive representations of this figure of the undead that Lucy Swanson's monograph challenges, by interrogating how and why the zombie is used in French Caribbean fiction.

Swanson grounds her study in contemporary fiction by authors writing from and about Haiti, Martinique, and Guadeloupe, arguing that the zombie functions as a 'complex, iconic and ever-evolving figure in the Caribbean imaginary' (p. 4). Structured around a consideration of what she identifies as the four avatars of the zombie—the slave, the figure of mental illness, the horde, and the popular zombie—Swanson traces the evolution of this literary symbol, highlighting how the zombie represents not only the memory and enduring legacy of French Caribbean enslavement, but also a prism through which writers can both comment on and critique the region's contemporary socio-political landscape. Her carefully chosen corpus spans the work of novelists such as Martinican Patrick Chamoiseau's *Chronique des septs misères* (1986), André and Simone Schwarz-Bart's Guadeloupean *La Mulâtresse Solitude* (1972), and most of all the work of Haitian writers, including Jean-Claude Fignolé (*Aube tranquille*, 1990), Frankétienne (*Les Affres d'un défi*, 1979), Dany Laferrière (*Down among the Dead Men*, 1996), and Gary Victor (*La Piste des sortilèges*, 1996, and his serialized *Le Revenant* novels, 2007 and 2009), to name but a few. While the focus of her monograph is the zombie in French Caribbean fiction, Swanson also embeds into her analysis a consideration of the various—and often limiting—representations of the zombie in American and European literature and film, exploring, for instance, the trope of the zombie as 'a figure of mental illness' in the work of writers and directors such as Jacques Tourneur, William Seabrook, and Zora Neale Hurston (p. 19). The inclusion of these Western imaginings of the zombie compellingly rubs up against those found in the French Caribbean texts, offering insight into the ways in which contemporary French Antillean authors both contribute to and contest what Swanson calls the 'global zombie imaginary'. Swanson's varied sample therefore allows her simultaneously to give a broad account of the zombie tropes that authors across geographically, culturally, and temporally diverse realms rely on, while also enabling her to pull apart the specificities of the literary treatment of the zombie in different contexts. This is particularly the case in Chapter 1, where the comparative framework that Swanson adopts sheds light on how, in Haitian literature, the zombie has often been invoked as 'walking Haitian history' or the 'living or "recently" dead' (p. 6), while in Martinique and Guadeloupe the zombie has been literarily imagined as a 'symbol of the dangers that confront the maroon or freedom runner' (p. 25).

As the first book-length study of the zombie in contemporary French Caribbean fiction, this monograph is a landmark publication in both francophone Postcolonial Studies and Zombie Studies. In challenging how the Caribbean zombie has heretofore been regarded as 'little more than a footnote or preface to analyses of the "cannibal", "modern" or "Romero" zombies' such as those found in George Romero's *Night of the Living Dead* (1968) (p. 4) and by showcasing the multifaceted and radical potentiality of this literary figure beyond Western imaginations, Swanson's work convincingly urges us to rethink how we conceive not only the Caribbean zombie, but also the region from which it emerged. The monograph is thus an exemplar of decolonial academic praxis, and marks a vital contribution to reframing how the French Caribbean is regarded in both academic and popular discourse.

QUEEN'S UNIVERSITY BELFAST   LAURA KENNEDY
doi:10.1353/mlr.00017

Manuscript Poetics: Materiality and Textuality in Medieval Italian Literature. By FRANCESCO MARCO ARESU. (William and Katherine Devers Series in Dante and Medieval Italian Literature, 22) Notre Dame: University of Notre Dame Press. 2023. xviii+509 pp; 19 plates. $150 (pbk $65; ebk $51.99). ISBN 978–0–268–20648–2 (pbk 978–0–268–20649–9; ebk 978–0–268–20647–5).

Francesco Marco Aresu describes this insightful and richly detailed book as 'both an investigation into the material foundations of literature and a reflection on notions of textuality, writing, and media in late medieval and early modern Italy' (p. 3). His approach builds on research into material and visual aspects of book history by scholars such as Donald M. McKenzie, Jerome McGann, H. Wayne Storey, and Armando Petrucci, but he also draws deeply on the study of medieval poetics. The three parts of the book examine how text and form, 'project' and 'product' (p. 11), were intrinsically bound together in different ways in the conception and publication of three major works: Dante's *Vita nova*, Boccaccio's *Teseida*, and Petrarch's *Rerum vulgarium fragmenta*.

No autograph manuscript of Dante's youthful autobiography survives, but the author thematizes its materiality from the outset. In the prose sections, he narrates his transcription of passages drawn from the book of his memory into a self-contained booklet, the selection and exegesis of his verse, and the reception of this verse by others both orally and in writing. Aresu begins his Part I by examining the metanarrative elements of the *Vita nova*, drawing on recent German narratological studies by Ansgar Nünning and others. He then suggests that Dante attempted to protect the form of his prosimetrum from alteration by subsequent scribes by including analyses of the structure of his poems—a device that can moreover 'mirror the dividedness of Dante's self' (p. 83)—and by determining the correct sequence of prose and verse. Dante's work also portrays some of its readers within the narrative and envisages other readers outside it. Aresu's survey of four of the earliest manuscripts shows that, notwithstanding Dante's precautions, the presentation of the *Vita nova* was soon modified by scribes, including Boccaccio, who moved Dante's exegetical *divisioni* to the margins, probably in order to bestow on the work the authority of a glossed classical text. 'The book form intended *for the text* is described *within the text*', writes Aresu (p. 127), and yet manuscript transmission proved only partly faithful to Dante's intentions.

Boccaccio's poem in ottava rima, conceived as an epic (as the classicizing title *Teseida* suggests) but also related to popular narratives in the same metre, is discussed in Part II. In a transcription of the work that Boccaccio made around 1348, several years after its composition, he incorporated his own interlinear and marginal glosses, imitating the way in which a manuscript that he owned presented his principal classical model, Statius's *Thebaid*, with the commentary of Lactantius Placidus. However, Boccaccio's self-exegesis appears to have been an afterthought, it refers to the author as a separate person, and it does not claim to provide the only correct interpretation of the work. Boccaccio thus allowed for a less scholarly reception of the *Teseida*. The presentation of some of the extant manuscripts, which are not necessarily descended from the known autograph, reflects the status of the *Teseida* as literature to be enjoyed as entertainment. Only one-third of the manuscripts include a commentary. Of two copies made by a friend and neighbour of Boccaccio's in Florence not long after the author's death, one does not have the author's glosses, while the other has a shortened version of them. However, the work was accorded a higher status in three fifteenth-century manuscripts associated with the court of the Este in Ferrara and in the first printed edition (1475), also from Ferrara. All these witnesses incorporate a new commentary by Pietro Andrea de' Bassi, an Estense courtier. Bassi may not have known Boccaccio's commentary, but Aresu speculates that the resemblance of the presentation of Bassi's commentary in the three Ferrarese manuscripts to that of Boccaccio's autograph commentary 'seemingly signals the kind of power of visual attraction often exerted by author's books within the manuscript tradition' (p. 210).

The last part of Aresu's book focuses on Petrarch's presentation of the nine sestinas within his collection of lyric verse in the partly autograph manuscript now in the Vatican Library (which can be consulted online at <https://digi.vatlib.it/view/MSS_Vat.lat.3195>). The sestinas are presented unusually and therefore prominently: each of the six lines of verse in a stanza is transcribed one above the other in two columns, whereas in all other poems each line of text is occupied by two consecutive lines of verse in a single column, as was normal in the mid-fourteenth century. A sestina is characterized by the use of only six rhyme-words, which move backwards and crosswise in successive stanzas. Aresu argues persuasively that Petrarch's visual disposition of the hendecasyllables, which highlights the tortuous rhyme scheme, 'performs for the reader the dilemmatic torments of a soul conflicted between ascesis and sensuality, between progression and retraction' (p. 257). Despite the extreme care taken by Petrarch in the preparation of this Vatican copy, only a few manuscripts from the late fourteenth and early fifteenth centuries respected his presentation of his poems. In printed editions of the early sixteenth century, Girolamo Soncino (1503) and Alessandro Vellutello (1525) even expressed varying degrees of doubt about whether Petrarch had transcribed this copy. In the end, as Aresu observes, readers and patrons 'often determined book forms more than authors did' (p. 16).

Aresu claims no radical innovation in methodology, but he rightly expresses the hope that his book will help to bridge two existing approaches to medieval texts with respective emphases on materiality and on theory and interpretation (p. 9). A dense appendix to Part I succinctly illustrates similarities between Dante's metanarrative strategies in the *Vita nova* and the *Commedia*, and a further study of this topic by Aresu would be very welcome.

UNIVERSITY OF LEEDS   BRIAN RICHARDSON
doi:10.1353/mlr.00018

Boccaccio and the Consolation of Literature. By GUR ZAK. (Studies and Texts, 229) Toronto: Pontifical Institute of Mediaeval Studies. 2022. x+216 pp. £74.96. ISBN 978–0–88844–229–1.

Gur Zak's latest monograph reflects on the late medieval concept of 'consolation' within Giovanni Boccaccio's extensive body of work, focusing in particular on his vernacular compositions.

The book is structured meticulously. In the Introduction (pp. 1–24) Zak provides a useful overview of the late medieval concept of consolation in the literary and intellectual contexts of the three Italian crowns (Dante, Petrarch, and Boccaccio), insisting on the relevance of the consolatory act as a literary, human, and ethical phenomenon, especially within Boccaccio's œuvre. Zak, who views Dante's *Commedia* as a work of consolation (p. 1), observes how Boccaccio's concept of consolation challenges this late medieval tradition, significantly influenced by Boethius's *De consolatione philosophiae* and by several of Dante's works. The Certaldese not only challenges but also contributes to the evolution of this tradition with innovative elements. For instance, in contrast to what happens between Dante and Virgil in the *Commedia* or between Boethius and Lady Philosophy in the *De consolatione*, the protagonist of Boccaccio's *Amorosa Visione* resists following the constant advice and behavioural guidance offered by his mentor. This initial attempt at emancipation by an individual, i.e. the protagonist, later transforms into a more inclusive representation of the entire readership in Boccaccio's mature work, the *Corbaccio*. In this text, both the protagonist character and the figure of the guide are entirely anonymized: this authorial choice allows readers to liberate themselves from the obligation to identify the narrative event with specific characters, enabling a personal appropriation of the consolatory journey's beneficial effects. This evolution facilitates a genuine and complete process of identification with the narrative's flow, as well as direct and free immersion on the part of readers into the psychologically relevant aspects of the story.

Zak's exploration also gains depth and richness by drawing essential reference points from the ideas and representations of consolation found in the works of classical literary masters such as Virgil, Ovid, and Seneca, all well known by Boccaccio himself. These classical influences contribute to a nuanced and comprehensive analysis of the consolatory themes in the works of the Certaldese.

An additional innovative aspect of Zak's Introduction lies in his intricate theorization of the four types of consolation found in Boccaccio's texts. These typologies can be categorized into two main groups: the first encompasses forms of consolation that offer partial relief from sorrow or pain to the reader or the protagonists; the second includes types of consolation that lead to a complete overcoming of sorrow or pain. Zak argues that partial consolation can be achieved through engaging in pleasurable activities (a diversion) or by empathizing with the suffering of others. On the other hand, a state of complete consolation can be reached through the attainment of the desired object (satisfaction of desire) or by distancing oneself from the source of suffering (escape from desire). Throughout his works, Boccaccio employs all four of these consolatory methods, constantly striving to make them function harmoniously. Zak thoroughly applies and discusses this theory in each subsequent chapter, rigorously and meticulously analysing numerous passages from Boccaccio's extensive vernacular corpus.

The first two chapters delve into Boccaccio's early works, unravelling the nuances of his theory of consolation within each context. Chapter 1, entitled 'The *Filocolo* and the Polyphony of Consolation' (pp. 25–56), explores the author's first attempts to merge in a single literary work the four forms of consolation listed and discussed in the introductory chapter, and highlights the intricate relationship between the *Filocolo* and those diverse typologies of consolation. Chapter 2, 'The *Filostrato*, *Elegia*, and the Consolation of Tragedy' (pp. 57–87), extends the exploration to Boccaccio's engagement with tragedy and its consolatory aspects in the *Filostrato* and the *Elegia di Madonna Fiametta*.

Chapter 3, entitled '"Il senno di consolazion sia cagione": The *Decameron* and the Consolation of Storytelling' (pp. 88–132), scrutinizes how the action of storytelling becomes a vehicle for consolation for the narrators and readers, mainly thanks to the power of identification proper of the genre of the short story. In a literary genre characterized by a high degree of verisimilitude and a deep propensity towards didacticism, Boccaccio's appropriation of the principles of Aristotle's *Nicomachean Ethics* allows the author to perfect an ever closer and more profitable interaction between the four different types of consolation already examined in the preceding works.

The last two chapters continue Zak's chronological exploration of Boccaccio's œuvre. Chapter 4, entitled 'The *Corbaccio*, Dante, and the Disavowal of Love' (pp. 133–53), examines Boccaccio's intricate relationship with Dante and their differences of opinion on the question of consolation. Zak delves into the works of Boccaccio's maturity (especially those in the vernacular, such as the *Corbaccio* and the consolatory letter to Pino de' Rossi, but also taking into consideration the *Genealogy of the Pagan Gods*), comparing them with Dante's *Vita nova, Convivio*, and, above all, the *Commedia*. Chapter 5, entitled 'Boccaccio after Petrarch: The Polyphony of Consolation in the Later Writings' (pp. 154–87), explores Boccaccio's relationship with the more introspective and contemplative side of Petrarch, as found in his Latin works, especially the *De remediis utriusque fortunae*, the *Epistulae ad familiares*, and the *Secretum*, as well as the most philosophical and intimate poems in the *Rerum vulgarium fragmenta*. These dialogues with Dante and Petrarch serve as a foundation for Boccaccio's development of a truly 'polyphonic' consolatory vision, sufficiently evolved for him to incorporate in the works of his maturity all four types of consolation theorized by Zak in the introductory chapter.

The Conclusion (pp. 188–93) synthesizes the book's findings, providing a cohesive understanding of Boccaccio's diachronic engagement with the theme of consolation. A highly up-to-date bibliography (pp. 194–209) ensures the study's academic relevance, while a meticulously crafted index (pp. 210–16) facilitates easy navigation through the monograph.

This study is a significant contribution that sheds light on the theme of consolation as it evolved throughout Boccaccio's literary career and across both his vernacular and his Latin writings. Zak's comprehensive and insightful research enriches our understanding of Boccaccio's engagement with the theme of consolation. The author's diachronic approach, his meticulous analysis of specific works, and his study of the influence that philosophical and classical texts had on the Certaldese, make his monograph an invaluable contribution to Boccaccio scholarship.

UNIVERSITY OF NOTRE DAME NICOLA ESPOSITO
doi:10.1353/mlr.00019

Interpreting and Judging Petrarch's 'Canzoniere' in Early Modern Italy. Ed. by MAIKO FAVARO. (Italian Perspectives, 49) Cambridge: Legenda. 2021. xii+177 pp. £85. ISBN 978-1-781885-72-7.

In years in which Dante Alighieri seems to be dominating a significant portion of research in medieval and early modern Italian Studies, the recent scholarship on Francis Petrarch is certainly to be welcomed. His intellectual and poetic legacy in the Italian Peninsula and beyond, in literature and art, has substantially contributed to shaping the modern idea of human being and subjectivity.

Maiko Favaro's edited volume addresses the reception of Petrarch's *Rerum vulgarium fragmenta*—the *Canzoniere* par excellence—through the lens of the commentary tradition from the fifteenth to the eighteenth century. The collection reviews and discusses with rigour the origins and later development of Petrarchan exegesis, from the first commentary offered by Luigi Marsili in the early fifteenth century to that of Lodovico Antonio Muratori in the early eighteenth century, via the golden age of Petrarchism marked by Pietro Bembo's canonization and the Venetian press industry. While recent scholarship has mostly focused on individual commentaries and commentators, this volume offers insight into the multifaceted phenomenon of the exegetical tradition of Petrarch's lyric production in early modern Italy. The nine essays presented here open up new perspectives on the early modern understanding of Petrarch's *Canzoniere*, with special emphasis on the variety of forms that constitute sixteenth-century exegetical practice: lectures, treatises, dialogues, letters, and paratexts. While these types of work are not commentaries in a traditional sense, each of them allows us to explore the multiple and widespread reverberations of Petrarch's legacy in Italian literary culture, especially in its golden age.

The first chapter, by Favaro himself, 'A Problematic and Contradictory Authority: Petrarch in the Love Treatises of the Sixteenth and Early Seventeenth Centuries', explores the reception and use of Petrarch's lyrics in theorizations of love, where quotations from the *Canzoniere* are employed to discuss issues revolving around the phenomenon. The rivalry between Girolamo Ruscelli and Ludovico Dolce, two of the most important editors in mid-sixteenth-century Venice, is instead explored in Cristina Acucella's chapter, 'Editing Petrarch in Venice: The *Canzoniere* in the Dispute between Ruscelli and Dolce', which also examines the different editorial and philological techniques deployed by Ruscelli and Dolce. Turning to the mysterious figure of Laura, Chapter 3 by Guglielmo Barucci, 'Laura's Nobility and Greatness in Two Sixteenth-Century Florentine Speeches by Simone della Barba (1554) and Francesco de' Vieri (1580)', investigates how Petrarch's beloved was depicted as a model of virtue in Renaissance commentaries and paratexts. Giacomo Comiati's essay in Chapter 4, 'Judging Petrarch in the Venetian Accademia della Fama: Celio Magno and his *Prefatione sopra il Petrarca* (*c.* 1558)', offers an exploration of the development of Magno's theoretical elaborations about poetry from the perspective of his own understanding of Petrarch's production. Moving from Venetian academies to Brescia, Simona Oberto's essay in Chapter 5, 'Anthological *Discorsi* as Means of "Doctrinization" of Petrarchism in the *Rime degli Accademici Occulti* (1568)', analyses a prosimetrum based on a moral and philosophical interpretation of Petrarch's *Canzoniere*. By shifting to issues belonging to the *Questione della lingua*, Lorenzo Sacchini's essay in Chapter 6, 'Reading Petrarch: Gregorio Anastagi's (1336/39–1601) Manuscript Writings on Petrarch's *Canzoniere*', explores Anastagi's lectures and position regarding Petrarch's idiom. Chapters 7 and 8 are both devoted to Alessandro Tassoni. In his essay 'Deconstructing Petrarch: Alessandro Tassoni's *Considerazioni sopra le Rime del Petrarca*' Andrea Lazzarini discusses the textual history of this work. Laura Benedetti's essay, 'Petrarch, Aristotle, and the Inquisition: The Controversy between Giuseppe degli Aromatari and Alessandro Tassoni', explores the terms of the debate on Petrarch's and Petrarchists' lyric production in the seventeenth century. With his closing essay, '"Nobiltà dello stile" and "grandezza e rarità del pensiero": Petrarch and the Petrarchists in Apostolo Zeno's *Giornale de' letterati italiani* (1710–18)', Giacomo Vagni concludes the volume by exploring the interpretation and promotion of Petrarch's lyric poetry through Zeno's journal, following in the steps of Lodovico Antonio Muratori and Giovan Mario Crescimbeni.

The recent AHRC-funded collaborative project led by Simon Gilson, Guyda
Armstrong, and Federica Pich, 'Petrarch Commentary and Exegesis in Renaissance Italy, c. 1350–c. 1650', with its online catalogue of manuscripts and prints
containing exegetical works on Petrarch's poetry, constitutes the most significant
milestone in recent years for Petrarchan Studies, providing a new foundation for
further research in this area. Favaro's edited volume situates itself in this strand and
successfully contributes to enriching the body of scholarship on the reception of
Petrarch's vernacular poetry in the early modern period.

UNIVERSITY OF CAMBRIDGE   NICOLÒ MORELLI
doi:10.1353/mlr.00020

*Drama, Poetry and Music in Late-Renaissance Italy: The Life and Works of Leonora
   Bernardi.* By VIRGINIA COX, LISA SAMPSON, ERIC NICHOLSON, EUGENIO RE-
   FINI, and DAVIDE DAOLMI, with a translation by ANNA WAINWRIGHT. London:
   UCL Press. 2023. xv+552 pp. £35. ISBN 978-1-80008-431-5.

Virginia Cox and her colleagues continue their excellent work of rediscovering
female writers of the Italian Renaissance, as this pioneering volume on Leonora
Bernardi—a Lucchese *literata* and singer praised by contemporary poets such as
Angelo Grillo and Ottavio Rinuccini—testifies. As its Introduction makes clear, this
volume is the fruit of many years of intensive and collaborative work put in by its
contributors. The result is a truly interdisciplinary and thorough presentation of a
hitherto understudied figure and her literary output, which sheds new light on the
cultural landscape in late Renaissance Italy.

Structurally, the book consists of three main sections, which respectively treat
Bernardi's life, her dramatic work *Clorilli*, and her lyric works together with their
musical settings. In the first part, Cox elegantly reconstructs in colourful detail the
life of Bernardi, in both its public and its private aspects. The second part (which
comprises the majority of the book's length) begins with Lisa Sampson's critical
study of *Clorilli* and the manuscript that includes the text of the drama itself. The
modern bilingual edition of *Clorilli*, with the Italian text critically edited by Lisa
Sampson and a modern English prose translation by Anna Wainwright, serves as
the central piece, followed by Eric Nicholson's retrospective account of the first
'modern' premiere of *Clorilli* in 2018. Finally, the third part provides us with Cox's
analysis of Bernardi's extant lyrics (with English translations) and Eugenio Refini's
discussion of their musical settings with modern editions of the musical scores (by
Refini and Davide Daolmi).

Given the eclectic range of its contributors and their disciplinary formations, the
volume is exemplary in maintaining both depth and variety of critical enquiry, deploying a diverse set of evidence and methods such as archival sources, manuscripts,
printed sources, and even musical sources to reconstruct Bernardi's biography and
the reception of her works. For example, Sampson's essay on the Marciana manuscript of *Clorilli* demonstrates how the nature of a particular work's reception could
be inferred through critical engagement with other texts found within the same

source. Through this methodology she is able to observe astutely how *Clorilli* 'potentially attracted prurient interest, criticism, and intentional obscuration' (p. 139) by contemporary audiences. Especially notable, too, is engagement with the more 'performative' aspects of Bernardi's literary works, which places them in theatrical and musical contexts (as in Nicholson's and Refini's contributions) and allows us to better understand the ambient court culture and musical world that enabled her agency as both a playwright and a performer.

As for Bernardi's *Clorilli*, which is her magnum opus, it is an intriguing work that is entertaining to read on its own, thanks to the meticulous critical notes and English translation provided. As a pastoral *tragicomedia* written by a female author, however, it is also an important work that invites us to re-examine the more renowned works in the genre (especially within the context of the Ferrarese court) by male authors, such as Tasso's *Aminta* and Guarini's *Il Pastor Fido*. In fact, as the critical study and notes reveal, *Chlorili* borrows or echoes many of the topoi found in *Aminta*. Therefore, the modern rediscovery of *Clorilli* potentially has a far-reaching impact on our understanding of late Renaissance Italian literature and the role played by female authors in its development.

Readable as self-contained articles, the chapters are organized and presented in a logical and seamless manner with appropriate headings and subsections. The writing style, too, while formal and academic, is easy to read and engaging throughout. All Italian texts are carefully curated and accompanied by modern English translations, which means that even readers with limited fluency in Italian can appreciate the captivating life and works of Bernardi. The authors have done a fine work of making this book accessible to a wider audience than specialists in early modern Italian literature. Musicians and musicologists (including the present reviewer) may also appreciate the modern transcriptions of music based on Bernardi's lyrics, many of which appear here for the first time. Overall, this volume sets a fresh standard for how modern scholarship should be done, and its contents will be of immediate interest to cultural historians, scholars working in Theatre Studies, musicologists, and Italianists interested in any humanistic aspect of the late Renaissance.

University of Oxford   Taro Kobayashi
doi:10.1353/mlr.00021

Staging the Soul: Allegorical Drama as Spiritual Practice in Baroque Italy. By Eugenio Refini. Cambridge: Legenda. 2023. xiv+256 pp. £85. ISBN 978–1–78188–437–9.

Eugenio Refini's research focuses primarily on the reception, translation, and forms of adaptation of medieval and early modern literary culture in Italy. In this, his third monograph, he returns to the subject of his doctoral dissertation—author, physician, and educator Fabio Glissenti—focusing on the morality plays written by Glissenti for the education of female orphans in the hospitals of Venice around 1600.

Like other transnational baroque themes, the *theatrum mundi* metaphor was common among many authors, including Pedro Calderón de la Barca and William Shakespeare. By analysing drama and theatre, the text and its performance, *Staging the Soul* looks at Glissenti's *theatrum mundi* not as a trope, but as an object brought on stage, arguing that Glissenti's morality plays move 'from the staging of the world to the staging of the soul' (p. 5), from *theatrum mundi* to *theatrum animae*. This is discussed in Chapter 1, which looks into the pedagogical uses of dramatic allegories to convey performative images (*imagines agentes*) as active metaphors of vices, virtues, passions, and other abstract entities, common during the post-Tridentine Counter-Reformation. Whereas tangible objects can be perceived, bodiless objects need to be visualized by an audience through the personification of their iconographic attributes. In classical and early modern rhetoric, poetics, and dramatic theory, personified allegories are invested with pedagogical purposes. Through Francesco Bonciani's 1578 *Lezione della prosopopea*, Refini surveys the creative process of prosopopeia, or personification, in poetry, and through Gabriele Paleotti's 1582 *Discorso intorno alle immagini sacre et profane*, on personified allegories in Counter-Reformation figurative arts, he highlights how the *theatrum mundi* helps visualization by the audience.

Glissenti's *Discorsi morali* (1596) is the focus of Chapter 2. Its alternative title, *Athanatophilia*, explains the twofold concern of the work with both 'love of immortality' and 'love of death'. These 'moral dialogues' are intended to be practical, providing spiritual care with a range of quotations, references, and proverbs. The iconographic apparatus of 117 woodcuts in the 1596 edition is analysed by Refini in this richly illustrated chapter. While the personification of Death seems to be inspired by Hans Holbein's drawings, these woodcuts are typically set in Venice, the stage or 'theatre of the world' for Glissenti. The city and the stage here are closely related.

Chapter 3 explores Glissenti's corpus of ten morality plays, written to educate both performers and spectators. The diffusion of the genre in Venice was promoted by confraternities and religious orders, including the Jesuits, for the spiritual well-being of orphans and foundlings. However, the circulation of these works beyond the occasions on which they were performed is more broadly linked to the Counter-Reformation, as they provided moral alternatives to the *commedia dell'arte*. This success and wider circulation is confirmed by the reprinting of many of these devotional works in the 1630s. Confession and self-examination are openly performed on a stage where, in spite of its ambiguity, the performance can be turned into a 'performative experience'.

Refini's Conclusion looks at the possible reasons why these plays have been forgotten. Glissenti's works, like those of his contemporaries, are still largely undiscovered, and Refini's research is based on the manuscript collection at the Marciana Library in Venice. The hope is that books such as *Staging the Soul* will contribute to the rediscovery of early modern Italian literature with a transnational perspective.

THE BRITISH LIBRARY VALENTINA MIRABELLA
doi:10.1353/mlr.00022

Psychoanalysis, Ideology and Commitment in Italy 1945–1975: Edoardo Sanguineti,
    Ottiero Ottieri, Andrea Zanzotto. By ALESSANDRA DIAZZI. Cambridge: Le-
    genda. 2022. xi+142 pp. £85. ISBN 978-1-781887-94-3.

Alessandra Diazzi introduces this work by referring to Antonio Tabucchi's *Requiem*
(1991), which declares that the unconscious is like a contagious disease: 'oramai
l'inconscio uno se lo prende, è come una malattia' (p. 1). A few questions can be
raised with regard to this quotation: when, and how, did the contagion happen
in Italy? What were the channels by which the 'plague of psychoanalysis' spread
through the country? Was there a time when Italy was reluctant to accept the
sphere of the unconscious, and if so, why? Psychoanalysis was regarded, especially
during the Fascist regime, as a threat to the nation's morality, but Italy witnessed a
dramatic rise of interest in the subject in the 1960s. Given the difficult relationship
between Italian culture and psychoanalysis, Diazzi underlines how an attempt to
rethink the cultural reception of the discipline, by looking specifically at its encounters with politics and ideology, is still missing. By adopting a socio-literary
approach, Diazzi focuses on 'a prism of three voices' (p. 10), Edoardo Sanguineti
(1930–2010), Ottiero Ottieri (1924–2002), and Andrea Zanzotto (1921–2011), to
detect and examine some of the major turning points that characterized the reception of psychoanalysis in Italy. In order to shed new light on psychoanalysis and
literature (a privileged domain for the cultural transmission of psychoanalysis) in
Italy, Diazzi offers a map of the encounter between psychoanalysis and Italy's leftist
culture, alongside investigation of the overlooked reception between intellectuals
and cultural circles.

    Diazzi analyses the reasons why in Italy the relationship between psychoanalysis,
society, and politics had such a fraught beginning. Indeed, leftist culture was scep-
tical towards psychoanalysis, as it was conceived to be a bourgeois science. Greater
resistance came from the Marxist intellectuals, who saw in psychoanalysis a form
of threat to the domain of reason. According to Diazzi, the roots of the 'explosive
diffusion' of psychoanalysis lay in the so-called *miracolo economico*, on account of
which the individual demand for therapeutic psychoanalysis developed in parallel
with an increasing openness to it. In need of consideration is also the role of the
sessantotto, a moment in which psychoanalysis shifted from being considered an
intrinsically reactionary discipline and a cure for bourgeois neuroses to becoming a
potentially subversive tool. This is the moment in which so-called Freudo-Marxism
arose, a designation which encompassed those thinkers who sought to demonstrate that Freudian doctrine was compatible with the principle of a materialist or
'Pavlovian' psychology.

    It is not surprising that Diazzi's first case study is the Marxist intellectual Edoardo
Sanguineti, one of the most influential leftist intellectuals of post-war Italy who,
refraining from personally subjecting himself to its clinical aspects, gave psychoanalysis a fundamental role within his 'committed' new avant-garde poetics. Diazzi
underlines how for Sanguineti psychoanalysis became a tool of political commitment in service to the Marxist praxis. In fact, Sanguineti employed psychoanalysis

as a critical instrument for debunking bourgeois ideology by means of literature and language. He attempted to reassess analytical psychology from an ideological perspective, elaborating a personal form of 'Jungian Marxism'. Crucial is the negotiation of those aspects of Jung's teaching that were perceived as 'inaccoglibili'—that is, a form of rethinking which consisted in a 'gestione materialistica' of the symbols and the archetypes which took shape especially in Sanguineti's work of poetry *Laborintus* (1956) and *Capriccio italiano* (1963), a novel which attempts to subvert the structures and value system dominating the social context that *Laborintus* criticized.

Ottiero Ottieri was an intellectual active both socially and politically. His interest in psychoanalysis was not exclusively theoretical; indeed, he himself undertook several psychoanalytic, psychotherapeutic, and psychiatric treatments. These experiences permeate Ottieri's literary production, the constant thematic focus of which is on alienation; in this way psychoanalysis is employed as an interpretative framework to explain both psychological and socio-political dynamics. In fact, for Ottieri, psychoanalysis (Freud) and politics (Marx) were considered to be inseparable, and this is particularly visible in his first novel *Memorie dell'incoscienza* (1954). His prose works are permeated by this tension between psychoanalysis and politics, as in *Donnarumma all'assalto* (1959) and *L'irrealtà quotidiana* (1966), a novel in which Ottieri took further his challenge to the dominant view of alienation as the neurosis of industrialization.

Andrea Zanzotto was one of the few Italian writers to adopt Jacques Lacan as a 'truly secret master' (p. 91). He used Lacan's psychoanalysis as a means of expressing the crisis of subjectivity in contemporary society, although Diazzi distances herself from a Lacanian interpretation of Zanzotto's œuvre; in fact, Zanzotto was suspicious of those aspects of Lacan's thought that seemed to him closer to a philosophical, rather than clinical, approach to the human psyche. Indeed, Diazzi looks at Zanzotto's encounter with the work of Lacan by considering his own experience with therapy. Her examination of the many ways in which Lacanianism influenced Zanzotto's writing is thus centred on the first collection of poems in which the poet employed a conscious assimilation of psychoanalysis as an explicit source of his poetics, *La beltà* (1968). By meticulously analysing its language, Diazzi demonstrates how Zanzotto's view of modernity as a collective and historical trauma is conceptualized in his work through quintessentially Lacanian paradigms.

As Diazzi's three case studies evince, the relationship between psychoanalysis and Italian culture can be more fruitfully understood in terms of reciprocal 'diffraction' than as a conflictual opposition. Diazzi creates a suitable environment for understanding the topic thanks to her ability to offer clear summaries of the sociocultural contexts in which the three authors worked. In fact, her analysis of these sociocultural contexts reveals how the several encounters between psychoanalysis, ideology, and politics led different appropriations of the discipline to stand for different ideological perspectives. In conclusion, this work shows how the assimilation of psychoanalysis into literature and culture implied a reduction and even, in some cases, a complete dissolution of its very traits of 'otherness' in an incessant negotiation between the intrinsic features of psychoanalysis itself and Italy's cultural identity.

DURHAM UNIVERSITY   ROBERTA PASSAGHE
doi:10.1353/mlr.00023

María de Zayas y la imaginación crítica: bibliografía razonada y comentada. By EN-RÍQUE GARCÍA SANTO-TOMÁS. (Bibliografías y catálogos, 56) Kassel: Reichenberger. 2022. vi+410 pp. €86. ISBN 978–3–967280–41–8.

Very little biographical material is available on María de Zayas, the early modern Spanish author of sadistic, blood-drenched, and sexually deviant *novelas*. The extant œuvre unwittingly mirrors this mystery, featuring as it does multiple characters whose identities are kept hidden. Furthermore, many such characters stand to gain from the epistemological upper hand of concealing their identity. Take, for example, Madame Lucrecia in Zayas's second collection of *novelas, Desengaños amorosos:* she is a financially secure widow who essentially pays an attractive man for regular sex, in which he is deprived of sight (first with a blindfold, and second by being placed in utter darkness). Lucrecia is secure in knowing his identity and being able to pay for services rendered. It is tempting to say that Zayas maintains an epistemological hold over contemporary twenty-first-century readers too, who can do little more than speculate about her life.

Enrique García Santo-Tomás engages with the biographical enigma in the opening prologue to his critical bibliography, surmising a tendency by scholars to oscillate between extremes: 'lo que para algunos ha sido una cautela que muchas veces acababa transformándose en olvido o exclusión del canon, para otros ha sido excusa para imaginar todo tipo de identificaciones, de causas y de reivindicaciones' (p. 1). This comprehensive and fruitful volume is useful for both Zayascan specialists and those encountering her work for the first time. In the second half, García Santo-Tomás offers one of the most useful strategies for categorizing Zayas's work. Rather than simply splitting her *novelas* into their two collections, the 1637 *Novelas amorosas y ejemplares* and the 1647 *Desengaños amorosos*, he sets out scholarship relating to each individual tale (twenty in total). In the process, he shows how and why each of Zayas's deftly crafted *novelas* is worthy of consideration in and of itself.

The preliminary section, 'La Creación de Zayas (1922–2022)', considers a century of Zayascan scholarship. Here, García Santo-Tomás successfully navigates the secondary literature to offer a well-balanced, state-of-the art study of her work and afterlife. Fittingly, this appears a century after the recuperation of Zayas's legacy by Lena Evelyn V. Sylvania in 1922. García Santo-Tomás takes this as a point of departure to provide a decade-by-decade analysis of how Zayas's work was received, tracing a transition from obscenity and revulsion to the deification of the author as a mouthpiece for female experience. This necessary critical bibliography facilitates Zayas's admittance to the canon of major male Golden Age authors such as Cervantes, Lope, Góngora, or Quevedo. A clear manifestation of Zayas's rising stock is the esteem in which her play *La traición en la amistad* is now held in comparison to its reception a hundred years ago. A labour of retrospective synthesis, García Santo-Tomás's book also constitutes an invitation and point of departure for new interpretations of Zayas's works.

UNIVERSITY OF LEEDS   HAYLEY O'KELL
doi:10.1353/mlr.00024

Empire of Objects: Iurii Trifonov and the Material World of Soviet Culture. By BEN-
    JAMIN M. SUTCLIFFE. Madison: University of Wisconsin Press. 2023. xii+
    170 pp. $79.95. ISBN 978-0-299-34400-9.

Born to a Cossack father who was executed in 1937 and a Jewish intellectual mother who managed to survive Stalin's forced-labour camps, Iurii Trifonov (1925–1981) is one of the central figures in Russian (Soviet) literature. He created a diverse literary corpus that depicted Soviet life from the post-war period to the late Brezhnev era. Despite his family background of political purges and repression, Trifonov surprisingly received the Stalin Prize in 1950 for his first novel, *Students* (*Studenty*, 1949). From this initial success, Trifonov constructed a considerable body of work that captured various facets of the Soviet era.

Challenging the common dichotomy of official versus unofficial literature in the USSR, which Trifonov himself contested, Benjamin M. Sutcliffe's monograph provides an extensively documented approach to one of the central aspects of Trifonov's literary œuvre: the significance of the material world in Soviet everyday life (*byt*) and its role in exploring 'the gap between ideals and reality in Soviet culture' (p. 4). As Sutcliffe argues, 'In Trifonov's prose, it is not ideas that shape existence but the overwhelming force of the material' (p. 17). In an Introduction that is as lengthy and substantive as the other chapters of the book, Sutcliffe delineates the main factors serving as the axes of his study: three key concepts in Soviet cultural history.

The first factor is corporeality (*telesnost'*), referring to the USSR's fixation on portraying the body. Whether used to signal subservience (p. 7) or as evidence 'that the body has its own memories and does not lie' (p. 75), *telesnost'* serves in Trifonov's works as a binding element between physique and ideological fitness or as a challenge to Soviet notions about perfecting human form and behaviour. According to Sutcliffe, although Soviet literature, dominated by the intelligentsia, 'mistrusted the material world' (p. 5), Trifonov's 'prose envisions the USSR's doomed effort to subordinate bodies and objects to ideas' (p. 3).

The second key component guiding Sutcliffe's study is consumption, a concept with a paradoxical nature in Soviet times. Despite the fact that the Soviet state and intelligentsia supposedly rejected admiration of objects as a manifestation of philistinism, policies promoting a 'modern' lifestyle through consumer behaviour were developed during Trifonov's lifetime. The state and ordinary citizens attempted to control the material world, while 'the Moscow inhabited by Trifonov's intelligentsia characters was a privileged exception' (p. 5).

The third concept underlying Sutcliffe's study is sincerity (*iskrennost'*), which for

Trifonov is an 'intangible deficit good', encompassing genuineness and truthfulness (p. 5). Whether seen as 'the product of a dishonest society' in the late Stalin era (p. 40) or as 'the force behind transformation through the material world' during the Thaw era (p. 45), the author argues that *iskrennost'* was to be found in a good work of literature. However, when discussing his final choice of narratives, Sutcliffe concedes that '*iskrennost'* seemed impossible within a society where sincerity was co-opted by consumption and the temptation to distort personal as well as national history' (p. 99), given that 'the nature of sincerity dramatically changed as society rejected the recent past' (p. 9).

Intertwining these key elements with memory, sociological and personal trauma, and history, and including a discussion of the critical reception of Trifonov's works both in the author's lifetime and from the start of perestroika until more recent periods, the book addresses, successively, Trifonov's Stalinist prose (Chapter 1), his Thaw works (Chapter 2), the Moscow novellas (Chapter 3), and the final narratives from the 1970s to 1981 (Chapter 4). Sutcliffe's study combines a chronological approach with a thematic one, and thus the overall tone has a very personal style, overlaid with an *iskrennost'* that makes his text compelling. The study also includes several considerations and comparisons of the sociocultural construction across different Soviet periods and its nature in contemporary Russia (referred to as 'Putin's Russia' by Sutcliffe). These reflections open an insightful dialogue that cannot be avoided in these rather troubled times. The book provides an excellent opportunity to delve into the legacy of one of the most prominent authors from the second half of Russian twentieth-century literature, one who influenced Vladimir Makanin, Liudmila Ulitskaia, Andrei Bitov, and Liudmila Petrushevskaia, among others. Sutcliffe's monograph offers an exceptional chance to become acquainted with the eloquent images of Soviet *byt*, or lifestyle, and to understand its major elements and characters.

Universitat de Barcelona   Miquel Cabal-Guarro
doi:10.1353/mlr.00025

How the Soviet Jew Was Made. By Sasha Senderovich. Cambridge, MA: Harvard University Press. 2022. xii+356 pp. $39.95. ISBN 978–0–6742–3819–0.

After I had read the final chapter of this wide-ranging study I was delighted to see in the Acknowledgments that the author had, during the course of a decade of research and writing, contributed the critical introduction and commentary to Hillel Halkin's English translation of the Yiddish novel *The Zelmenyaners: A Family Saga*, by Moyshe Kulbak (New Haven: Yale University Press, 2013). In Chapter 2 of Sasha Senderovich's monograph this work receives an engaging exploration, which has left me keen to read Kulbak's text. Detailed and close reading is at the heart of Senderovich's book: he brings his attentiveness to bear on nuance, echo, and omission in all the works considered here. The title, nodding in the direction of Boris Eikhenbaum's 1918 essay 'How Gogol's *Overcoat* Was Made', offers a clue about the author's approach. As Senderovich explains in his Introduction, his analysis of the texts (literary and cinematic) under discussion focuses on literary qualities such as alliteration and sentence structure, or, when it comes to the films, the use of sound and gesture (p. 13). Imaginative and attentive readings are to be found in every chapter, where examination of apparently insignificant details reveals layers of meaning, whether drawn verbatim from Russian translations of conversations that must have taken place in Yiddish, or from the sudden inability of a Jewish worker, 'returned' to the USSR after years of living in the United States, to find the words with which to announce his embrace of the Soviet project.

These layers of meaning are carefully unpacked and explained as part of the book's demonstration of what went into the process of making the Soviet Jew, considered as a figure in the cultural landscape of the first two decades after the Bolshevik Revolution. Senderovich is at pains to distinguish this pre-Second World War figure from later versions that featured in the Stalin-era and Cold War imagination, noting in the Epilogue that some literary texts of the 1920s and 1930s have been overlooked because they did not lend themselves to being read as a prelude to the trauma of the Holocaust that was to follow. The Soviet Jew who is the object of Senderovich's investigations 'came into being within an idiosyncratic and culturally rich response to the Soviet state's attempt to reform Jews [. . .] into model Soviet citizens' (p. 277). As his study shows, this programme of transformation of Jewish citizens into a version of the New Soviet Man, as reflected in the texts under analysis, was not uniformly successful, and indeed, the trajectory followed by Jewish figures represented in these texts was far from uniform, being 'layered, indeterminate, and fluid' (p. 2).

The transition between old and new worlds was a particularly complicated one for Jewish citizens of the USSR. In the five chapters of his book, Senderovich guides readers through texts which confront, even if obliquely, these complexities. He begins with a chapter exploring the lasting trauma of violent pogroms—under imperial rule and in the chaos of civil war—which haunt the text of David Bergelson's 1920 novel *Judgement*. A second Yiddish text, *The Zelmenyaners*, portrays an extended family's ultimate dispersal from their traditional home, the *shtetl* in microcosm, but cannot, as Senderovich shows, easily be read as a straightforward tale of their transformation to 'Soviet-ness'. The third chapter considers a selection of journalistic and fictional texts ostensibly about Birobidzhan, created as a homeland for Jews in the Soviet Far East. The present-day life of Jews in the region is all but absent from texts which emphasize instead an imagined future of productive labour, or the lives of the non-Jewish population. This is followed by an examination of the figure of the Jew who settles in the USSR after years spent abroad, as portrayed in films of the early 1930s, and, in the final chapter, a guided tour through the labyrinths of Isaac Babel's prose, following the thread of allusions to the trickster Hershele Ostropoler, a real character immortalized in Yiddish folklore and a shaping force in Babel's creative world.

Admirably, Senderovich manages to keep this apparently disparate array of texts and characters under control, never losing sight of his understanding of the Soviet Jew as 'a figure of indeterminacy that emerged from within the Soviet project, was defined by it, and, on occasion, defined it in turn' (p. 8). It is not hard to see why several years were needed to complete the task of marshalling this material into a coherent structure through which to contemplate this indeterminate figure of in-between-ness; the author's efforts have given us a thoroughly readable and thought-provoking book.

University of Exeter   Katharine Hodgson
doi:10.1353/mlr.00026

In Search of Tito's Punks: On the Road in a Country that No Longer Exists. By Barry
      Phillips. (Global Punk) Bristol: Intellect with Punk Scholars Network. 2023.
      xviii+256 pp. £29.95. ISBN 978–1–78938–731–5.

In 1981, Barry Phillips played bass guitar for the punk band Demob. Hailing from Gloucester, situated nearly two hundred kilometres from punk's London epicentre, Demob recorded the song 'No Room for You' for the independent Bristol label Round Ear Records. Eventually, the song gained popularity in Yugoslavia's alternative punk music scene, an arena that emerged after popular music's 'essential incandescent pomp' associated with the Clash and the Sex Pistols (p. 36). Phillips became aware of the song's impact on the punk scene in the former Yugoslavia when Saša Mijatović, a Croatian musician, contacted him on Facebook in 2011, a situation Phillips describes as 'baffling and intriguing' (p. 2). He examines the song's evolution and relevance in the former Yugoslavia over the ensuing twelve years. The book uses an ethnographic method, drawing on a series of meetings and discussions with gatekeepers within the former Yugoslavian punk movement during the Tito era to illustrate the influence of both the song 'No Room for You' and punk more generally.

The book consists of twenty-one chapters, a discography, and a timeline. The main text resonates with Rebecca West's travelogue *Black Lamb and Grey Falcon: A Journey through Yugoslavia* (first published in 1941), which the author uses as 'scaffolding and reference point' (p. 13) for his search, building upon West's narrative of 'big' and 'small' pictures (p. 24). In the context of the book, the author's quest for one song aligns with the dialogue centred on his journey from his home in the Netherlands, as he travels around Croatia, Serbia, and Slovenia, and the UK. Underneath this lies a micro-historical approach, namely his series of interviews with leading punk and avant-garde pop-culture exponents. Philips also visits the former Demob band member and composer of 'No Room for You', Robert 'Miff' Smith, who saw the 'emergence of punk as a response to "that arrogance of the musical elite"' (p.144).

Each chapter contains one of the fifteen interviews, opening with a narrative outline of the arrangement for the interview location and an explanation of the interviewee's place within the former Yugoslavian music scene. The second part of each chapter contains the interview, usually in the form of an unbroken monologue from the interviewee. The detailed recollections of their social and personal circumstances of living in a country that allowed and encouraged their continued musical activity, both during Tito's regime and after his death, deliver a powerful message to the reader. Additionally, these candid, in-depth interviews offer insight into how punk musicians are still tackling modern problems by drawing on the past. Their shared history began with Tito's unique style of socialism, which disintegrated in the late 1980s and eventually ended in the 1990s when each newly established post-Yugoslav nation state began the process of self-revelation and restructuring. Different social and political actors have the ability and often the will to take part in creating public memory, even though nation-state officials may use the resources and authority of the state's hegemonic power to advance an official historical narrative. The interviews reaffirm that those original punks, influenced by Demob and other less familiar groups, are still active and still reinventing music by incorporating elements of their past to strengthen their original ethic of political resistance.

Throughout the book, those interviewed remind the reader that socialist former Yugoslavia was not behind the Iron Curtain, so that they had freedom to travel. Punks regularly travelled to 'Graz, Vienna, or Trieste for gigs and to buy records' (p. 20). State-owned record labels not only supported local punk bands by letting them use cultural channels and venues to schedule shows and get media attention; they even licensed foreign punk and rock records for release. Moreover, to further punk authenticity, the Welsh mail-order record store Cob Records fed the demand for 'originals' (p. 232). American and British bands regularly performed at major venues in the former Yugoslav Republics. Accordingly, the Gang of Four's performance at the 1981 Zagreb Biennale is recalled as an influence on the Yugoslav punk scene and as a concert legendary in punk memory.

This book is part of the increasingly varied portfolio issued under the umbrella of the Punk Scholars Network. Phillips presented the topic of the book at the Fourth Punk Scholars Conference at Bolton in 2017, an experience that convinced him that 'punk is not dead; it just got a PhD' (p. 5). *In Search of Tito's Punks* will appeal to academics interested in the origins and dissemination of punk beyond the United States and the United Kingdom; the fall of socialist Yugoslavia; and anthropological Memory Studies.

University of East Anglia   Christopher Spinks
doi:10.1353/mlr.00027

Cabbage and Caviar: A History of Food in Russia. By Alison K. Smith. London: Reaktion. 2021. 352 pp. £27.50. ISBN 978-1-78914-364-5.

Alison K. Smith's monograph delivers 300 pages (seven chapters, including an Introduction and Epilogue) of rich culinary history, accessible in style and interspersed with colourful illustrations (including menus), cultural references, and fascinating facts ('the largest female beluga ever recorded [. . .] weighed 1,143 kilograms (2,520 lb)—and 408 kilograms (900 lb) of her weight was roe', we learn on p. 41). The Introduction—a concise overview of Russian history which defines Smith's concepts of 'Russia' and Russian cuisine—prepares the way for the more detailed chapters that follow. Beginning with Kyivan Rus, Smith steers the reader through five hundred years of feast and famine: the Qipchaq Khanate; starvation during the 'Time of Troubles'; Eastern expansion and Ivan the Terrible; Petrine curiosity about and affection for the West (extending to its food); autocracy and serfdom; the collapse of tsarism and birth of the USSR; the Second World War; post-war and post-Communism supply issues; and post-Soviet border tensions. All these periods had both geopolitical and culinary effects (where and when did *shchi* become *kapusniak*, then *kapusta*; where do *pelmeni* diverge from *vareniki* and *pierogi?*). Smith's historical overview makes readers realize both the multiple components of Russia's cuisine and the sheer difficulty of feeding the people of such a vast nation. Chapters 1–7 explore these issues in detail, frequently drawing on primary sources such as the work of Russian ethnographer Ivan Snegirev, cookbook authors (Vasilii Levshin, Katerina Avdeeva, Elena Molokhovets), various international visitors (Sigismund von Herberstein, Giles Fletcher, Paul of Aleppo), and, not least, writers (Ivan Boltin, Vladimir Burnashev, Afanasii Fet, Lev Tolstoy).

Chapter 1 unpacks the fundamentals of Russian food, from *zakuski* and salads, to soups, grains (liquid and solid), through to traditional festive fare and gastronomic ceremonies. Chapter 2 focuses on the practicalities of using nature's store cupboard: the terrain, infrastructure, and technologies of food supply, and cooking practices. Using medieval sources (*The Tale of Bygone Years* and *Paterik*) and tenth-century archaeological discoveries (such as mortars and pestles, walnut shells, cucumber seeds, dill, apples, cherries, and plums), Smith constructs in Chapter 3 an account of everyday life and food in medieval Rus, including the impact of the Mongol invasion and the Black Death, and the influence of the *Domostroi* manual on household regulation. Chapter 4 explains how food played a role in Russian territorial expansion, and vice versa (as the movement of peoples introduced new foodstuffs and cooking methods). It examines Boris Godunov's efforts to control famine and the consequences of the unpopular salt tax. Smith shines a sobering light on the arrival of vodka, a drink that reappears in the book as it flows from one generation to the next. Chapter 5 engages with the contrast between deprived peasants and fine-dining nobles, recreating some of scenes most widely imagined in classic nineteenth-century Russian literature with facts, figures, and ethnographic detail. Chapters 6 and 7 move from serfdom and tsarism to revolution and the Soviet era. The latter brought both horrors and successes: collectivization, dekulakization, man-made famines (in Ukraine, Kazakhstan, and of course the Gulag camps). But Soviet society also entailed culinary multiculturalism, aspirations to *obshchepit* (public catering), and public protest at the reality of food shortages. Smith's evocative Epilogue, 'Russia Again', spoke to my own experiences as a language student in 1990s Krasnodar, recapturing days of buying fruit and vegetables from the market, spicy Korean carrot, hot *pirozhki*, and *lavash* flatbreads. This period saw the arrival of McDonald's, followed by Russian fast-food outlets (*Teremok*, the rebirth of the *stolovaia* or cheap, basic restaurant), and native grocery chains (*Perekrestok, Azbuka Vkusa*). Smith's gastronomic journey ends with the international sanctions which punished Russia's 2014 annexation of Crimea as well as Russian attempts to make Camembert and Brie. Sadly, the sanctions continue, as does the evolving story of Russia's food—since Smith produced her book, McDonald's has left Russia, replaced by the home-grown *Vkusno i Tochka*—but we must wait for analysis of this latest chain restaurant. *Cabbage and Caviar* is a joy: from the assiduousness and engaging delivery of Smith's research, to the glossy production and quality illustrations. It will appeal to Slavic, social, and food historians.

University of Exeter   Cathy McAteer
doi:10.1353/mlr.00028

ABSTRACTS

'More Love Letters, Please!': Portuguese Love and the Literary Legacy of Sincere Feeling
   by Manuela Mourão

This essay traces the formation of the myth of **Portuguese Love**, and demonstrates both its transcultural reach and its importance for **literary history**. Sparked by the tragic love of **Pedro and Inês de Castro**, the notion of Portuguese Love was crystallized in seventeenth-century France by *Lettres portugaises*, influenced **European letters** for centuries, and became an enduring **myth** in **Portuguese culture**. Anchored by **Roland Barthes**'s critique of the contemporary disparagement of **sentimental love**, the essay argues that Portuguese Love's continued affirmation, from nineteenth-century literary iterations to current manifestations, demonstrates the power of a discourse of genuine feeling to counter ideological appropriation.

The Nation on Trial: Tengiz Abuladze's *Repentance* (1987) and Christian Frosch's *Murer* (2018)   by Katya Krylova

This article compares the Soviet Georgian film *Repentance* (Tengiz Abuladze, 1987) with the contemporary Austrian film *Murer: Anatomy of a Trial* (Christian Frosch, 2018), arguing that, through their **courtroom scenes**, these films put their respective **nations on trial**. Drawing on scholarship related to the **trial film genre** as well as on discourse related to **law and justice** (Hannah Arendt, Shoshana Felman), I show how, whether dealing with the crimes of **Stalinism** or **Nazism**, these films seek to confront their audiences with hitherto repressed aspects of their countries' **historical legacies**.

'The contents o'th' story': The Diana and Actaeon Myth in Shakespeare's *Cymbeline*
   by Martina Zamparo

Moving from the rich Ovidianism that characterizes **Shakespeare**'s *Cymbeline* and from the retrospective and 'valedictory' character of this late play, the aim of this essay is to explore how the **Diana** and **Actaeon** myth from **Ovid**'s *Metamorphoses* serves to connect several motifs that are at the core of the drama: from sexual exposure and illicit viewing to matters of reading, writing, and publishing. As will be demonstrated, references to this myth also contribute to reinforcing the **imagery of birth** and of **reunion** that is so central in the final part of the play.

James L. W. West on F. Scott Fitzgerald: A Review Article   by William Blažek

Over a twenty-five-year period, James L. W. West III was the general editor of the **Cambridge Edition of the Works of F. Scott Fitzgerald**, an eighteen-volume series that was completed with the Variorum Edition of *The Great Gatsby* in 2019. His new collection of essays provides important insights into **Fitzgerald's professional writing career**, the complexities of **scholarly textual editing**, and especially the creation and legacy of *The Great Gatsby* as we approach the 2025 centennial of its original publication.

All the Islands the Island: The Crafting of Cortázar's 'La isla a mediodía'   by Dominic Moran

This essay aims to achieve a better understanding of how **Julio Cortázar** came to write one of his most iconic stories, '**La isla a mediodía**', as and when he did by identifying the various literary sources on which he may have drawn, including **D. H. Lawrence**'s story '**The Man Who Loved Islands**', various works by **Aldous Huxley**, and, above all, **William Golding**'s novel *Pincher Martin*.

Between Waste Studies and Postcolonial Theory: Wasted Lives, Necropolitics, and Environmental (In)Justice in Marcos Herrera's *La mitad mejor*   by Lucy Bell

This essay bridges a gap between **Waste Theory, Postcolonial Studies,** and **Environmental Justice** through a new reading of **Marcos Herrera**'s *La mitad mejor* (2009). Set in Buenos Aires' clandestine underworld, the narrative stages acts of extreme cruelty that reduce its marginalized characters to 'wasted lives' (**Zygmunt Bauman**), 'living dead' (**Achille Mbembe**), and 'less than human beings' (**Maria Lugones**). Attending to Herrera's 'unplots', racialized 'uncharacters', and wasted settings, I argue that violence flows deeper than these spectacular acts, and read *La mitad mejor* as a fictionalized response to Rob Nixon's pressing question: how to narrate the '**slow violence**' of environmental injustice.

THE
MODERN LANGUAGE REVIEW

VOLUME 119

2024

THE
MODERN LANGUAGE REVIEW

Edited by

L. O'MEARA   A. HISCOCK/S. ROGERS/A. HANSEN
C. MORAN   G. BONSAVER
D. WHEELER   F. FINLAY   M. MAGUIRE

VOLUME 119
2024

Modern Humanities Research Association

The Modern Language Review

is published by

THE MODERN HUMANITIES RESEARCH ASSOCIATION

For details of ordering and subscription see www.mhra.org.uk/journals/MLR
For online publication see https://muse.jhu.edu/journal/822
(older volumes at https://www.jstor.org/journal/modelangrevi)
For institutional subscription rates and information,
contact subscriptions@mhra.org.uk

ISSN 0026-7937 (Print)
ISSN 2222-4319 (Online)

DISCLAIMER

Views expressed in the content of the *Modern Language Review* are those of the respective authors and contributors and not of the journal editors or of the Modern Humanities Research Association (MHRA). MHRA makes no representation, express or implied, in respect of the accuracy of the material in this journal and cannot accept any legal responsibility or liability for views expressed or for any errors or omissions that may be made.

TYPESET BY JOHN WAŚ, OXFORD

CONTENTS

REVIEWS

Contents   vii

Contents   ix

Contents   xi

Contents   xiii

Milton Keynes UK
Ingram Content Group UK Ltd.
UKHW021045021024
449145UK00008B/133